Alexandra Reed Lajoux
Empowering Municipal Sustainabili

MW01482465

The Alexandra Lajoux Corporate Governance Series

Edited by
Alexandra Reed Lajoux

Alexandra Reed Lajoux

Empowering Municipal Sustainability

A Guide for Towns, Cities, and Citizens

DE GRUYTER

ISBN 978-3-11-068981-5
e-ISBN (PDF) 978-3-11-068986-0
e-ISBN (EPUB) 978-3-11-068990-7
ISSN 2629-8155

Library of Congress Control Number: 2021946660

Bibliographic information published by the Deutsche Nationalbibliothek
The Deutsche Nationalbibliothek lists this publication in the Deutsche Nationalbibliografie;
detailed bibliographic data are available on the Internet at http://dnb.dnb.de.

© 2022 Walter de Gruyter GmbH, Berlin/Boston
Typesetting: Integra Software Services Pvt. Ltd.
Printing and Binding: LSC Communications, United States

www.degruyter.com

Acknowledgments

My first acknowledgment goes to McLean, Virginia. If I had not grown up there, I may never have written this book. For it was there that I saw how a town can lose its identity in a single generation if the townspeople and their leaders fail to preserve it.

During my childhood in the 1950s, we lived in Chesterbrook Woods, next to Reed's Farm (no relation), with a deep and hilly forest on the other side. We were on the edge of the more urban Arlington, Virginia, but to the west just a few miles way was a small grocery store called Tyson's Corners at the intersection of Route 7 and Route 123. By the time I went to college, the farmlands and woodlands were entirely gone, and Tyson's Corners was on its way to becoming one of the largest shopping malls in the world.

My next acknowledgment goes to my parents – Stella Swingle Reed and Stanley Foster Reed, who chose McLean as their home because of its rural charm. My father dreaded and mourned all the changes. Once he led me up to a high hill and we looked down on forests. "Someday, all these forests will be gone," he said solemnly. Sadly, he was right. And more than once he observed that "The American businessman would chop down the last cherry tree." On one occasion, I invited a Pikestaff restaurant coworker to a family barbecue, and my father refused to shake his hand. (This was no ordinary developer, but one who had been involved in a scandal pertaining to the environment. Scofflaw developers demolished protected historic buildings and legacy trees under cover of night without a permit and some officials took bribes to look the other way. I don't recall his role, but he had gone to jail – "the pokey" – for it.)

Since growing up in McLean, I have made my home in many towns and cities – sometimes for a decade or more, sometimes for only a season. Municipalities that have sheltered me include Alexandria, Arlington, and Fairfax, VA; Avignon, France; Bennington, VT; Berlin, Germany; Oswego, NY; Paris and Poitiers, France; Philadelphia, PA; Princeton, NJ; Oswego, NY; Washington, DC; San Jose, Costa Rica; and since 2017, Fernandina Beach, FL – where I first became aware of the difference engaged citizens can make in municipal policy. Fast forward to 2020, when my lifelong love of nature and longtime engagement in policy fused into a campaign for City Commission. Although I lost, I treasure every one of the 2,307 votes I got! To see how I campaigned for the environment, visit LajouxforCi tyCommission.com.[1]

Special thanks to the more than 100 neighbors in Isle de Mai who signed petitions to save trees, and who later signed my petition to get on the city ballot. Campaigning on a green platform took away from my home and work life, so I thank my family (Bernard, Franklin, and Romero Lajoux), my research colleagues

https://doi.org/10.1515/9783110689860-202

at the National Association of Corporate Directors (especially Peter Gleason, Friso van der Oord, and Judy Warner as well as Hon. Cari Dominguez and her predecessor in the indispensable director role Dr. Reatha Clark King), and all my colleagues at Capital Expert Services, LLC (especially John Hotta and our advisor Hon. Carlos C. Campbell).

Organizations helpful in endorsing or informing my campaign included Conserve Amelia Now, The Amelia Tree Conservancy, and the North Florida Central Labor Council, including the International Brotherhood of Electrical Workers.

I would also like to acknowledge the following individuals for their civic leadership: Dr. Eric Aguilar, Bryn Bryon, Julie Ferreira, Beth Foster, Samir Gupte, Lowell Hall, Lauree Hemke, Arthur and Diane Herman, Frank Hopf, Betsie Huben, Kristin Huben, Margaret Kirkland, Tammi Kosack, Al Laub, Christie LeLait, Mary Libby, Paul Lore, Wendall McGahee, Mac Morriss, Benjamin Clark Morrison, Chuck Oliva, Taylor Owenby, Sarah Pelican, Wayne Peterson, Marian Phillips, Faith Ross, Ron Sapp, Eric Schmidt, Megan Stewart, Hon. Patricia Thompson, Rev. Bernard Thompson, and the venerable Robert Weintraub.

Big shout out also to the many who signed my petition to be on the ballot, who made financial and sign-waving contributions to my campaign, or just encouraged me along the way. These include many of the individuals listed above, as well as Christine Bottka, Loretta Parker Brown, Richard Cain (treasurer par excellence), Francesca Caramagno, Steven Crounse, Brian and Mary Downey, Kenneth Daly, Barbara Ellrich, John Hotta, James Jyz, Karen Kane, Daniel Parra, George and Jane Polinksi, Perry Rae, Greg Shurman, Kathryn Harris Tijerina, Lisa Leonard Timm, and my sisters Nancie Chang and Beryl Wolfe. Your support has inspired me to continue my advocacy rain or shine. Other environmentalists who inspired me for this book included Kathleen Anderson Steeves, Gail Pfoh, Stephanie Mooney, and Dr. Pat Foster-Turley. Special thanks to Geoffrey Charles Henny, Abdul Quayum, and Elizabeth Lwanda Rutsate, environmental scholars; to René Smith and Dr. Anton Endress for advising on Chapter 6 and to Jesse Rhodes for his good counsel on Chapter 9. Chapters 10 and 11 benefited from reviews by Ben G. Price, Kai Hutchke, and Tish O'Dell of the Community Environmental Defense Legal Fund. Scholars around the world linking on academia.edu, including Barbara A. Coe, Arturo Herman, David McRobert, Mokgerwa Makoti, Anu Pande, John Payne, Manoj Pumer, and Dmitry Pozhidaev have provided helpful commentary.

Special shout out to Billy Robinson, a friend and "doubting Thomas" on the environment, who helped me clarify my ideas.

Also appreciated are the current City Commission of Fernandina Beach: Mayor Mike Lednovich, Vice Mayor Len Kreger, Dr. Chip Ross, Bradley Bean, and David Sturges.

Thanks also to Dale Martin, city manager; Tammi Bach, city attorney; Caroline Best, city clerk; and Kelli Gibson, city planner; and members and leaders of the City's volunteer advisory committees. Appreciation also goes to SuAnne Thamm and all members of our local free press, as well as Island representatives John Martin and Aaron Bell of the Nassau County, Florida, Board of County Commissioners, and our Florida legislative representatives Sen. Aaron Bean and Rep. Cord Byrd. Thank you for all you do to keep Fernandina and Florida sustainable.

Finally, I want to thank De Gruyter for giving me the opportunity to publish this book. Sincere thanks go to Stefan Giesen, editorial director; Jaya Dalal, content editor; Suruthi Manogaran, project manager; and Denise Pangia, copy editor, proofreader, and indexer. Thanks also to David Repetto who recruited me to De Gruyter. Finally, kudos and thanks to Jeffrey Pepper, who launched the governance and sustainability series that will be the home for this book.

Alexandra R. Lajoux
August 2021

A.M.D.G.

Note

1 Passcode, if needed, is Fernandina 2022.

About the Author and Series Editor

Alexandra Reed Lajoux is chief knowledge officer emeritus (CKO) at the National Association of Corporate Directors (NACD) and founding principal of Capital Expert Services, LLC (CapEx), a global consultancy providing expert witnesses for legal cases. Dr. Lajoux is a Series Editor for Walter De Gruyter, Inc. The series has an emphasis on governance, corporate leadership, and sustainability. She has served as editor of *Directors & Boards, Mergers & Acquisitions, Export Today,* and *Director's Monthly,* and has coauthored a series of books on M&A for McGraw-Hill, including *The Art of M&A* and eight spin-off titles on strategy, valuation, financing, structuring, due diligence, integration, bank M&A, and distressed M&A. For Bloomberg/Wiley, she coauthored *Corporate Valuation for Portfolio Investment* with Robert A. G. Monks. Dr. Lajoux serves on the advisory board of Campaigns and Elections, and is a Fellow of the Caux Round Table for Moral Capitalism. She holds a B.A. from Bennington College, a Ph.D. from Princeton University, and an M.B.A. from Loyola University in Maryland.

https://doi.org/10.1515/9783110689860-203

Foreword

Don't Fight City Hall; Make It Work for People and Nature

In *Empowering Municipal Sustainability: A Guide for Towns, Cities, and Citizens*, Alexandra Lajoux presents an extensive review of tools available to citizens and to locally elected officials in their quest to respond to constituent demands for community sustainability.

The book has global reach but is made in America, where citizen empowerment is sorely lacking. Most Americans seem to believe that all the governing that matters happens in state capitols and in Washington D.C.—and those centers of power are far beyond our reach and influence. The reason for this outward-looking stance toward government, and perhaps for Lajoux's presentation of options for the governments located in our own hometowns, is that community residents have generally given up hope that local authority exists to set policy and respond to quality of life and existential challenges, such as the relationship between local industrial and extractive projects and cancer rates, habitat loss, and climate change.

When it comes to decisions being made about our communities—all without public input or consent—the general consensus seems to be, as the saying goes, *you can't fight City Hall.* People don't bother asking anymore *why does it so often have to be a fight?* They just don't bother. What may be mistaken for apathy and disengagement from the public life of community is in fact a general malaise and resignation stemming from once vibrant local engagement that was met by downward looks and shaking heads, as municipal officials intoned again and again, *we wish we could help, but our hands are tied.*

Most Americans not only wouldn't think to try using their municipal government to vindicate local interests and aspirations; they just flat-out don't think seriously about the government closest to them. They've been trained to stay away from public meetings of the local government, with the imposition of three-minute public comment sessions—before municipal meetings address substantive issues; and with often-conflicted citizen advisory committees that have no power and amount to a repository for tabled issues where all good ideas go to die. The setting aside of their aspirations for the future of their community has been normalized by the routine granting of conditional uses and variances to the comprehensive plans and the zoning laws intended to realize those aspirations. The threat of unbudgetable litigation from corporate applicants for permits at-odds with local aspirations account for the constant recommendations from municipal

https://doi.org/10.1515/9783110689860-204

attorneys to grant variances and ignore toothless, aspirational documents like comprehensive land use plans.

I'll be honest: my long experience working with municipal leaders and fed-up residents has taught me that many of the tools reviewed here by Alexandra Lajoux don't work and were never intended to work when the interests of the community conflict with the commercial interests of large corporations. When People try to use municipal government to protect their community and local environment from, for instance, state chartered and permitted waste disposal and resource extracting businesses, they discover how thoroughly the law has been crafted to eliminate local governing authority over corporate behavior within a municipality's nominal jurisdiction.

So, why this emphasis on municipal government as the last, best hope for achieving sustainability? Lajoux makes clear that it's within our municipally organized hometowns that all the living and dying, all the industrial assaults on our environment and all the first-hand encounters with the challenges of modern life occur. It's where we live and laugh and love, and for each of us, it's the place that matters most in the world.

Alexandra Lajoux is an optimist, trying to uncover every possible avenue for municipal governments and their citizens to achieve local sustainability. From assessing challenges to sustainability, to making an inventory of available assets, to developing a practical plan to realize a community's sustainability aspirations, Lajoux charts an idealistic path, using tools like comprehensive land use planning, zoning, land trusts, equitable taxation and budgeting. It is hard not to notice that the author touches on these and many other tools and processes in her exploration of the role municipalities might play in achieving sustainability goals, but in the end her recommendation is for a less traditionally constrained strategy.

In fact, in chapters 10 and 11, Lajoux minces few words as she advocates for the two cornerstones of the Community Rights strategy: The Right of Local, Community Self-Government, and the Rights of Nature. These two legal concepts depart radically from the deprivations of democratic governance that are laced throughout the highly restricted menu of hierarchically administered legal codes and regulations proffered as the outer contours of municipal authority.

This volume can serve as a civics lesson worth getting familiar with. It is a necessary addition to the collective knowledge of local self-government and a guidebook, as the title suggests, for "Towns, Cities and Citizens," which covers traditional authorities and processes your hometown can try-out in the quest for real sustainability. But it's necessary to say, as Lajoux's concluding chapters suggest, that the pathological relationship between municipal, state, and federal power makes local sustainability all but illegal when the interests of the public come into conflict with the interests of the so-called "private sector." The whole of the US judiciary has privileged that "private sector" with legal rights that immunize corporate actors from public governance. Hence the need for a radical approach to living well, democratically, and justly, in the face of a received system of law that does violence with impunity to our families, our natural environment, our civic lives and our most cherished values.

Because federated nations and united kingdoms are built on property-favoring constitutions, and the US Constitution is explicitly property and commerce oriented, and because the US. Supreme Court has usurped the citizenry as the final arbiter of legality, basic tenants of democratic governance have been transformed into insurmountable authoritarian obstacles that benefit incorporated wealth at the expense of People and Nature. The very structure of law—the parameters that allow legislators and courts to define the limits of popular political society—have been constricted to the point of a singularity—the continuing counterintuitive belief that democracy exists in these states.

Commerce Clause preemption at the national level, and state invocations of the democracy-killing judicial precedent known as Dillon's Rule and the imposition of illiberal preemptions on municipal law-making, disenfranchise community-level government in general, and are activated by the courts in defense of privileged wealth whenever the prompting of corporate lobbyists alerts the system to their benefactors' particular needs.

Fortunately, an increasingly less-quiet insurrection against the mooting of municipal sovereignty is stirring. A global quest for local community self-government, what Murray Bookchin has called *Global Municipalism* and some refer to as *Fearless Cities*, is setting roots in places widespread, from Barcelona, Spain; to Chiapas, Mexico; to Grant Township in Pennsylvania.

A parallel and symbiotic movement for the Rights of Nature is gaining momentum. Transforming the legal status of ecosystems from that of mere property to that of rights-bearing entities promises a social/cultural revolution that could change everything for the better.

Underneath this two-pronged revolution is a growing global alignment of communities against empire, colonialism, racism, privilege, hierarchy, divisiveness and perpetual war. The right of ecosystems to survive, thrive, replenish and regenerate, is being recognized in real places around the world. With this change, there is also the accompanying rejection of the so-called enlightenment ideology that argued human superiority over Nature and those elitists believed were *lesser People*. It was high-class propaganda that propelled European empires to rove the globe committing genocide and ecocide with equal measures of self-righteousness.

The trend toward local community empowerment and liberation from central government dictates is, quite simply, a visceral recognition that humans evolved to gather in communities of limited size, to inhabit natural environments from which they gained sustenance, not surpluses, and that the community, when they thought of it, included the local ecosystem and their neighbors. It was the coerced amalgamation of communities into states, and states into empires, and the intentional separation of People from the land and solidarity with their neighbors, that has led to the multiple global crises that frighten us today and make large, unmoored populations of insecure People vulnerable to manipulation and submersion in the nightmare of technological "progress" that continues to create, not lessen, those dangers that frighten us.

The Community Rights Movement, rightly understood, includes the Rights of Nature Movement, and suggests a way out of the stifling desert of life-opposing lies that pass for political discourse. Like a vast expanse of dunes, the horizon in the direction of the future defined for us by corporate colonial totalitarianism appears as an endless landscape of unassailable deception and diminishing quality of life, but only because we've been led to believe that barren vista is the only option available. No wonder the general sense of despair has grown palpable.

To use the strongest yet truest language, this was a colonial-settler-genocidal-ecocidal cultural mandate, and its premises are more than flawed. They are maladaptive and have spawned a cultural pathology whose *cause célèbre* was once summed up by Richard Grossman as *the endless production and consumption of more*. The false premises of the corporate colonial culture are these:

1. Humans are inherently apart from and superior to Nature, not a part of and dependent upon it.
2. Superiority over the natural world, including People who will not separate themselves from it, justifies conquest, subjugation, and dominion over both natural and human communities.
3. Reason and law are to be the governing principles of the corporate-colonial hegemony, with both reason and law rooted in the axiom that the hegemony is superior to and deservedly governs over biological persons and Nature.
4. The law, by premising its legitimacy on the corporate-colonial ideology, finds it rational to elevate legal rights attached to accumulated property (wealth), that is, conquered and possessed land, labor and resources, above all other rights and interests. It is an ideology with its pedigree in the Doctrine of Discovery and the Law of Conquest.
5. Any posited rights pertaining to People, communities and Nature are subordinate to rights attached to property ownership and conveyed to the owner through that property.

6. Since all the legal rights and social privileges that matter in the eyes of the law are conveyed via ownership to the owner of property, the greater the accumulated property (wealth), the more legal rights and social privileges are accrued by the owner.
7. All necessary laws and institutions will be devised to sustain this arrangement as the perpetual status quo.

Certainly, this is not the kind of sustainability Alexandra Lajoux is proposing here. That's why she brings the crescendo of this book, arriving at chapters 10 and 11, to a full-on fanfare for Community Rights and the Rights of Nature.

These are legal concepts that challenge the notion that whoever possesses the greater exclusive control over Planet Earth and its riches deserves to govern, by virtue of that material wealth. We should be howling that their social Darwinian-styled culture can't pretend to be playing by the law of the jungle when the laws they've made let corporations protected against public control clear cut the jungle and suck its water and minerals and soils for every monetizable element possible—while making it illegal for us to stop them. Let's keep in mind that Rights of Nature advocates, not neoliberal corporate colonists, are on the side of the jungle.

The Right of Local, Community Self-Government challenges black-letter law that allows the central government to veto community rights-protecting local laws in order to privilege the priorities of corporate wealth accumulation and criminalize community self-defense. Rights of Nature proponents challenge bedrock corporate-colonial law that says that Nature has no other legal status than that of property, whose owners may do as they wish to ecosystems in their possession. Community Rights advocates challenge the big lie that says People are not part of their local ecosystems. It does so by recognizing the unity of People and Nature as a community, indivisible and rights-bearing. The People, neither individually, nor collectively can "own" Nature, any more than they can own their neighbors.

The violation of these principles for more than six hundred years has cursed humanity on a global scale, inflicted what historian Gerald Horne calls *The Apocalypse of Settler Colonialism*, upon indigenous people worldwide, and brought us to a realization of the multiple existential crises confronting us today. To reverse, or at least halt the momentum, of these rolling catastrophes requires that we do more than try to make "work" the nominal and wholly inadequate tools given to municipalities. They won't. They can't. Not without ending the dictatorship of property and the concomitant privileges that accompany its gluttonous accumulation by the smallest of narcissistic and parasitic minorities.

We all have to start from where we are, of course. If reading this book is your taking-off point, then welcome to the struggle. Keep learning, Keep asking questions. But remember: it's going to take more than becoming informed. They say that *knowledge is power*, but it's not true. Knowledge fuels our actions and our actions are power. If aimed in the right direction, if our knowledge is informed by integrity and not deceit, then our *actions* are where our power lives. Read and learn. Then discern. Then act. Your neighbors and your planet are counting on you.

Ben G. Price

National Organizer, Community Environmental Legal Defense Fund
Author, *How Wealth Rules the World: Saving Our Communities and Freedoms from the Dictatorship of Property*
May 31, 2021

Contents

PART I: Setting Sustainability Goals

PART II: Using Environmental, Economic, and Engineering Tools to Advance Sustainability

PART III: **Beyond Taxes: Green Financing**

PART IV: **Dealing with Conflict Over Sustainability**

Appendices

Introduction
Municipalities at the Crossroads of Change

The earth's many sovereign nations garner much attention and allegiance for their powers to shape human destiny through their founding constitutions and their just laws.[1] Yet within each of these are smaller self-governing units – from regional provinces, to states, to counties, to cities, to boroughs and towns, as well as the lands of self-governing tribes.

While historians record the rise and fall of nations, they often overlook these smaller jurisdictions, where so many important aspects of our lives take shape. This book offers guidance to local municipalities – called "cities" or "towns" for short throughout this book[2] – that seek sustainability in their environment, their economy, and their engineering.

"Sustainability" in this book means capable of enduring and adapting over time. Without the qualities of endurance and adaptability, cities can see their assets and even their identities erode over time. The role of a good local government is to prevent such erosion, whether it be of natural habitat, human communities, or engineering infrastructure.[3]

Global versus Local Village

No matter how large or small a city is, its government can make a vital difference in the lives of its citizens – protecting the environment that contributes to the public safety and enjoyment of life, while attending to the economic and engineering needs of residents. In fact, one of the sustainable development goals (SDG) of the United Nations specifically calls out the sustainability of cities.[4] (See Goal 11 in Appendix 1: SDG at the end of this book.) The UN's Agenda 21 initiative looked to local governments as a key to climate change response.[5]

This book's emphasis on local governments – even the smallest ones – may seem quaint in this highly globalized world, but in fact this is where our common vigilance belongs. The ever-zooming post-COVID-19 world may well be, in the words of sociologist Marshall McLuhan, a "global village," but *where we live still matters*. In nations that grant powers to them, our local governments have a greater impact on our day-to-day lives than more distant units of government such as states, provinces, or countries.

Around the world, local governments affect the lives and fortunes of the citizens within their boundaries, because they have the power to pass ordinances and levy taxes. The Council of European Municipalities and Regions (CEMR)

https://doi.org/10.1515/9783110689860-206

notes that up to 80 percent of public investments in Europe are made by local and regional authorities.[6]

Local governments play a key role in advancing and protecting our quality of life. Consider the many beneficial effects of nature – whether in the form of dunes, wetlands, rivers, lakes, forests, parklands, or preserves. Local ordinances can make the difference between conservation and destruction. Consider also that we are living creatures, who need to consume food and water and dispose of waste. Local governments often provide our only water, sewer, and sanitation services. Furthermore, we need to be safe, and towns and cities often provide local police and fire fighters. Clearly, for many citizens, the blessings and benefits we want and/or need are typically provided by the local governments duly elected by the citizens of a municipality. In some countries, the role of local commissions or councils is even greater, taking charge of public education and social services, as well as the aforementioned services typically provided by local authorities.[7]

Municipal Definitions

This book defines a municipality (whether it calls itself a "city," "town," or other name) as *any boundaried population empowered to elect local representatives to serve on a governing body* such as a commission, council, or other such structure. In US legal terms, these are called "incorporated" areas. In the US they total approximately 79,000, not counting tribal councils.[8] Many of these are large enough to participate in public policy. The National League of Cities has a membership of 19,000 US cities, towns, and villages.[9]

This book uses the terms "city" or "town" as shorthand for a local self-governing community but acknowledges that such communities may go by a variety of names, such as township or borough. In some cases, a local community may legitimately define itself as a sovereign nation to be guided by a council of tribal elders.

For the purposes of this book, if a municipality calls itself a "city," it is one, no matter what its size. This identity-based definition of the term "city" differs from the population-based approach adopted by the United Nations in March 2020.[10] Under that definition, the term "city" is reserved for areas with a population of at least 50,000 living in contiguous grid cells with a density of greater than 1,500 inhabitants per square kilometer,[11] which equates to 2,414 inhabitants per square mile – a size typical of many US cities.[12] The United Nations defines a town (or semi-dense area) as having a population of at least 5,000 inhabitants with a density of at least 300 inhabitants per square kilometer. Other places with a lower population and density are considered rural. These definitions are based on size and density of population, not on governmental identities.[13]

This book defines municipalities by their governments. Size and density matter, but they are not the defining characteristics of the places we live. An area may be designated by population counters as a "city" or "town," but unless an area has a name, a government, and ultimately an identity, the power of its people to affect – or absorb – lasting social change will be low. Indeed, local sustainability depends on the influence of a local government and engaged citizens. As one recent empirical study of small municipalities noted, "the governmental structure, local interest groups, and growth pressures of a municipality jointly determine the likelihood that sustainability planning efforts will result in policy adoption."[14]

For their citizens, these places are home – a place to forge a personal identity; a place to defend and protect; a place to make a difference through public service and activism. Therefore, the focus of this book will be on how to advance the sustainability of the place we call home, by whatever name, through either public service or through activism. Understanding how local governments work – and in particularly the degree to which they can be self-governing – will be key to this approach.

From Magna Carta to COVID-19: Municipal Self- Determination

According to the principle of subsidiarity (see Appendix 2: Subsidiarity), government action is best taken at the level nearest to the citizen.[15] As such, the smaller the entity, the greater the potential it may have for understanding and resolving local issues.

During the COVID-19 Crisis of 2020, as the entire world tried to cope with a global pandemic, we saw how important local governments can be – whether by enforcing, exceeding, or protesting the standards of higher national or regional authorities. Some towns and cities helped to enforce mandates from higher authorities, while some set even stricter local policies to save lives. Still others tried to assert their own, less restrictive rules to save their economies. The long-term medical and financial repercussions of these local decisions remain to be seen, but one lesson is clear: local governments play an important role in our lives, in both the best and worst of times.

The history of human civilization includes many struggles of local governments to determine their own standards. An early example of this impulse is captured in the Magna Carta, signed in 1215 in England, where a group of barons successfully demanded that a higher authority, King John, respect their rights, as enumerated in their grand charter.[16] After perpetual revisions, the charter became official in 1297 (see Figure 1).

Figure 1: The 1297 Magna Carta.
Source: Courtesy of the David M. Rubenstein Magna Carta Collection, Creative Commons
License. https://www.archives.gov/exhibits/featured-documents/magna-carta

Another classic example is the European Charter of Municipal Liberties, passed in 1953.[17] With inspiring eloquence, this document sets forth standards on several topics of perennial importance to municipalities everywhere.

- On citizen participation: "Municipalities should be conscious that they constitute the very foundation of the nation. Their citizens, members of the community, have the right to work together for their development. Municipalities must therefore strive to enable them to participate in the town's life."
- On municipal self-determination: "A true municipal freedom can flourish only if it is beyond all kinds of arbitrary authority. It exists only where the citizens possess the firm will to safeguard local self-government . . .. The law must be applied in such a way that safeguards the rights of the local community toward the higher authorities, just as it must also guarantee the rights of the citizens in the local community itself."
- On municipal taxation: "Municipalities have the right to create their own resources, by voting local taxes that are sufficient to cover the costs of their administration, as well as all expenses necessary to meet the needs of their inhabitants."
- On inter-municipal relations: "A system of compensation between municipalities shall be established, which will have effect in case of proven inadequacy of resources, without imposing any constraint on the management of the municipality."[18]

We will explore these and other governance concepts in subsequent chapters.

The Threefold Importance of Self-Determination Today

The issue of local self-determination is no mere civic abstraction, but rather an urgent priority today, considering the most critical environmental, economic, and engineering issues of our time. The United Nations has defined a sustainable city as one "where achievements in social, economic, and physical development are made to last,"[19] with environment an integral part of all these goals (see Appendix 1).[20]

Around the world, cities large and small are facing major *environmental* risks. While global, national, and other external sources may be helpful in identifying and facing those risks, nothing can help a city more than local awareness and engagement. If cities and towns can exercise their rights of self-determination to protect their environments from destruction, they can help slow the negative trends observers have charted for global warming, rising sea levels, and loss of biodiversity. Engaged cities, and citizens need not be experts in such matters, but they would do well to understand some key trends. As of mid-2021, the steady rise in earth temperature is unbroken, with 2020 registering record-breaking heat, being the warmest year ever since 1896.[21] The month of June 2020, for example, measured 2.3 degrees above preindustrial levels – close to the limit set by the Paris Climate Agreement.[22] As for sea level, it is rising at an eighth of an inch per year, increasing the chance of flooding – a relevant concern for many cities, as eight of the world's 10 largest cities are near a coast.[23] Meanwhile, the loss of biodiversity has reached critical levels, with one million plant and animal species currently doomed to likely extinction, many within our lifetime.[24]

At the same time, the global *economic* system is experiencing unprecedented changes. A January 2021 report from the World Bank predicted a modest 3.8 percent global growth rate in gross domestic product (GDP) for 2022, as the world continues to be "weighed down by the pandemic's lasting damage to potential growth."[25] This was after the world experienced what the World Bank described as "the deepest global recession in eight decades."[26] In the US government sector (including local governments), total contributions to GDP declined in 2020, reports a March 2021 report from the Bureau of Economic Analysis.[27]

GDP – calculated as the total market value of goods and services produced in a country (or in the collective case, all countries) during a given time – is a broad indicator of both human industry and human confidence. When GDP is low, it means that fewer people or properties are engaged in the economy, and/or the economy is not placing as high a value on these assets. A recessionary economy shrinks a city's tax base at the very time when it may need to deliver more in social services due to poverty and its effects – including crime. New research shows that criminal activity in cities is highly localized by neighborhood, and that the most effective long-term solutions include not merely law and order, but economic opportunity.[28]

Finally, *engineering* issues are also coming to the fore as a threat to city life. The world's infrastructure is aging, and local officials know best what is broken where. More than 47,000 bridges in the US are in poor condition and require repairs, according to a 2019 report from the American Road and Transportation Builders Association. While many projects involve state or national purchases, local governments often have a role in infrastructure projects. Green thinking, such as preference for composite materials, including biological materials,[29] can help with both environmental and financial sustainability.[30]

It goes without saying that all of the issues covered in this book should be a topic for training of municipal staff, and areas for potential support from consultants. This book should be useful in the support of such efforts.

Over 10,000 Mayors

The number of towns and cities in the world can not easily be tallied but it is safe to say that they number in the hundreds of thousands. While the Global Covenant of Mayors for Climate and Energy alone has more than 10,000 signatories,[31] they represent only a small part of the municipal world.

Europe, for example, has more than 100,000 municipalities and regions. The CEMR has a membership of 54 national associations of municipalities and regions from 40 European countries, representing over 100,000 local and regional authorities.[32]

The US claims 19,495 incorporated cities and towns, in addition to its counties and states. Most of these incorporated areas, which are also known as townships and districts, are small. Three-fourths of the nation's cities and towns have a population of less than 5,000, and of these, more than half have fewer than 500 people; only 4 percent of all US cities have a population of more than 50,000.[33]

The Municipal Hierarchy

One conundrum in municipal life is the relationship of towns or cities to the next level of government above them, such as a province or county.

In Europe, most countries have a complex government that involves not only cities but higher authorities.[34] The terminology of governance varies from country to country. In a study of 39 European countries, the CEMR identified these unique combinations, ranging from villages to regions.[35]

In the US, city government exists in tandem with county government. As of mid-2021, in the US, according to the latest data from the US Census, the US has 3,141 counties and equivalent jurisdictions.[36] In most US states, cities are part of counties or their equivalents.[37] In Maryland, Missouri, Nevada, and Virginia some cities are independent from counties and entirely self-governing. In Connecticut and Rhode Island, counties have no governmental power. In some rare cases, city and county governments combine. Hawaii has only counties.

Civic Activists

Every hometown has its issues, and no one knows them better than the citizens, both old and new. Those who have been in the locality for generations will know the past and how to avoid repeating its mistakes. Those moving to the area in recent years may be able to perceive problems and solutions with a fresh perspective. While there may arise a culture clash between locals and newcomers,[38] common values – and common enemies – can bring a truce and common action.[39]

Civic activism may arise spontaneously from a purely local issue, or it may take its inspiration from a national movement. Through social media, local movements can quickly become national – even global – and vice versa. In the spring of 2020, many US towns held marches to protest police brutality, including towns where de-escalation policies had prevented this problem. In such towns, however, the marches were often followed with formation of local task forces to identify and resolve specific local problems.[40] Another example is the America the Beautiful initiative of the Biden Administration in the US, named after a beloved national hymn.[41] This movement, setting a 30 percent conservation goal by 2030, is animating similar local efforts, for example in Silver City, New Mexico.[42]

Another cross-cutting theme in civic activism is protest versus politics. When local citizens want change, they can act as citizens by various civic actions – holding protests, speaking out at council meetings, collecting petitions, and so forth. As an alternative, they can run for office, or support someone who does. It is expensive to run for office[43] and victory is not guaranteed but win or lose this is a good way of getting out a sustainability message. Another venue for change is service on a local advisory board. Many local candidates and activists concerned about sustainability have read the practical wisdom of Eben Fodor's *Better Not Bigger: How to Take Control of Urban Growth and Improve Your Community*.[44] The present book, hopes to be equally useful as a greenprint for change.

A Greenprint for Municipal Change

The four main sections of this book can help cities and citizens prioritize their environmental assets as part of a larger plan for sustainability. The Nature Conservancy sees a greenprint as "a strategic conservation plan and/or tool that reveals the economic and social benefits that parks, open space, and working lands provide communities." Building on that concept, this book guides the reader through setting sustainability goals, financing those goals, implementing the goals, to resolving conflicts over the goals.

Part 1 addresses goal setting, as readers will identify key environmental, economic, and engineering issues; map their municipalities; and write a sustainability plan.

Part 2 covers the important subject of city financing, including land trusts, municipal bonds, and various kinds of grants.

Part 3 covers the environment, the economy, and engineering. (A compatible framework for this is the Global Development Research Center (GDRC) framework of the natural environment, the social environment, and the built environment.[45])

Part 4 faces the issues of rights, conflict, and identity, covering the rights of nature, environmental litigation, and the issue of municipal boundaries and identity.

Concluding Reflections

This book is being published at what we can only hope is the waning of the COVID-19 pandemic. Around the world city leaders are forming groups to meet the challenges ahead. One such group is the C40 initiative engaging the globe's megacities.

At a recent meeting of the group, the mayor of one of the world's oldest cities struck a positive note: "Historical Athens begins its recovery phase from the epidemic with an array of green initiatives . . . treating this challenge as nothing more – and nothing less – than a unique opportunity. An opportunity to help our cities and our citizens grow, prosper and enter a new era of environmental awareness and involvement."[46]

As these words show, it is important for governments and citizens alike to play an active role in advancing the sustainability of their communities. This book sets forth guidance in doing just that.

Notes

1 As of mid-2021, the world counts 195 nations, including the 193 members of the United Nations, plus observer states of Palestine and the Vatican. Some estimates have a higher count.
2 The term city is used here to mean any municipality with its own government. This is consistent with usage by the US Green Building Council, developer of the LEED standards. The USGBC defines a city as "political jurisdictions or places defined by their municipal public sector governance (e.g., mayors or town manager)." https://www.usgbc.org/leed/v41#cities-and-communities
3 As noted later in this chapter, the United Nations has defined a sustainable city as one "where achievements in social, economic, and physical development are made to last." Source: United Nations Centre for Human Settlements (UNCHS) Sustainable Cities Programme (UN-Habitat), 2002, p. 6. See the discussion in note 19.
4 Goal #11 of the United Nation's 20 sustainable development goals is to "make cities and human settlements inclusive, safe, resilient, and sustainable." https://sdgs.un.org/goals/goal11
5 https://sustainabledevelopment.un.org/content/documents/Agenda21.pdf

6 Local and Regional Government in Europe: Structures and Competences (CCRE, 2020). https://www.ccre.org/docs/Local_and_Regional_Government_in_Europe.EN.pdf

7. Sweden is an example of a country that grants municipalities broad-based powers of self-determination. https://eacea.ec.europa.eu/national-policies/eurydice/content/main-executive-and-legislative-bodies-80_en

8 https://fas.org/sgp/crs/misc/R40638.pdf

9 National League of Cities – Cities Strong Together; https://www.ncl.org

10 https://blogs.worldbank.org/sustainablecities/how-do-we-define-cities-towns-and-rural-areas

11 1 km = (1/1.609344) mi, so about 2,414 people per square mile.

12 US cities with approximately this size and density include Durham, North Carolina; Pearland, Texas; Rockford, Illinois; and Wichita, Kansas. "Population Density for U.S. Cities Statistics" Governing.com, November 29, 2016. https://www.governing.com/gov-data/population-density-land-area-cities-map.html

13 A recent UN booklet on the world's cities specifically states that "The designations employed and the presentation of the material in this publication do not imply the expression of any opinion whatsoever on the part of the Secretariat of the United Nations concerning the legal status of any country, territory, city or area or of its authorities, or concerning the delimitation of its frontiers of boundaries." Global State of Metropolis 2020 – Population Data Booklet, United Nations Human Settlement Program, 2020. https://unhabitat.org/sites/default/files/2020/07/gsm-population-data-booklet-2020.pdf

14 Vanessa R. Levesque, Kathleen P. Bell, and Aram J. K. Calhoun. "Planning for Sustainability in Small Municipalities: The Influence of Interest Groups, Growth Patterns, and Institutional Characteristics," *Journal of Planning Education and Research 37*(3) (2017): 322–333. https://journals.sagepub.com/doi/pdf/10.1177/0739456X16655601

15 For the European Union's discussion of subsidiarity, see "The Principle of Subsidiarity," at Eur-Lex, accessed July 19, 2020. https://eur-lex.europa.eu/legal-content/EN/TXT/?uri=LEGISSUM:ai0017

16 https://www.archivesfoundation.org/documents/magna-carta/

17 https://www.ccre.org/docs/charter_municipal_liberties.pdf

18 https://www.ccre.org/docs/charter_municipal_liberties.pdf, correcting "guaranteed" to read "guarantee."

19 United Nations Centre for Human Settlements (UNCHS) Sustainable Cities Programme (UN-Habitat), 2002, p. 6).

20 For the full text, see https://unstats.un.org/sdgs/report/2020/The-Sustainable-Development-Goals-Report-2020.pdf. Note especially this quote from p. 50 at Goal 13 on Climate: "Governments and businesses should use the lessons learned and opportunities arising from this crisis to accelerate the transitions needed to . . . redefine our relationship with the environment, and make systemic shifts and transformational changes to become low-greenhouse-gas emission and climate-resilient economies and societies."

21 Climate at a Glance | National Centers for Environmental Information (NCEI), https://www.noaa.gov

22 At the Paris climate agreement, policy makers agreed to limit global warming to less than 3.6 degrees Fahrenheit (or 2 degrees Centigrade) above preindustrial levels by 2100, with an aspirational goal of a rise no less than 2.7F (1.5C). The accord does not define this baseline and commentaries vary. The oldest temperature covered by the National Oceanic and Atmospheric Administration was in 1895: 50.34 F or 10.19 C. Source: NOAA National Centers for Environmental

Information, Climate at a Glance: National Time Series, March 2021, https://www.ncdc.noaa.gov/cag/For a report as of August 2021, see https://www.ipcc.ch/report/sixth-assessment-report-working-group-i/ For more history, see Matthew Capucci, "Unprecedented heat in Siberia pushed planet to warmest June on record, tied with last year," *Washington Post*, June 7, 2020. https://www.washingtonpost.com/weather/2020/07/07/warmest-june-siberia-planet/

23 https://oceanservice.noaa.gov/facts/sealevel.html

24 Sustainable Development Goal 15: Life on Land. United Nations, https://www.un.org/sustainabledevelopment/biodiversity/

25 Global Economic Prospects, https://www.worldbank.org

26 World Bank, Global Economic Prospects (June 2020). https://www.worldbank.org/en/publication/global-economic-prospects

27 "Gross Domestic Product (Third Estimate), Corporate Profits, and GDP by Industry, Fourth Quarter and Year 2020," gdp4q20_3rd.pdf, https://www.bea.gov

28 Robert Muggah and Sameh Wahba, "How reducing inequality will make our cities safer," *World Economic Forum*, March 2, 2020.

29 "Bio-based composite bridge in The Netherlands," *Composites World*, October 1, 2018. https://www.compositesworld.com/articles/a-bio-based-composite-bridge-in-netherlands-

30 "The markets: Civil infrastructure," Composites World, January 10, 2020. https://www.compositesworld.com/articles/the-markets-civil-infrastructure

31 https://www.globalcovenantofmayors.org/about/

32 https://ccre.org/en/actualites/view/4058

33 Amel Toukabri and Lauren Medina, "America: A Nation of Small Towns," May 21, 2020. https://www.census.gov/library/stories/2020/05/america-a-nation-of-small-towns.html

34 Local and Regional Government in Europe: Structures and Competences (CCRE, 2020). https://www.ccre.org/docs/Local_and_Regional_Government_in_Europe.EN.pdf

35 See Box 12.1 in Chapter 12.

36 h Ch4GARM.pdf (census.gov). https://www2.census.gov/geo/pdfs/reference/GARM/Ch4GARM.pdf

37 In Louisiana, the primary governmental divisions are called parishes; in Alaska, they are called boroughs, municipalities, or census areas. Source: https://www.census.gov/programs-surveys/popest/guidance-geographies/terms-and-definitions.html

38 See "Culture Clash? Predictors of Views on Amenity-Led Development and Comm," by Jessica D. Ulrich-Schad and Hua Qin; https://www.usu.edu Rural Sociology, June 2017.

39 See Jessica D. Ullrich-Schad and Hua Qin, "Culture Clash? Predictors of Views on Amenity-Led Development and Comm," https://www.usu.edu

40 See, for example, Citizen task force to advise Laguna Beach police on use of force – Laguna Beach Local News https://www.lagunabeachindy.com and City of Fernandina Beach Police Chief announces Police Department Advisory Board | Fernandina Observer

41 Biden-Harris Administration Outlines "America the Beautiful" Initiative | The White House, https://www.whitehouse.gov/ceq/news-updates/2021/05/06/biden-harris-administration-outlines-america-the-beautiful-initiative/

42 'America the Beautiful' initiative supports outdoor rec, conservation plans here – Silvercity Daily Press (scdailypress.com), https://www.scdailypress.com/2021/05/19/america-beautiful-initiative-supports-outdoor-rec-conservation-plans/

43 What Does It Cost to Run for City Council (And Win)? – Campaign in a Box. http://www.campaigninabox.us/blog/2018/1/28/what-does-it-cost-to-run-for-city-council-and-win

44 Eban V. Fodor, *Better Not Bigger: How to Take Control of Urban Growth and Improve your Community* (New Catalyst Books, 2007). See also Jeff Speck, *Walkable City Rules: 101 Steps to Making Better Places* (Island Press, 2018).
45 https://www.gdrc.org/uem/doc-intro.html
46 Kosta Bakoyannis, mayor of Athens, Greece, quoted in "No Return to Business as Usual: Mayors Pledge on COVID-19 Economic Recovery," May 7, 2020: C40.

PART I: **Setting Sustainability Goals**

Chapter 1
Identifying Key Issues for Your Municipality

By being both enduring and adaptable, a sustainable city or town "meets the needs of the present without compromising the ability of future generations to meet their own needs," exemplifying the famous definition advanced by the Brundtland Report of the United Nations four decades ago.[1] To achieve sustainability in this sense, a municipality must face, prioritize, and resolve a full range of challenges.

- *Environmental sustainability* ranks high as a concern for leaders who want their cities to remain livable for future generations. Given our basic biological needs as humans, as well as the ultimate fragility of the structures we build to protect ourselves from the elements, our cities need to protect the natural resources that provide multiple benefits to our safety and enjoyment.
- *Economic sustainability, including social equity,* is also important for every town or city – both for the citizenry and the city. A city must know and serve its long-term tax base, including any businesses within its boundaries that provide for residents and/or generate more tax dollars.
- *Engineering* stands as a third critical element in city sustainability. The physical infrastructure of a city – its buildings, roads, sidewalks, and bridges – must be built to last,[2] and must be supported by ongoing maintenance.

These three issues are fundamental for all cities, yet how they rank and interconnect will vary from one municipality to the next, based on a city's social realities and political values. As noted by one political scientist after an extensive review of research on sustainable cities: "There is an essential role for local government to play: that is to (1) create an environment in which citizens empower themselves by collaboratively making the rules for participation, and (2) identify key individuals who connect the various networks and involve them in the development of sustainability strategies; thereby expediting the process of reaching the stage where local government and citizens share the same sustainability goals."[3] The practical ideas presented in this book work best when there is such a foundation of empowerment and involvement.

This chapter discusses these "three Es," drawing from current (2021) data and examples. At the end of the chapter is a ranking tool to help a municipality identify and prioritize issues for any city's environment, the economy, and engineering.

https://doi.org/10.1515/9783110689860-001

Environmental Issues

Enlightened city leaders strive to advance the well-being of citizens, both for their physical safety and for their personal happiness. Setting environmental goals can foster both aims.

Reduction of Risk: Mitigating Effects of Climate Change

A critical goal for any city today is to prepare for and mitigate the effects of climate risk. When cities develop their strategic plans, their land development codes, and their future land use maps, they need to factor in the particular environmental threats that face them. Existing plans, codes, and maps from neighboring municipalities can provide good models.

Depending on their location, cities face many different climate threats and must plan ahead to mitigate them. Cities in North America face threats that differ from those faced by their neighbors to the south, or by Europe, Asia, and Australasia. Each of these continents faces a different set of perils. For example, generally speaking, the change of major flooding is higher in cities located in Africa than in those based in North America.[4]

And within each region there is additional variation. For example, in the US, according to the US National Aeronautics and Space Administration (NASA),[5] and based on the Fourth National Climate Assessment,[6] climate threats vary by region:[7]

Northeast. Heat waves, heavy rain, and *sea level rise* are stressing agriculture,[8] fisheries, ecosystems, and infrastructure. The Northeast has some of the nation's oldest infrastructure and it is highly vulnerable to flooding.[9]

Southeast. Sea level rise poses widespread and continuing threats to the region's economy and environment. Flooding is a part of this risk. For example, coastal cities in Florida must have comprehensive plans and these may identify an adaptation action area (AAA).[10]

Meanwhile, *extreme heat* in this region is affecting agriculture, energy, and health. Decreased water availability including *draught* is having economic and environmental impacts.

Southwest. Increased heat, drought, and *insect outbreaks,* all linked to climate change, have increased wildfires. Declining water supplies reduced agricultural yields, health impacts in cities due to heat, and *flooding* and *erosion* in coastal areas are additional concerns, especially during hurricane seasons. The City of Houston, Texas, is still recovering from Hurricane Harvey.[11]

Northwest. In this region, changes in the timing of *streamflow* are reducing water supplies. Streamflow is the amount of water flowing in a stream or river and is an important part of the water cycle. It can change due to both natural and manmade causes.[12] *Sea level rise, erosion, flooding,* and *ocean acidity* pose major threats. Increasing *wildfires, insect outbreaks,* and *tree diseases* are causing widespread tree die-off.

Midwest. *Extreme heat, heavy rain,* and *flooding* are affecting agriculture, air and water quality, forestry, transportation, and infrastructure. Heavy rains and flooding stress storm water management systems and other critical infrastructure[13] (see Figure 1.1).

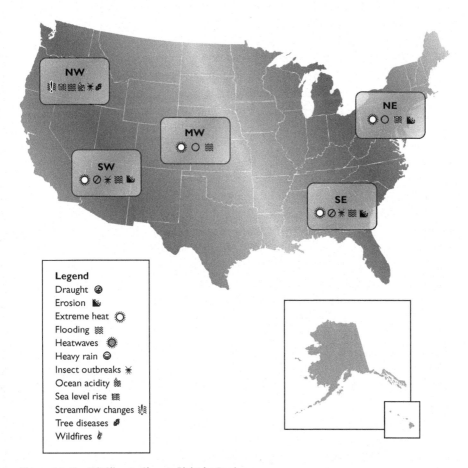

Figure 1.1: Key US Climate Change Risks by Region.
Source: Art by Chris Smith, quarternative.com

Quality of Life: Ensuring Public Access to Nature

Another city goal related to the environment is the quality of life experienced by all residents, rich and poor. When municipalities provide and/or protect free public access to nature, they provide an important benefit. Exposure to nature is associated with positive mental and physical health.[14]

In some cases, city leaders must make a conscious effort to even out an environmental imbalance that correlates to an economic imbalance. When local economies are left to run according to their own devices, with no commitment to shared public natural spaces, there can be a winner-take-all trend. The rich may get richer not only economically but also environmentally. For example, because their wealth affords them greater choice of location, the wealthy may be protected from heat by living ogn large, treed lots. By contrast, the poor may be forced to live on inner-city "heat islands" due to the absence of trees and the presence of paved surfaces that absorb and radiate solar energy.[15] This situation can mean that the effects of global warming are experienced more miserably by the poor.

As observed by Pope Francis in his 2015 encyclical *Laudato Si'*, the devastation caused by climate change falls most heavily on the poor. Throughout the encyclical he points but "intimate relationship between the poor and the fragility of the planet."[16] He documents the unequal effects with several examples, including atmospheric pollution.[17] Therefore the work that cities do to address environmental risk can also have a positive effect on social equality.

The vulnerability of the poor to climate change is addressed by the United Nations in the Cities and Climate Change initiative, which supports cities in developing nations in assessing their vulnerability to climate change.[18] For example, the CCI's work in cities located in Burkina Faso, Nepal, and Sri Lanka included not only strengthening climate resilience, reducing greenhouse gas emissions and protecting the environment, but also ensuring food security and supporting of livelihoods.[19]

Economic Issues (Including Social Equity)

Every year, city governments must approve a budget for the following fiscal year. Because the budget will include a millage rate that directly affects how much citizens will pay in taxes, the budget is often a very public event, with outcry over tax rates. Also, the addition or elimination of specific programs or services can generate public comment. A city with excellent budgetary reporting might report each expenditure by indicating not only the budget amount, but also the purpose, justification (citing the city's comprehensive plan), and duration of the expenditure (see Box 1.1).[20]

Box 1.1: Sample Explanation of a Green Purchase Line Item in City Budget
Environmental Improvements
   Budget: $250,000
   Purpose: Purchase and install wet dust collector for the tripper floor area on JTEC Unit 2.
   Justification: These projects are required to comply with operating permits and environmental regulations and are needed to improve safety of our employees in the plants that have been problematic in the past. (*Strategies 3.1 Responsibility and 3.3 Environmental Awareness)
   Duration: Most of the purchase of the wet dust collector will have occurred in 2020. The final purchase and installation cost will occur in 2021.
   SOURCE: *2021 Operating Budget,* City Utilities, Springfield, Missouri (2020).
   https://www.cityutilities.net/wp-content/uploads/cu-budget-proposed.pdf
   *References are to the City Utilities Strategic Plan

Budgetary line items affect quality of life and do merit this level of meaningful reporting, as described here. Yet as important as budgets are, they should not distract attention from the larger issue of long-term city solvency. Municipal governments need to understand the economic drivers of their city so they can promote financial health – both for their citizens and for the city that serves them.

Clearly, it is in the city's interest to have a tax base – whether this comes from individuals who are employed and/or retired, or from businesses. A city will build its tax base by levying taxes on the income, assets, and/or purchases of citizens and businesses. These taxes enable cities to provide services such as police, fire, and emergency services (including COVID arrangements), as well as infrastructure support such as water, sewer, and roads. Another important use of taxes – and one closely associated with sustainability – is historic preservation and environmental conservation especially through the purchase and support of open natural spaces for conservation and recreation. In some cases, the tax revenue generated by a new development is not enough to pay for the ongoing public services the development requires. This so-called cost of growth needs to be calculated so that developers pay an impact fee.

Municipal tax bases vary widely. One city may depend on tourism; another on a local factory; yet another on the wealth of retirees. Understanding such economic dependencies is crucial to a city's economic sustainability. At the same time, city leaders must anticipate trends. While in the current economy, much work is via internet, in many places residents still need nearby brick-and-mortar jobs. Not every city can attract residents who are retired or who work remotely.

Reducing Tax Burden

In cities with rising property values, it takes determination to keep taxes flat, as the rising values provide a rationale for increasing taxes. The property tax amount for each property (also called the ad valorem tax) is the result of multiplying the assessed value of the property times the millage rate, which is how many dollars per $1,000 in assessed value will be charged. So, for example, if the millage rate is 5.0, this means that the ad valorem tax is $5 per thousand, so on a $200,000 property the tax would be $1,000. If the millage rate stays the same while property values go up, then taxes go up – a trend called tax creep.

To avoid tax creep, property appraisers in some jurisdictions also calculate a rollback millage rate that will cause taxes to be flat. For example, if the property in the above example is now appraised as being worth $220,000, the rollback millage rate would have to be reduced to 4.545 to keep taxes at $1,000. (For more on rollback rates, see Chapter5.)

Reconciling Private Property with the Public Good

"Property rights" is a value often invoked by landowners and developers pushing back against conservation ordinances in cities undergoing hyperdevelopment. The claim that property rights are sacred is often backed by constitutional arguments in countries where the founding legal documents uphold such rights. A different perspective is offered by Pope Francis in his newest encyclical, *Fratelli Tutti* (October 2020).

> The right to private property can only be considered a secondary natural right, derived from the principle of the universal destination of created goods. This has concrete consequences that ought to be reflected in the workings of society. Yet it often happens that secondary rights displace primary and overriding rights, in practice making them irrelevant.[21]

The economy of a town or city, much like its natural environment, is a complex adaptive system composed of many elements. As town and city leaders assess the strength of their economy, they need to understand city financial statements, but also see the big picture – the "macro economy," if you will.

Accounting for City Finances

Many (but not all) aspects of a city's economic information will be included in the financial statements of the town or city. These must follow accounting rules for the home country. Here is a brief discussion of global standards followed by an example of US standards.

International Public Sector Accounting Standards

Accounting theorists have long advocated for a single framework for public sector accounting based on accrual methods of accounting. The result is a body of literature supporting International Public Sector Accounting Standards (IPSAS). Unlike national or regional standards, however, these standards are not generated by a particular institution with accountability and transparency, but rather exist as a series of academic articles. Unless and until these standards are adopted by some official body, they are primarily important as a guide for accounting authorities in the process of setting standards.[22]

US Government Accounting Standards

In the US, the federal, state, and local governments must follow the accounting standards of the Government Accounting Standards Board (GASB). The main standards in the US for city government accounting are the National Council on Governmental Accounting (NCGA) Statement 1, *Governmental Accounting and Financial Reporting Principles*, as amended, and GASB *Statement No. 34, Basic Financial Statements – and Management's Discussion and Analysis – for State and Local Governments*, as amended.[23]

In use now for more than two decades, this standard revolutionized municipal accounting by requiring reporting of infrastructure as its own category of asset, by requiring a management discussion and analysis to preface the financial statements, and by introducing a separate reporting protocol for government activities (showing revenues and costs for taxes and city services) versus enterprise funds (showing revenues and costs for business-type activities such as public golf courses, publicly-owned marinas, and the like).

Some financial statement preparers and users have complained that the information in the separate fund statements was too short term and focused on financial resources rather than economic resources.[24] From mid-2020 to mid-2021 the GASB worked on updating these standards by studying financial reporting in 465 cities. In 2020, GASB issued a 258-page exposure draft, *Sample Reporting Model Improvements*, detailing possible changes to government accounting and asking for comments.[25]

The 2020 GASB exposure draft includes a sample municipal report that includes *Selected Notes to the Financial Statements*. Such notes can be helpful to city leaders and activists in understanding the meaning behind the main financial statement (the statement of net position, or the balance sheet), which gives the value of "Capital Assets" (see Box 1.2).

Box 1.2: Sample City's Net Position

Table A-1
Sample City's Net Position
(in thousands of dollars, rounded)

	Governmental Activities		Business-Type Activities		Total		Total Percentage Change
	20×5	20×4	20×5	20×4	20×5	20×4	20×5-20×4
Current and other assets	$ 849,249	$ 760,540	$ 96,025	$ 100,640	$ 945,274	$ 861,180	9.8%
Capital assets	1,845,379	1,781,939	576,876	566,000	2,422,255	2,347,939	3.2%
Total assets	2,694,628	2,542,479	672,901	666,640	3,367,529	3,209,119	4.9%
Deferred outflows of resources	89,902	70,018	3,994	3,130	93,896	73,148	28.4%
Long-term liabilities	975,103	922,831	103,694	104,502	1,078,797	1,027,333	5.0%
Other liabilities	40,321	46,197	23,601	24,955	63,922	71,162	-10.2%
Total liabilities	1,015,424	969,028	127,295	129,467	1,142,719	1,098,495	4.0%
Deferred inflows of resources	35,295	27,322	1,204	1,226	36,499	28,548	27.9%
Net position							
Net investment in capital assets	1,216,106	1,209,700	489,610	474,914	1,705,716	1,684,614	1.3%
Restricted	734,441	711,690	17,514	14,985	751,955	726,675	3.5%
Unrestricted	(216,736)	(305,243)	41,272	49,178	(175,464)	(256,065)	31.5%
Total net position	$ 1,733,811	$ 1,616,147	$ 548,396	$ 539,077	$ 2,282,207	$ 2,155,224	5.9%

Source:https://gasb.org/jsp/GASB/Document_C/DocumentPage?cid=1176174965673&acceptedDisclaimer=true

As Box 1.2 shows, the assets are not broken out by type. Notes are needed for that. A good example of an explanatory note is the report's "Illustrative Disclosure of Information About Capital Assets," breaking out assets by type such as "land" and "buildings." Such a breakdown enables city leaders and citizens to see just exactly how much valuable real estate their city owns (see Box 1.3).

Box 1.3: Illustrative Disclosure of Information about a City's Capital Assets

SELECTED NOTES TO FINANCIAL STATEMENTS

Note 1—Illustrative Disclosure of Information about Capital Assets

Capital asset activity for the year ended June 30, 20X5, was as follows (in thousands):

	Primary Government			
	Beginning Balance	Increases	Decreases	Ending Balance
Governmental activities:				
Capital assets not being deprciated:*				
Land and improvements	$ 544,021	$ 27,652	$ —	$ 571,673
Construction in progress	182,756	145,861	(182,676)	145,941
Total capital assets not being depreciated	726,777	173,513	(182,676)	717,614
Depreciable capital assets:				
Building and improvements	318,405	20,981	(111)	339,275
Vehicles and equipment	208,460	13,677	(1,099)	221,038
Infrastructure	3,448,611	106,388	(3,456)	3,551,543
Leases—vehicles and equipment	12,986	—	—	12,986
Total depreciable capital assets at historical cost	3,988,462	141,048	(4.666)	4,124,842
Less accumulated depreciation/amortization for:				
Building and improvements	(146,913)	(8,134)	111	(154,936)
Vehicles and equipment	(133,953)	(13,134)	852	(146,235)
Infrastructure	(2,651,137)	(45,535)	3,360	(2,693,312)
Leases—vehicles and equipment	(1,297)	(1,297)	—	(2,594)
Total accumulated depreciation/amortization	(2,933,300)	(68,100)	4.323	(2,997,077)
Other capital assets. net	1,055,162	72,946	(343)	1,127,765
Governmental activities capital assets. net	$ 1,781,939	$246,459	$ (183,019)	$1,845,379

⊤Depreciation/amortization expense was charged to functions as follows:

Governmental activities:		
General government	$	1,132
Public safety		9,298
Public works, which includes the depreciation of infrastructure		51,284
Social and economic development		1,013
Culture and recreation		4,958
In addition, depreciation on capital assets held by the City's internal service funds (see Exhibit 8) is charged to the varous functions based on their usage of the assets.		415
Total geovernmenta; activities depreciation/amortization expense	$	68,100

Source:https://gasb.org/jsp/GASB/Document_C/DocumentPage?cid=1176174965673&ac ceptedDisclaimer=true

Notes about assets can be as detailed as the municipality wishes.

The astute guardian of city value will know – or learn – the location of the assets in question, and work to safeguard and maintain them. For example, the illustrative note shown in Box 1.3 discloses amounts for land, infrastructure, and buildings. Members of the city council or the general public can request more detail if needed – for example, location and condition of these assets.

The Big Economic Picture

Clearly, based on the above examples of municipal accounting, a city's financial reports contain valuable clues to the economic vitality of a city. But it is also true that financial statements do not tell the whole story. For a real economic analysis, one must go beyond accounting statements and conduct analysis. Environmentalist Martin Westerman, writing on "The Value of Green Urban Assets and the True Cost of Development," proposes a "soft asset" value system that values the natural assets in green spaces, to offset the "hard asset" approach that only looks at land and buildings.[26] The Seattle Green Spaces Coalition has calculated that "natural capital" – which is not treated as an asset under municipal accounting – provides more than $3 billion a year in benefits and savings to the city.[27]

Engineering Issues

Engineering needs underlie the day-to-day needs of every city.

Roads and bridges. Every town or city has means to enter and exit, so roads and bridges deserve key consideration. For larger municipalities, public transit may be an issue, and the city may have a dedicated commission to develop policies and resources.[28] Here intergovernmental coordination comes into play because municipalities may contain thoroughfares that are owned and maintained by higher-level government entities such as counties, states, or federal governments. The average locality spends only about 4 percent of its budget on roads and bridges.[29] This level is fairly low because within any city or town, there can be roads that classify as county, state, or federal roadways. Also, contiguous municipalities may have formal agreements to cooperate on roads.[30] City leaders and activists concerned about roads in their communities need to determine jurisdiction before taking action. When it comes to roads, intergovernmental coordination will be an essential area of any policy.

Trash collection and recycling. Some cities collect taxes for waste disposal and recycling services as direct suppliers or as agents. Other cities leave it up to citizens to find their own waste management services. In all cases, however, the city typically has a say in the type and frequency of recycling that will occur in city boundaries. This is a hot topic globally, since under its National Sword Policy, China has restricted its purchases of recycled material.[31] The two main approaches in recent decades have been single stream, where the consumer puts all recyclables into one bin and the vendor does the sorting; and dual stream, where the consumer separates out types of recyclables. There are pros and cons to each approach, says a recent report the Solid Waste Association of North America's Applied Research Foundation.[32]

Sanitation/sewer. Sanitation systems have tremendous importance to cities – often defining a city's map. Where a city's sewage system ends, the city's boundaries may end, with annexation into the city being the only way to access a sewer system. Design of such systems requires a long-term mindset. As the Stockholm Environmental Institute (SEI, in Stockholm, Sweden) has stated, "Few urban infrastructure decisions cast as long a shadow as designing a sewerage network." A current design issue for cities involves single source versus dual source sanitation streams.

Water. The United Nations has recognized water as a basic human right, and as the subject of one of its sustainable development goals.[33] City water quality can affect public health, which is why health authorities address the issue as part of their mandates.[34] Engineering as well as economic issues play a critical role in the delivery of safe drinking water, as the well-known example of Flint, Michigan, shows.[35] When an auditor for the city projected a $25 million deficit for the city, the state took over the city's finances. Intending to increase revenues to its water fund, the state began to build a pipeline to the city from Lake Huron. While the pipeline was under construction, the state and city turned to the Flint River as a source, generating complaints about water quality, which had deteriorated for two main reasons. First, the river was polluted. Second, the state and city failed to add an anticorrosive chemical to the water supply, which allowed metal from the iron and lead pipes to leech into the already polluted water supply.

Utilities (as a group). In a typical accounting case, a city will have a separate utilities fund. The utilities in question may be electricity, gas, sewer, and/ or water depending on whether the city has its own services or outsources. No matter what kind of utilities a city provides, it is important to communicate with voters concerning the reliability and pricing of services. A good example is the Springfield, Missouri, utilities function, which covers a wide range of utilities.[36] The *2021 Operating Budget* of the city of Springfield, Missouri (approved by Board of Public Utilities and a City Council as required by Illinois law) states the purpose for the city utilities function in Springfield (see Box 1.4). City utility functions looking to improve their communications to customers can employ this kind of language. (See also the discussion earlier in this chapter of how Springfield Utilities communicates budgetary line items to stakeholders.)

Box 1.4: Sample Disclosure for a City's Utilities Fund

"City Utilities' planning process is deliberate with a focus on enabling sustainable financial strength while safely providing reliable services at the lowest possible long-term costs for customers. The process is dynamic and incorporates the impact of changing variables such as customer demands, fuel prices, regulatory changes, and the economic climate . . . .

Capital improvements are necessary to maintain and rehabilitate aging infrastructure in order to provide safe and reliable services to our existing customers, to prepare for future demand, and to meet environmental and regulatory requirements."

Source: *2021 Operating Budget,* City Utilities, Springfield, Missouri (2020). https://www.cityutilities.net/wp-content/uploads/cu-budget-proposed.pdf

---

Setting Priorities

Local governments and residents today clearly face a range of environmental, economic, and engineering issues. Individuals who are new to the role of public servant or activist must maintain awareness of all of them to be effective. Some may find it useful to create a checklist of risks and solutions. They may wish to use a global checklist like the one developed by LEED (see Appendix 3: LEED-ND Scoring Tool at the end of this book). Or they may wish to create one of their own, as shown in Box 1.5.

Box 1.5: Customizable Template for Ranking City Risks/Solutions

Rate the importance of the following risks and check all viable solutions:

ENVIRONMENT

Flooding HIGH MEDIUM LOW
- Develop/improve storm management system
- Add/repair storm walls
- Other

Loss of trees, wetlands, dunes and/or wildlife HIGH MEDIUM LOW
- Revise key city documents[37] to preserve natural habitat
- Map and protect wildlife corridors
- Other

Poor air quality
- Revise key city documents to improve ratio of conservation and recreation land use to other land use
- Pass ordinances affecting operations of local manufacturers
- Other

Other Environmental Risks/Solutions

_____
—
_____

ECONOMY AND SOCIAL EQUITY
High rate of failure for local small businesses
- Review, reduce costs of permits
- Review, reduce regulations
- Other

Lack of affordable housing HIGH MEDIUM LOW
- Revise key city documents to require set asides for affordable housing
- Develop partnership with Habitat for Humanity
- Other

Underfunded pension funds HIGH MEDIUM LOW
- Improve investment strategy for better ROI
- Increase level of employee contributions
- Other

Other Economic/Social Risks/Solutions

_____
—
_____

ENGINEERING
Limited or Aging Public Facilities HIGH MEDIUM LOW
- Repair/replace police station/s
- Repair/replace fire house/s
- Other

Limited or Aging Transportation Infrastructure HIGH MEDIUM LOW
- Build/repair sidewalks and/or bike paths
- Build/repair streets and/or bridges
- Other

Limited or Aging Sanitation System HIGH MEDIUM LOW
- Replace/repair sewage pipes
- Increase septic to sewer conversions
- Other

Other Engineering Risks/Solutions

_____
—
_____

Source: Alexandra R. Lajoux ©2021.

There are advantages to both global and local sustainability checklists. As the American Planning Association has noted, "National, international, and NGO indicators, checklists, and metrics help allow easy comparisons with national and international norms, especially for larger communities," and further, "More interesting, and most important, are the indicators, checklists, and metrics that judge how a community is implementing its own sustainability planning. These measures should help identify how the community rates on measures of community health as defined by its residents in terms that they can understand – and if collected over time, they can allow for longitudinal comparisons."[38]

Concluding Reflections

Focus on issues in the order that they are killing you.

Anonymous

City leaders and activists share the awesome responsibility of making their local communities a better place to live. The first step in doing so is awareness of the most critical local environmental, economic, and engineering issues – the subject of this chapter. But awareness alone is not enough. The next step in ensuring municipal sustainability is assessment – or mapping. Exactly what assets does a local community have and where are they located? This is the subject of the following chapter.

Notes

1 The Brundtland Commission, led by Gro Harlem Brundtland, former prime minister of Norway, produced the *Report of the World Commission on Environment and Development: Our Common Future* (United Nations, 1987), which was issued in Brundtland, Belgium. https://digitallibrary.un.org/record/139811
2 Durability is a key value in civil engineering. See Halperin, et alia, Building for Infrastructure Durability, Construction Specifier, June 5, 2020. https://www.constructionspecifier.com/building-for-infrastructure-durability/
3 Emiko Kusakabe, "Advancing sustainable development at the local level: The case of *machizukuri* in Japanese cities," *Progress in Planning*, February 2013: 1–65. The author explains: "*Machi* literally means a local community and its physical setting, and *zukuri* means the act of making with care. . . *machizukuri* has the positive connotation of residents building their own living environment, reflecting their own values and lifestyles, and is seen as a radical departure from the conventional centralised, top–down, 'civil engineering' approach of Japanese urban planning. . . ." https://www.sciencedirect.com/science/article/pii/S0305900612000803. See

also https://www.researchgate.net/publication/333443175_Planning_Urban_Futures_With_Refer ence_to_Sustainable_Cities

4 Nigel Arnell, et al., "Global and regional impacts of climate change at different levels of global temperature," *Climatic Change 155,* July 2019: 13. https://www.researchgate.net/publica tion/333017679_Global_and_regional_impacts_of_climate_change_at_different_levels_of_ global_temperature

5 US Regional Effects, https://climate.nasa.gov/effects/

6 Fourth National Climate Assessment | GlobalChange.gov

7 The following regional descriptions are based on the NASA source, with occasional examples provided by the author. It is beyond the scope of this chapter to explain the diverse and interconnected effects of climate change, but the reader is referred to sources such as the following: Climate Science and Effects | USDA.

8 Heavy rain in the spring causes a delay in planting, and extreme moisture can weaken root systems. See Unique challenges and opportunities for northeastern US crop production in a changing climate | SpringerLink.

9 Northeast | US Climate Resilience Toolkit.

10 https://floridadep.gov/sites/default/files/CRI_AAA_Planning_Guidebook_for_Florida% 27s_Local_Government.pdf

11 City of Houston – Recovery from Hurricane Harvey (houstontx.gov).

12 See "Streamflow and the Water Cycle," US Geological Survey, https://www.usgs.gov/special-topic/water-science-school/science/streamflow-and-water-cycle?qt-science_center_objects=0#qt-science_center_objects

13 https://nca2018.globalchange.gov/downloads/NCA4_2018_FullReport.pdf, p.150.

14 Two-higg Bennett et al., "The Health Benefits of the Great Outdoors," *Environmental Research 166* (October 2018): 628–637. https://www.sciencedirect.com/science/article/pii/S0013935118303323?via%3Dihub

15 https://www.nytimes.com/interactive/2019/08/09/climate/city-heat-islands.html

16 Laudato Si' Introduction, Paragraph 16. http://www.vatican.va/content/francesco/en/en cyclicals/documents/papa-francesco_20150524_enciclica-laudato-si.html

17 "Exposure to atmospheric pollutants produces a broad spectrum of health hazards, especially for the poor, and causes millions of premature deaths." Laudato Si' Chapter 1, Paragraph 20. http://www.vatican.va/content/francesco/en/encyclicals/documents/papa-francesco_20150524_enciclica-laudato-si.html

18 https://unhabitat.org/programme/cities-and-climate-change-initiative

19 https://unhabitat.org/programme/cities-and-climate-change-initiative

20 https://www.cityutilities.net/wp-content/uploads/cu-budget.pdf

21 Fratelli Tutti, http://www.vatican.va/content/francesco/en/encyclicals/documents/papa-francesco_20201003_enciclica-fratelli-tutti.html

22 Lisa Schmidthuber, Dennis Hilgers, and Sebastian Hofmann "International Public Sector Accounting Standards (IPSASs): A systematic literature review and future research agenda," *Financial Accountability and Management: In Governments, Public Services, and Charities*, June 24, 2020. https://onlinelibrary.wiley.com/doi/full/10.1111/faam.1226v

23 https://www.gasb.org/st/summary/gstsm34.html

24 https://gasb.org/jsp/GASB/Document_C/DocumentPage?cid=1176174965673&acceptedDis claimer=true, pp. 24, and 52.

25 Financial Reporting Model Improvements (June 2020). https://gasb.org/jsp/GASB/Docu ment_C/DocumentPage?cid=1176174965673&acceptedDisclaimer=true

26 Martin Westerman, "The Value of Green Urban Assets and the True Costs pf Development," *The Nature of Cities*, August 12, 2020. https://www.thenatureofcities.com/2020/08/12/the-value-of-green-urban-assets-and-the-true-costs-of-development/

27 Ibid.

28 For a sample engineering checklist from such a commission, see https://catc.ca.gov/-/media/ctc-media/documents/programs/atp/workshops/feb-10-2020/engr-checklist-attach-b-ally.pdf

29 "Highway and Road Expenditures," https://www.urban.org/policy-centers/cross-center-initiatives/state-and-local-finance-initiative/state-and-local-backgrounders/highway-and-road-expenditures#Question2Highway

30 For an example of an inter-municipal agreement among three townships in the form of an ordinance, see Township of Lower Nazareth, Northampton County, Pennsylvania, Ordinance No. 226-07-18. https://lowernazareth.com/pdf/forms/Ord%20226-07-18%20-%20Intergovern mental%20Cooperation%20Agreement.pdf

31 https://www.epa.nsw.gov.au/your-environment/recycling-and-reuse/response-to-china-national-sword

32 https://www.biocycle.net/swana-report-analyzes-curbside-recycling-options/

33 https://www.un.org/en/sections/issues-depth/water/

34 In the US, see the water resources at the Centers for Disease Control and Prevention, "Importance of Quarter Quality and Testing," https://www.cdc.gov/healthywater/drinking/pub lic/water_quality.html; and "Policy and Recommendations," https://www.cdc.gov/healthy water/drinking/policy.html

35 "Flint Water Crisis Fast Facts," CNN, October 14, 2020. https://www.cnn.com/2016/03/04/us/flint-water-crisis-fast-facts/index.html

36 "The term 'public utilities' by way of description, but not as a limitation, shall include electric systems (and appurtenant steam heating apparatus and piping), gas systems, water systems, transit systems, and public communications systems (including all plants, apparatus, equipment, and distribution facilities related to any such system), or any other service or facility commonly considered to be a public utility or so declared to be by any statute, ordinance or court decision." https://library.municode.com/mo/springfield/codes/code_of_ordinances?no deId=PTICICH_ARTXVIBOPUUT_S16.8BUPR

37 Key city documents would include the Comprehensive Plan, Land Development Code, and Future Land Use Map.

38 American Planning Association, *Assessing Sustainability: A Guide for Local Governments* https://www.cityofpa.us/DocumentCenter/View/7378/PAS-Report-565

Chapter 2
Mapping Your Municipality: Identifying Key Environmental Assets

Municipal leaders, both elected and appointed, can play an important role as stewards of the key assets in their communities – ranging from the assets that are accounted for in city financial statements to those that lie outside traditional financial reporting, such as natural resources. Through ordinances, resolutions, and policies, cities and towns have the power to protect the resources that matter most to their people. Local activists can also play a stewardship role by monitoring the safety of specific assets, and by sounding an alarm when they are under threat.

In many cities, however, awareness of such key assets comes in fits and starts. In some cities, assets may be valued only after they are gone – as communal grief sets in over the environmental, cultural, and architectural loss when an old farmhouse on expansive acreage gives way to a mini-mall. Many communities recognize only in retrospect that they could have done more to protect their heritage.

Inventory

The best approaches begin with an inventory: the first step in protecting a municipalities' assets is to identify them. Some cities, such as Madrid in Spain, have invested in the identification of their assets and have created means to track their status. In Madrid, an IBM technology platform called Madrid iNTeligente (MiNT) – Smarter Madrid – is used for this purpose. The platform tracks the 5 million assets owned by the city.[1] While most of these are traditional material assets, such as traffic lights and fire hydrants, the technology can include assets such as heritage trees. Some cities use citizen advisory groups to help them track and protect city assets.[2]

So, what are a city's key assets? Some of them, such as cash on hand or government buildings, can be listed on a balance sheet. Other assets exist outside the realm of traditional accounting – such as a river flowing through town, a centuries-old oak tree, or the collective cultural memories of longtime residents.

One particularly useful tool for thinking about a city's assets is the list of 162 City Indicators created by 2thinknow, a think tank founded by Christopher Hire. The Index, which measures "conditions for innovation" has resulted in rankings for 500 major cities around the world.[3] Even smaller cities and towns can benefit

https://doi.org/10.1515/9783110689860-002

from matching themselves against the Index. It features a wealth of items municipal leaders can consider as they serve in their guardian roles (see Box 2.1).

Box 2.1: Environmental Assets as Indicators for Innovation
According to 2thinknow.com
From "Cultural Assets"
Air cleanliness. Measuring the city air cleanliness, and potential for air quality in each geography.
Nature. Natural environmental assets such as beaches, parks, wetlands, which may affect life quality, and drive tourism/eco-tourism.
Public green areas. Measuring city park protection, and natural and wildlife preservation areas within immediate metropolitan area and inner-city.
Water features. The major water features in terms of importance (e.g., major river), range of amenity, and cleanliness.
From "Human Infrastructure"
Public water supply. Water supply quality and purity, and process of water supply
From "Networked Markets"
Physical location. How favorable is the geographic position of the city, and how favorable is the traditional geographic features?
Source: 2thinknow – 162 Indicators 2thinknow – Innovation Cities™ Index (innovationcities.com)

The index element "Nature" covers many assets, including the ones covered in this chapter, from dunes to wildlife. It can be valuable to account for these in some detail. A helpful tool in this regard is the green mapping done in 65 countries by adherents of the greenmapping movement[4] (for a checklist using Greenmap Icons, see Figure 2.1: Green Checklist).

Green Checklist

☐ Dunes	☐ Sidewalks	☐ Reservoirs
☐ Forests	☐ Parks	☐ Rivers
☐ Trees	☐ Recreation	☐ Watersheds
☐ Medians	☐ Open Space	☐ Wetlands
☐ Roadsides	☐ Lakes/Ponds	☐ Wildlife

Figure 2.1: Green Checklist.
Source: Concept by Alexandra R. Lajoux. Art by Chris Smith, quarternative.com

Of course, not all assets can be protected forever. Some depreciate due to the passage of time or acts of nature. And there can be tradeoffs between and among assets – for example, the tradeoff between the need to increase the amount of cash held in a special reserve fund for marina repairs versus the need to purchase scenic land to prevent it from being developed. Such choices are not always easy. This said, however, community leaders do have a responsibility for identifying and locating the assets that most matter to their communities, and for developing policies that protect them in a sustainable manner.

This chapter will identify some possible categories of environmental assets and help leaders learn how to assess their location, condition, and value to the community. This chapter will also make occasional reference to economic and engineering assets, as these categories intersect. For example, the key economic assets of many municipalities (often accounted for through enterprise funds) include airports, convention centers, golf courses, marinas, museums, ports, and utilities (water and sewer). These are all ways for cities to make money, to be financially sustainable, yet their value is not merely financial. They can also have tremendous environmental value. A golf course may be the only open space in a community, for example (see Box 2.2).

Box 2.2: Beacon Hill's Gas Lights
Sometimes the efforts to preserve key municipal assets can clash.

For example, an inventory of Boston's cultural assets might include the colonial-style gas lamps on Beacon Hill, which have been in place for nearly half a century. Some residents want to preserve them. "The gas lights are just as important as the brick sidewalks, which are as important as our quiet streets, and our little cute alleyways here and there," opined Robert Whitney, chair of the Beacon Hill Civic Association, speaking to the *Boston Globe* in November 2020.[5]

At the same time, however, an inventory of Boston's environmental assets might include the trees on these same streets, which some residents claim is being harmed by the infrastructure for the gas lamps. "Gas leaks have either killed or severely weakened the 16 trees planted the same year as the gas lamps were installed on Temple Street (1977)," said 32 citizens in an open letter.

The City of Boston seeks a compromise: "The Public Works Street Lighting Division is currently in the exploratory phase to locate ideal locations that would maintain the character of the existing lights while also reducing overall maintenance costs and improving the carbon footprint," a spokesman for the Public Works Department told the *Globe*.

Ecosystems

The most valuable assets for many municipalities are their natural assets – such as a seashore in a small beach community, a central park in a major city, or a wetland that serves as a scenic bird sanctuary on the edge of a small town. These are dynamic ecological contributions to a city – ones that can be valued through a technique called "ecosystem services valuation."[6] Adding the estimated economic value of all these assets together for the entire planet, a team of economists led by Robert Costanza once estimated their value to be in the trillions[7] – amounting to nearly $54 trillion in 2020 dollars.[8] For a large city, the value can be in the billions. The Seattle Green Spaces Coalition estimates its own natural capital to be worth some $3 billion.[9]

In some cases, the town or city may own the assets. In other cases, the assets may be protected by a higher authority such as state or federal law. And in yet other instances, the assets may be under private ownership, which may or may not have restrictions on use via easement or ordinance. But no matter what their status, all these assets – whether protected by statute, and whether owned publicly or privately – need to be recognized so that a municipality can strive to protect them from damage or loss.

Environmental or geographic assets can be mapped – literally. One good way to map natural assets is a geographic information system (GIS). Such a system can collect, store, and manage the geographic (spatial) data in a particular location, such as a city.[10] GIS technology can be used to create story maps that identify natural assets and show vulnerability – for example, wildfire risk in the wildland-urban interface.[11] Cities and citizens who wish to set or advocate for policies to protect natural assets can use GIS systems to account for their existence. For some examples of GIS in use, see Box 2.3.

Box 2.3: GIS in Use: The US Geological Survey (USGS)

USGS is a primary source of geographic information system (GIS) data used by municipalities and others. USGS uses a variety of formats, including The National Map, Earth Explorer, GloVIS, and LandsatLook. Here are just a few examples out of hundreds:

Hydraulic Conditions (Draught) Network for New York State[12]

The National Map Viewer[13]

National Biogeographic Map[14]

Principal Aquifers of the US[15]

The following sections of this chapter describe the environmental assets that might be considered in an inventory aided by GIS, story maps, or otherwise.

Dunes

Sand dunes at the borders of seacoast cities provide an important environmental value as a buffer against storm surge from oceans. Naturally formed dunes are worth preserving and manmade dunes are often worth building. A municipality can exercise eminent domain to build a dune. A case in point is the Borough of

Harvey Cedars in New Jersey, which won a protracted legal battle to do so in the aftermath of Hurricane Sandy.[16] The state's acting attorney called the case "an important outcome for the citizens of New Jersey, for our precious natural resources along the coast, and for the rebuilding of our Jersey shore communities."[17]

To preserve dunes, cities can take several actions, including the following:[18]

1. Plant dune vegetation.[19]
2. Install fencing.[20]
3. Build and maintain beach crossovers and/or walkways.

Implementation should align with state and national laws.[21]

Forests and Trees

Many of the world's forests span geographic areas well outside the reaches of cities or towns – aka "unincorporated" areas. Yet some do have woodlands within or surrounding their borders – often called "urban forests."

Despite their ecological and economic benefits, forests often fall prey to clear-cutting for development – a phenomenon known as deforestation. The most well-known example of deforestation is taking place in the Amazon in Brazil,[22] but other continents are affected by the phenomenon. Some nonprofit groups engage in public education campaigns to increase public knowledge about the value of trees – and even specific types of trees. In America, there is the American Chestnut Foundation,[23] which has won an award for public education.[24]

Even when cities do not have forests, they can preserve and plant trees, which have distinct economic value for cities, as mentioned earlier.[25]

If cities want to preserve the trees within their borders, they need to be proactive in conserving them through urban forestry – managing trees inside and bordering cities to optimize their ecological, economic, and social benefits. Trees in cities require protection. As noted by the United Nations, "Many urban trees may have established naturally, although in an environment in which competition for land is high, they are unlikely to survive long unless actively cultivated and managed."[26] For Tree City USA standards, see Appendix 6.

The resistance against deforestation can involve many parties, including national governments, state governments, municipalities, tribal governments, and the philanthropic sector. As a good example of successful resistance, consider the Ekuri Initiative organized for the New Ekuri village in Nigeria.

The Ekuri Initiative was launched by tribal leaders to protect the forest from being compromised by a superhighway. For this people, the forest has been a source for medicinal plants, water for drinking and washing; vegetables, fruits, and seeds for food; and other products such as timber for housing and furniture. The initiative, which was supported by the Ford Foundation, started with a mapping of the forest to determine its size and boundaries. The plan then created different zones, including a protected area, a stream buffer zone, an animal movement corridor, a nontimber forest product zone, and an ecotourism area.[27]

In cities that have been affected by deforestation, city governments can direct resources to planting trees. Belfast, North Ireland; Tokyo, Japan; and Washington, DC, are notable in this regard. Although none of these three cities appear in the World Economic Forum's ranking for the top 20 most forested cities in the world (see Box 2.4), their histories remain impressive according to one account from the World Resources Institute.[28] In 1872 the governor of the District of Columbia ordered the planting of 60,000 trees; today the city has some 2 million trees.[29] Following World War II, the City of Tokyo had only 7,000 street trees, but by 1980 that number had increased to 235,000.[30] The city of Belfast created a Forest of Belfast by planting 200,000 trees following the Troubles of 1998.

BOX 2.4: Urban Forests
The 20 Most Forested Cities in the World
Showing percentage of land with trees
1. Tampa, Florida – 36.1%
2. Singapore – 29.3%
3. Oslo, Norway – 28.8%
4. Vancouver, Canada – 25.9%
5. Sydney, Australia – 25.9%
6. Montreal, Canada – 25.5%
7. Durban, South Africa – 23.7%
8. Johannesburg, South Africa – 23.6%
9. Sacramento, California – 23.6%
10. Frankfurt, Germany – 21.5%
11. Geneva, Switzerland – 21.4%
12. Amsterdam, Netherlands – 20.6%
13. Seattle, Washington – 20%
14. Toronto, Canada – 19.5%
15. Miami, Florida – 19.4%
16. Boston, Massachusetts – 18.2%
17. Tel Aviv, Israel – 17.5%
18. Turin, Italy – 16.2%
19. Los Angeles, California – 15.2%
20. Buenos Aires – 14.5%
Source: World Economic Forum https://www.weforum.org/agenda/2018/03/the-12-cities-with-the-most-trees-around-the-world. Also "Exploring the Green Canopy in Cities Around the World." http://senseable.mit.edu/treepedia/

Medians, Roadsides, and Sidewalks

Median strips and roadsides are another type of city asset worth cultivating. While the amount of land they involve is minor, they play an important role in the safe mobility of citizens by separating roadways going in opposite directions, and by providing a midway point for pedestrians travelling or crossing along busy roads. Medians and roadsides also play an important aesthetic role, supporting grass, flowers, bushes, and/or trees. Medians and roadsides may be under municipal control, or they may be the responsibility of the state, provincial, or federal government, depending on who controls the roadways. Nonetheless, it is important for city leaders to attend to their condition and act when needed. Municipal leaders should be aware of any policies regarding vegetation and maintenance.[31]

Sidewalks offer an opportunity for innovation in green engineering. While sidewalks themselves are generally required to be made of impermeable materials, they can be part of a "green street" system. In the US, the EPA defines green streets as "stormwater management approach that incorporates vegetation (perennials, shrubs, trees), soil, and engineered systems (e.g., permeable pavements) to slow, filter, and cleanse stormwater runoff from impervious surfaces (e.g., streets, sidewalks)."[32] Furthermore, some municipalities have experimented with permeable pavements, and performance data on these is generally promising, even in cold climates, where freezing can be a problem.[33] Competition for cities as clients is strong. One global company (located in Australia, Canada, and the US) offers a $50,000 "green grant" to cities willing to work with them to improve their urban forests and sidewalks.[34]

Parks, Recreation, and Open Spaces

Many cities and towns devote a considerable amount of their budget to parks (sometimes referred to as open spaces) and recreation, typically combining the two into one department – although there are exceptions.[35] It is important to distinguish between the two. Parks and open spaces refer to land – often the only conserved natural territory in city boundaries. Recreation may occur on some of the open spaces, such as baseball, football, and soccer fields, but it is also associated with recreation centers that include swimming pools, gymnasiums, and fitness rooms.

While these facilities have value for the health of citizens, they can at times conflict with a city's green goals if they take over natural space that is equally important for a city's environmental sustainability (see Box 2.5). Cities that combine parks and recreation do enjoy certain efficiencies when it comes to hybrid elements, such as sport fields (which can be described as both parks and recreation); this said, however, the combination of the two administratively requires a green advocate for the "parks" aspect of the department's work. Given humanity's naturally anthropocentric thinking,[36] "recreation" can dominate "parks" in the typical "parks and recreation" model.

In one case, a city's plan to build a park for recreational purposes ran into citizen resistance. Activists protested the park for reducing tree canopy and endangering wildlife (see Box 2.5).

Box 2.5: Environmental Battles on a Barrier Island

"You win a few, you lose a few," as the old expression goes. That is certainly the case for activists in the City of Fernandina Beach on Amelia Island, which hosts many significant environmental assets, including mature tree canopy throughout the island as well as extensive sand dune systems and river wetlands. Following a period of hyperdevelopment on Amelia Island, groups such as Conserve Amelia Now, Amelia Tree Conservancy, and Nassau County Sierra Club emerged to protest specific development projects on the island, including the City of Fernandina Beach, with a mixed record of success.

Amelia Bluff. In 2019, an administrative challenge to the City of Fernandina Beach and developer of Amelia Bluff failed in court[37] despite litigation support from the Sierra Club. The contested site was located on land designated as conservation land on the City's Future Land Use Map, but the developer made the case that the zoning was due to an error in the Fernandina Beach Future Land Use map.

Racetrack. On the winning side, a 2019 citizen drive to collect hundreds of petitions, accompanied by a massive campaign on social media and numerous speeches at City Hall, succeeded in driving away a planned "autocentric development" to replace the Amelia River golf course, which the City had been leasing to a private company. The developer responded to public backlash by withdrawing his bid. A local businessman took over the lease.

Simmons Park. In 2020, the Fernandina Beach City Commission approved plans to build a park on forested recreation land owned by the City, drawing many protests from the conservation community. The approved site for the park was a wildlife corridor with hundreds of mature trees, and was home to gopher tortoises, which are protected under the Endangered Species Act.[38] Ironically, the City had set up a land conservation trust to purchase private properties and put them into conservation, in part to save trees and protect wildlife. Why, then, was the City planning to develop its own forested land into a park?

Social media lit up with protests, and citizens wrote letters and spoke out against the park at City meetings. The architect reached out to one of the most vocal protesters and asked her to arrange a meeting with environmental activists; she in turn reached out to a senior environmentalist who in turn recruited his network.[39] Working together, the group was able to obtain the proper approvals to reduce the park's footprint, eliminating two detention ponds and saving 47 trees in the process.

Ponds, Lakes, and Reservoirs

A full accounting of a city's environmental assets should include any bodies of water within or bordering the municipality, including ponds, lakes, and reservoirs. A pond is an inland body of water shallow enough to enable photosynthesis for its plant life. A lake is like a pond, but deeper – too deep to support sun-dependent plant life at its bottom. When the city takes control of a natural lake (or builds an artificial lake) for use as a water system, it becomes a reservoir. Of the more than 100,000 lakes in the US, nearly half are artificial.[40] Any lakes used as reservoirs are likely to be recognized on the city's balance sheet as an asset. Natural lakes, by contrast, will not be recognized. But while municipalities may not recognize natural lakes or ponds as assets, they may regulate the quality of their water.

As noted by Christopher Hassall of the University of Leeds, urban ponds can give rise to "conflicting priorities over hydrological, geochemical, ecological, aesthetic, and cultural functions."[41]

A key *hydrological* use for a pond is its use in retaining storm water – hence, the term retention pond. Urban planners often include a second pond to detain extra runoff water, known as a detention pond or dry pond.

In populated areas, ponds can have *geochemical* consequences. Ponds often receive organic and chemical pollutants from various sources ranging from road salts to pesticides, considered to be "synanthropic."

Ecological tradeoffs can occur in pond placement. In awarding construction permits, some authorities require such ponds to compensate for impermeable surface that might cause runoff. But when construction sites include trees that will be cut down to create the ponds, this creates a pond-versus-forest tradeoff. Trees have roots that can absorb storm water as well. Removing them simply to accommodate runoff is not always the best option. Some codes require ponds to complement parking lots, but the reason for that is that parking lots are assumed to be impermeable. For parks that use crushed granite an exemption may be possible.

When it comes to *aesthetics* and *culture*, ponds and lakes are generally considered additive to communities, but this depends on what they replace. In one community, a developer added a viable pond to a community but to do so, the company removed a forest and a mature pond ecosystem (with fish, turtles, and lily pads). To maximize terrain for building, the developer eliminated these and replaced them with buildings, pavement, and a smaller retention pond located to the west. The developer drained the original pond and dug a new one, removing even trees to do so.[42]

Communities need to be aware of the presence of ponds, lakes, and reservoirs so they can take full advantage of their presence and prevent them from being compromised.

Rivers

Rivers constitute a particularly important aspect for municipalities, due to their important legal status as navigable. Their navigability ensures public access, and places them within the reach of federal protection and regulation.[43]

In the US, the Environmental Protection Agency (EPA) and the US Army Corps of Engineers (Army Corps) have Clean Water Act Jurisdiction. They have issued guidance on this jurisdiction based on the US Supreme Court's decisions in *Rapanos v. United States* and *Carabell v. United States*, called the Rapanos-Carabell Guidance.[44] The guidance, which takes into account extensive public commentary,[45] based on commentary from some 66,000 commenters representing a range of stakeholders, affirmed that EPA and the Army Corps will continue to assert jurisdiction over all "waters which are currently used, or were used in the past, or may be susceptible to use in interstate or foreign commerce, including all waters which are subject to the ebb and flow of the tide."[46] The guidance called these "traditional navigable waters," that included all the "navigable waters of the United States," as defined in Title 33 of the Code of Federal Regulations Part 329[47] and by numerous decisions of the federal courts.

In the US, there is a National Organization for Rivers formed to ensure continued public access to rivers. This group has noted that if a river can be navigated – not only by a boat but also by a canoe, kayak, or raft, then by law the right for such navigation is protected. All states (and thus municipalities within them) must hold their navigable rivers in trust to ensure that they offer public benefits such as navigation, recreation, and fishing. As for additional non-navigable streams and rivulets, state standards vary.[48]

Watersheds and Wetlands

Another asset in cities and towns is water in the ground, such as a watershed system or wetland that contributes to the town's water source. As in the case of many environmental assets, city financial authorities rarely if ever claim these natural water sources as assets when it comes to collateral for financing, although in theory they could. As one source opines, "Fossil-fuel industries can report the value of gas, oil and coal assets sitting in the ground, but public utilities cannot account for water in the ground – it counts for zero. While the watershed is a more resilient, less risky asset than water filtration facilities, lenders and bonding agencies look more favorably on financing a potential grey asset than on letting Seattle's water utility to take on debt for financing the real green asset."[49]

Watersheds and wetlands host water differently, but the two are connected within a hydrological system.

A *watershed* is the path for movement of water through waterway, such as streams or creeks and into larger bodies of water such as lakes and oceans. Despite its name, watersheds can run dry.

A *wetland* by contrast is a more stable body of water. Its role is not to move water along but rather give it a place of repose, collecting the water in one location between the watershed and the larger body of water and acting like a filter.

Wetlands are protected under the laws of many nations and in some cases subsidiary jurisdictions – such as states. In the US, some states require the mapping and protection of wetlands, with responsibility falling first on local governments unless they default to higher authorities.[50]

Wildlife

Cities are more likely to count their human populations than the animals they host, but both are important. One of the main reasons to preserve trees, underbrush, dunes, wetlands, and other natural assets described in this chapter is that they host animal life.

The Wild Cities nonprofit has developed five principles for cities committed to fostering wildlife:

The principles[51] are as follows:

- Increase and improve the quality of wild nature in the city.
- Measure, value, and restore healthy and abundant ecosystem benefits to humans and nature alike.
- Ensure access to wild nature by all socioeconomic, ethnic, and cultural groups, and increase relevance of wild nature to urban quality of life.
- Recognize, promote, and act upon the positive role the city can play in the ecoregion of which it is a part and improve wild nature connectivity through the city.
- Look first to wild nature-based solutions to urban challenges and economic opportunity.

The group also proposes for each of the principles and supports these principles with suggested policies, ordinances, practices, and financing mechanisms.

Concluding Reflections

The great environmentalist Rachel Carson author of Silent Spring (1968), once wrote that the "real wealth of the Nation lies in the resources of the earth – soil, water, forests, minerals, and wildlife." Their preservation for the present and future "requires a delicately balanced and continuing program . . . and cannot be, a matter of politics."[52]

Local governments have the right to protect their natural assets through such tools as comprehensive plans, land development codes, future land use maps, and ordinances. A court can uphold such documents unless they are unreasonable – in which case they can be challenged as unconstitutional. In the US, the fifth amendment says, in part, that private property shall not be taken "for public use, without just compensation." When governments do that, it is considered illegal – specifically, under constitutional law, an "illegal taking."[53] For more on the concept of taking, see Chapter 11 on Environmental Litigation.

Over time, courts have issued many opinions affirming the rights of local jurisdictions to develop and approve comprehensive plans that set forth protections of the natural environment, such as the various environmental assets listed in this chapter. At the same time, they have also issued opinions upholding the rights of private property owners against government overreach. The key is the standard of reasonableness.[54]

This standard will apply as municipalities create and update their plans – the subject of the next chapter.

Notes

1 City of Madrid Implements Large Smarter Cities Environmental Analytics Project, July 7, 2014. https://www-03.ibm.com/press/us/en/pressrelease/44328.wss#release
2 The City of Ann Arbor, Michigan, has instituted a volunteer council to support its asset management department. Council of the Commons (a2gov.org), https://www.a2gov.org/departments/systems-planning/programs/Pages/Council-of-the-Commons.aspx
3 Innovation Cities™ Index 2019 – Global City Rankings by 2thinknow (innovation-cities.com), https://www.innovation-cities.com/index-2019-global-city-rankings/18842/
4 GreenMap.org | Think Global, Map Local!, https://www.greenmap.org

5 "Beacon Hill Goes Green. Pilot Program Aims to Swap Gas Lights for LEDS." https://www. boston.com/news/local-news/2020/11/30/beacon-hill-pilot-program-led-gas-lamps

6 "Ecosystem service value assessment of a natural reserve region for strengthening protection and conservation," *Journal of Environmental Management 244* (August 15, 2019): 208–227. https://doi.org/10.1016/j.jenvman.2019.04.095

7 "The value of the world's ecosystem services and natural capital," *Nature 387*(15), May 1997: 253–260. https://www.researchgate.net/publication/229086194_The_Value_of_the_World%27s_Ecosystem_Services_and_Natural_Capital

8 Martin Westerman, "The Value of Green Urban Assets and the True Cost of Development," August 12, 2020. https://www.thenatureofcities.com/2020/08/12/the-value-of-green-urban-assets-and-the-true-costs-of-development/

9 Westerman, Ibid., note 3.

10 https://researchguides.library.wisc.edu/GIS

11 The New Normal (arcgis.com), https://landscapeteam.maps.arcgis.com/apps/Cascade/index.html?appid=cd69320c00384d8094d83b45e84fd5aa

12 Drought Network Map (ny.gov), https://www.drought.gov/states/new-york

13 The National Map – Advanced Viewer, http://https/apps.nationalmap.gov/viewer/

14 National Biogeographic Map (usgs.gov), https://maps.usgs.gov/biogeography/

15 USGS Map of the Principal Aquifers of the US, https://water.usgs.gov/ogw/aquifer/map.html

16 Acting Attorney General, DEP Commissioner Announce Settlement of Lawsuit Over Beachfront Sand Dune Easement, Sept. 25, 2013. https://nj.gov/oag/newsreleases13/pr20130925b.html

17 Acting Attorney General, DEP Commissioner Announce Settlement of Lawsuit Over Beachfront Sand Dune Easement, Sept. 25, 2013. https://nj.gov/oag/newsreleases13/pr20130925b.html

18 This list is adapted from one offered by the City of Kitty Hawk, North Carolina. https://www.kittyhawknc.gov/departments-and-services/planning-and-inspections/dune-protection-improvement/

19 Recommended vegetation includes sea oats, seashore elder, saltmeadow cordgrass, and bitter panicum (planted April through September) and American beach grass (November through March). Source: City of Kitty Hawk, North Carolina. https://www.kittyhawknc.gov/departments-and-services/planning-and-inspections/dune-protection-improvement/

20 The City of Kitty Hawk cites North Carolina's Coastal Area Management Act, enacted in 1973 in response to the federal government's Coastal Zone Management Act of 1972, which called upon coastal states to work with the federal government and municipalities to "develop policies, criteria, standards, for land and water use decisions of more than local significance." STATUTE-86-Pg1280.pdf (govinfo.gov).

21 For example, in its dune guidance the City of Kitty Hawk cites North Carolina's Coastal Area Management Act. See note 19.

22 Ceslo H. L. Silva, Junior, et alia, The Brazilian Amazon deforestation rate in 2020 is the greatest of the decade.| Nature Ecology & Evolution, December 21, 2020. https://www.nature.com/articles/s41559-020-01368-x

23 Saving the American Chestnut Tree | The American Chestnut Foundation (acf.org), https://acf.org/the-american-chestnut/history-american-chestnut/why-american-chestnut/

24 Arbor Day Award Winner Highlights: Public Awareness of Trees Award | Arbor Day Blog.

25 Martin Westerman, "The Value of Green Urban Assets and the True Cost of Development," August 12, 2020. https://www.thenatureofcities.com/2020/08/12/the-value-of-green-urban-assets-and-the-true-costs-of-development/

26 E. Jane Carter "The potential of urban forestry in developing countries: A concept paper." Forestry Department, Food and Agriculture Organization of the United Nations Rome, DATE. www. fao.org/3/t1680e/T1680E00.htm#TOC Carter defines urban forestry as the "planned, integrated and systematic approach to the management of trees in urban and peri-urban areas for their contribution to the physiological, sociological, and economic well-being of urban society."
27 Linus Unah, "Ekuri Initiative: Inside a Nigerian community's battle to keep its forest," Mongabay.com, August 15, 2019. http://1https//news.mongabay.com/2019/08/ekuri-initiative-inside-a-nigerian-communitys-battle-to-keep-its-forest/
28 Sarah Weber, "Three Cities Taking Urban Forestry to the Next Level," March 21, 2016. https://www.wri.org/blog/2016/03/3-cities-taking-urban-forestry-next-levelsara
29 Sarah Weber, "Three Cities Taking Urban Forestry to the Next Level," March 21, 2016. https://www.wri.org/blog/2016/03/3-cities-taking-urban-forestry-next-levelsara
30 Sarah Weber, "Three Cities Taking Urban Forestry to the Next Level," March 21, 2016. https://www.wri.org/blog/2016/03/3-cities-taking-urban-forestry-next-levelsara
31 For a recently comprehensive state policy see Policy: 6755-9 – Policy for Landscaping and Enhancements on GDOT Right of Way Section: Permits – Miscellaneous Reports To: Division of Permits & Ops Office/Department: Office of Traffic Operations, 6755–9 (ga.gov), http://mydocs.dot.ga.gov/info/gdotpubs/Publications/6755-9.pdf
32 Learn About Green Streets | Green Streets, Green Jobs, Green Towns (G3) Program | US EPA, https://www.epa.gov/G3/learn-about-green-streets
33 Green Streets Basics and Design, Water Environment Research Foundation. https://www.werf.org/liveablecommunities/toolbox/gst_design.htm
34 Grant Application Pack | City Green, https://www.epa.gov/G3/learn-about-green-streets
35 Sumter, South Carolina, separates the two. It has a department for Parks and Gardens. The Recreation department is separate. See https://www.sumtersc.gov/parks
36 Anthropocentric by Default? Attribution of Familiar and Novel Properties to Living Things – Arenson – 2018 – Cognitive Science – Wiley Online Library, https://onlinelibrary.wiley.com/doi/pdf/10.1111/cogs.12501
37 Administrative Law Judge Sides with City on Amelia Bluff, but Criticizes Approach | NCFL Independent September 2019 re Case 19–2515GM (Amelia Tree Conservancy and the Sierra Club vs. City of Fernandina Beach and Amelia Bluff, LLC). https://fernandinaobserver.com/city-news/breaking-news-alj-finds-against-amelia-bluff-petitioners/September2019
38 Endangered Species | Laws & Policies | Endangered Species Act (fws.gov), https://www.fws.gov/endangered/laws-policies/
39 The architect was Benjamin Clark Morrison of Eight Flags Playscapes. The activist was Alexandra Lajoux, author of this book. The veteran environmentalist was Robert Weintraub.
40 National Highlight – Comparing Natural Lakes and Manmade Reservoirs | National Aquatic Resource Surveys | US EPA, https://www.epa.gov/national-aquatic-resource-surveys/national-highlight-comparing-natural-lakes-and-manmade-reservoirs
41 Christopher Leeds, "The ecology and biodiversity of urban ponds," https://www.research gate.net/publication/260306757_The_ecology_and_biodiversity_of_urban_ponds
42 Lakeside, FB, FL.
43 https://www.epa.gov/sites/production/files/2017-05/documents/app_d_traditional_navi gable_waters.pdf; Microsoft Word – Appendix D_Traditional Navigable Waters.doc (epa.gov)
44 Legal Definition of "Traditional Navigable Waters," Environmental Protection Agency, Appendix D (undated), https://www.epa.gov/sites/production/files/2017-05/documents/app_d_traditional_navigable_waters.pdf

45 The EPA and Army Corps reviewed "over 66,000 comments submitted by tribes, states, environmental and conservation organizations, regulated entities, industry associations, and the general public," https://www.sas.usace.army.mil/Portals/61/docs/regulatory/rapanosrevisedg uidancepoints.pdf

46 33 C.F.R. § 328.3(a)(1); 40 C.F.R. § 230.3(s)(1).

47 https://www.law.cornell.edu/cfr/text/33/part-329

48 http://www.nationalrivers.org/river-fact-or-fiction.html

49 Martin Westerman, "The Value of Green Urban Assets and the True Cost of Development," August 12, 2020. https://www.thenatureofcities.com/2020/08/12/the-value-of-green-urban-assets-and-the-true-costs-of-development/

50 https://www.dec.ny.gov/docs/wildlife_pdf/wetart24a.pdf

51 https://wildcities.readme.io/docs/getting-started

52 Letter to the editor, *Washington Post* (1953); quoted in *Lost Woods: The Discovered Writing of Rachel Carson* (1999) edited by Linda Lear, p. 99.

53 See Stimmel, Stimmel, and Roeser, *Eminent Domain: The Basic Law.* https://www.stimmel-law.com/en/articles/eminent-domain-basic-law (undated).

54 For more on this issue, see Chapter 11: Environmental Litigation Involving Municipalities.

Chapter 3
Planning (and Protesting) for Sustainability

Of all responsibilities owed by cities to their citizens, planning may be the most important – and the most challenging. Long-term trends such as climate change are giving rise to new problems that require new solutions. And the answers that work for one city may not work for another. For example, the large city that struggles with massive downtown vacancies from taxpayer flight has environmental, economic, and engineering problems different from those facing small towns crowded from hypergrowth. Whatever their issues, city leaders must envision a better future and work toward it. After all, a city's elected representatives serve as guardians of the future.

All city planning is local, by definition, especially when it comes to the tangible issues involved in a city's environmental, fiscal, and engineering sustainability.

Yet city planners can and do learn from examples around the world. We know about such examples, thanks in part to global planning organizations large and small. Examples range from major nongovernmental organizations (NGOs) like the World Bank or World Economic Forum to smaller grassroots organizations like ISOCARP, the International Institute for Sustainable Development, or the Symbiotic Cities Network, or the Doughnut Economic Action Lab,[1] advocating a new and holistic approach to city planning. All such organizations explicitly include sustainability or related terms (such as the environment) in their mission statements. And some provide further links to regional, national, and local organizations devoted to sustainability. For a list of global green city planning organizations, see Appendix 4: Planning Resources.

This chapter presents a variety of planning resources for city leaders, as well as the people who work for, vote for, or advise them. This chapter will describe the who, what, where, when, and why of municipal planning and its relationship to development and zoning. Also considered will be the role of protests as a valuable part of the planning cycle. The chapter includes examples from a representative variety of examples, including Brazil, the European Union, Japan, and the US.

Who: Planners and Protesters

"Planning" may be a single line on a city's organization chart, with a single director, but it is in fact a multilayered activity. A city commission will typically delegate the planning process to a city manager, who oversees a department for planning and zoning, with help from appointed volunteer committees. In many

https://doi.org/10.1515/9783110689860-003

cases, cities will engage consultants to conduct studies of population trends and other aspects of municipal life. The planning process thus extends from the dais at City Hall to the farthest street corner under its watch.

Key roles include the following:

Chief Resilience Officer. The role of chief resilience officer (CRO) is a relatively new one first envisioned by the Rockefeller foundation in its pioneering 100 Resilient Cities Initiative (see Appendix 4). That six-year initiative, which concluded in 2019, is now continuing though the Global Resilient Cities Network.[2] As a result of such initiatives, the CRO is on the payroll for more than 100 cities, including Paris and Mexico City.[3] The City Council of Jacksonville, Florida, included a detailed CRO role description in its final March 2021 report on city resiliency, with hiring in progress in mid-2021.[4]

Planning director. This person directs planning as an employee of the jurisdiction. There may also be an assistant planning director as well as a planning coordinator (at the clerical level) supporting this role. Municipal planners will often have degrees and/or certification in urban planning with a variety of specializations (see Box 3.1).[5] The planning profession is well established in developed economies. In the US the number of employed urban and regional planners is approaching 40,000.[6]

Planning and/or zoning commission member. This body, which may be appointed or elected, may have a dual role: it may combine or separate planning and zoning. For the planning function, an important duty is to maintain and follow the city's comprehensive plan. For the zoning function, an important responsibility is to maintain and follow the city's future land use map (FLUM). In some cases, in addition to a planning and/or zoning commission, there may be a zoning board of adjustments and appeals to deal with variances.

Planning consultant. The best plans are based in facts and reasonable projections. Cities often retain consultants to provide this kind of support to their planning efforts and working with consultants may be baked into staff job descriptions.[7]

Protesters. Even the most painstaking plans can not prevent projects that go against the grain of a community. This is especially true in cities where private interests such as residential or commercial developers have strong influence on local governments, staff, and advisory boards. In such locations, plans tend to emphasize growth over conservation and preservation. In response, citizens who care about saving natural habitat typically mobilize to advocate for sustainable outcomes, speaking out at council and board meeting, and even holding protests. In some regions, groups work together to protect large geographic areas that cover multiple jurisdictions.[8] The wise public servant will view protesters as valuable voices and resources rather than as nuisances.

Box 3.1: Municipal Planning Specializations
Agriculture/Food Systems
Architecture
Civil Engineering
Coastal Planning
Community Development
Construction
Economic Development
Environmental Sustainability
Geodesign
Geography
Geoinformatics
Geomatics
Growth Management
Hazard Mitigation/Disaster Planning
Healthy Cities/Public Health
History/Preservation
Housing
Indigenous Planning
Infrastructure Planning
International Development
Land Use/Physical Planning
Land Use/Planning Law
Landscape Architecture
Parks and Recreation Planning
Planning
Public Policy
Public/Nonprofit Administration
Real Estate Development
Regional Planning
Rural/Small Town Planning
Social Justice
Social Planning/Demographics
Spatial Planning
Sustainable Agriculture
Sustainable Design
Technology/GIS
Tourism/Cultural Planning
Transportation
Urban Design
Urban Informatics
Urban Studies
Urban City Planning
Urbanism
Zoning Administration

What: City Plans and Land Use Codes

All towns and cities, at any given time, are operating under plans that in turn determine land use codes (unless national laws determine the latter). At the financial level, municipalities collect revenues and make expenditures and investments according to a budget set the previous year. These budgets must be approved by the municipal government and often attract widespread public comment, since they are linked to the rate of taxation. (For more on municipal budgets, see Chapter 8.) Budgets, however, are not the most important kind of plan a city generates. Cities make budgetary choices according to broader plans – called comprehensive plans, master plans, or strategies, among other names – created for the public good. Both types of plans may be required under law. The themes covered in these plans range from philosophical goals such as enhancing public trust[9] to concrete objectives such as reducing carbon emissions – known to be a cause (along with nature) of global warming.[10]

Official and Ancillary City Plans Around the Globe

Most cities have a broad plan that defines their development goals – following guidelines from higher authorities such as state or national guidelines. The names for such plans vary. In Brazil, they are called master plans; in the US, comprehensive plans; in Canada, official community plans or municipal development plans.

Generally speaking, a city plan is not a law itself (not legally binding); rather, it is the enabler of local laws. Any ordinances that a city passes must conform to the plan; a city can not pass an ordinance that contradicts its comprehensive plan. Conversely, if a plan sets a new standard, then the community must amend its ordinances to implement it.

One of the main outcomes of an official comprehensive plan for a city is zoning. Ideally, planning comes before zoning; zoning is determined by planning. For this reason, the emphasis of this chapter is on plans. But as one city planner notes, "in practice, zoning codes are often the de facto plans for many cities."[11]

Land development codes, also called land use or zoning codes, put into statutory form the directives given in comprehensive plans. Land use plans may be national, state-based, and/or municipal. The municipalities that develop their own codes typically use a geographic information system (GIS) to develop their policies. Both municipalities and higher authorities may monitor changes in land use with the help of GIS technology – a practice called land accounting.

Cities may also develop ancillary plans that are separate from and complementary to their official comprehensive plans. For example, cities with a tree canopy to protect, such as San Francisco, California,[12] have developed urban forest plans.[13]

Master Plans in Brazil

In Brazil as in most countries, there is the usual combination of city plans and city zoning codes, both of which are generally informed by national law.[14] The legal basis for both city plans and land development codes comes from a national law called the Forest Code, created in 1965 and updated in 2012.[15] To monitor compliance with the new Forest Code, Brazil has been successfully using satellite-based monitoring.[16]

The Brazilian Constitution (in effect since 1988) grants municipalities authority to set urban policy, recognizing the social function of property located within city boundaries, as well as the social function of the cities themselves – a concept translated as "right to the city."[17] The Constitution grants to cities, as well as the nation and its states, several powers, including powers to "to protect the environment and to fight pollution in any of its forms" (23:6) and to "to preserve the forests, fauna and flora" (23:7).[18]

Brazil's 2001 City Statute gave cities and activists a tool for such protection and preservation.[19] (For an excerpt from the statute, see Appendix 5: The City Statute of Brazil, at the end of this book.) It builds on the Constitution by requiring cities with more than 20,000 inhabitants (about 1,600 cities or one-third of the country's municipalities) to develop master plans. The City Statute asserts the right and responsibility of city governments to solve local social and environmental problems, and treats urban property as a public rather than an entirely private matter. Under the statute, city plans may protect the right to own property but not necessarily the right to build on it.

Brazil's City Statute "establishes norms for public order and social interest which regulate the use of urban property in favor of the common good, safety and well-being of citizens, as well as environmental equilibrium" (Article 1). It furthermore states that when Brazilian cities develop and implement their master plans, they must "guarantee the right to sustainable cities, understood as the right to urban land, housing, environmental sanitation, urban infrastructure, transportation and public services, to work and leisure for current and future generations" and states that land use policy must avoid "pollution and environmental degradation" (Article 2).[20] The law also allows cities to take action to preserve real estate when it is "of historic, environmental, landscape, social or cultural interest" (Article 35). The planning process must engage "the significant participation of the population and of associations that represent various segments of the community" (Article 45).[21] The 2001 statute, hailed as a "huge achievement in the area of urbanism, law and social justice,"[22] can be a model for other countries.

At the voluntary level, Brazil has a 12-Goal initiative based on goals advocated by the United Nations (see Appendix 1). One of the Brazilian goals, called Common Natural Resources, puts into action a variety of UN environmental goals. The initiative has made a difference for several Brazilian cities. In Quatro Puntes, PR, A partnership between the city and the citizens prioritized the recovery of springs in the region as an environmentally healthy and sustainable consensus for water collection and supply; and in Lyon Franca, cities and citizens have worked together to convert vacant lots into urban parks, and to revitalize riverbanks.[23]

City Strategies in Europe

Europe is one of the most intensively developed continents on the globe. As noted by the European Environment Agency, it has the highest proportion of land (some 80 percent) used for settlement, production systems (e.g., agriculture and forestry), and infrastructure.[24] With a shrinking amount of undeveloped land there is a rising consciousness of the need to conserve the natural environment, pitting commercial interests against citizens in the development of many land use codes. The data used for land use codes in Europe comes from the Copernicus Land Monitoring Service.[25] The Copernicus system is also used for land accounting and "ecosystem" accounting.

Unlike other jurisdictions (such as Brazil or other countries discussed in this chapter) cities in the European Union are under no legal obligation to develop official municipal plans – sustainable or otherwise. Instead, the European Union has encouraged the development of strategies through various policies promulgated by its governing body, the European Commission.[26]

City strategies in Europe are quite varied. As noted in the *Handbook of Sustainable Development Strategies* published by the European Union in 2020, "the

EU approach to urban development when implemented on the ground, leads to different interpretations, depending on local planning cultures, as well as on the wide typology of actors involved in its implementation."[27]

One reason for the lack of a single directive for city planning in the EU may be the multiplicity of urban policy requirements in the European Union. Notably, however, the European Union's new "cohesion policy 2021–2027" states that in the future, "a single instrument, the European Urban Initiative, will replace several different instruments and initiatives in urban policy."[28] If the aspirational document known as the European Green Deal[29] results in a central law for sustainability, this future law may include requirements for city strategies. The European Green Deal includes a Climate Pact that aims to strengthen EU guidance and support to cities: "It will continue to work to empower regional and local communities, including energy communities. The urban dimension of cohesion policy will be strengthened, and the proposed European Urban Initiative will help cities make best use of opportunities to develop sustainable urban development strategies."

Some guidance for strategies comes from the European Regional Development Fund (ERD Fund), established by the European Commission, which provides support for cities with "strategies that that set out integrated actions to tackle the economic, environmental, climate, demographic and social challenges affecting urban areas."[30] Furthermore, the European Commission, through the ERD Fund, gives awards for innovative urban initiatives.[31]

In September 2020, the EU launched an initiative to achieve "100 Climate Neutral Cities by 2030."[32] The 100 cities signing the Climate City Contracts will develop and implement the strategies reflecting innovation in governance, transport, energy, construction, and recycling, supported by digital technology. Each contract will be signed by the city's mayor on behalf of the local government and local stakeholders, by the Commission, and by national or regional authorities. These cities can then serve as "Innovation Hubs" for other cities, says the EU, "meaning that hundreds of European cities will be inspired by, learn from and replicate the ideas and solutions emerging from the initiative."[33]

National Land Use Plan in Japan

In Japan, there is a National Land Use Plan that provides directives to be implemented at the local level – for example, in Tokyo, by the Tokyo Metropolitan Region plan.

Comprehensive Plans in the US

In the US, state laws essentially "enable" their cities to plan. They authorize municipalities to create ordinances that zone land by use (e.g., commercial, conservation, residential). In addition, they establish a uniform regulatory framework to be carried out by two distinct regulatory bodies, a zoning commission, and a board of zoning adjustment, to ensure due process by separating ordinances from their administration.

In addition, to ensure that municipal action is constitutional (does not violate the US Constitution or the state's constitution) passage or amendment of the zoning ordinance may be subject to public notice and comment or hearings. Furthermore, hearings held by the zoning commission and/or the board of zoning adjustment are typically subject to "due process" requirements, including the right to receive notice, the right to cross examine witnesses, and the right to appeal a decision.[34]

Many states require their cities to have comprehensive plans (also called development plans, general plans, growth plans, master plans, and even "smart growth plans" – although many conservationists view that term with skepticism). In some cases – typically for plans of extremely broad scope – a plan may be called a "strategy." To create and maintain plans, municipalities typically follow the requirements of state law, which is generally based on standards developed nearly a century ago.[35] The Standard State Zoning Enabling Act of 1928 is still the basis for most US state law today on municipal planning.[36]

In the US, each state has developed its own requirements for municipal planning – many based on Standard State Zoning Enabling Act of 1928 mentioned earlier. Most comprehensive plans for cities in the US cover the same or similar areas, namely economic development, transportation, housing, open space and recreation, historic preservation, and the environment, but some plans add other categories, such as the problem of "sprawl" or special areas such as culture, heritage, healthcare, tourism, or youth. State statutes, while setting minimums, generally permit such options. For examples of state statutes enabling city comprehensive plans in the US, see Box 3.2.

Language for Plans and Codes

Plans and codes in English-speaking countries have traditionally used the word "shall" to indicate both requirements (must) and aspirations (should). In recent years, however, some parties to legal actions have successfully argued that the term "shall" is more aspirational than mandatory.

For example, in *People v. Geiler* (2016), the Illinois Supreme Court reversed a lower court order that had interpreted as mandatory a rule that used the term "shall." Noting that the rule did not include consequences, the Illinois high court interpreted the language as "directory" rather than mandator.[37] To cure this problem, many plans now use the word "must" instead, for elimination of any doubt.

Significantly, the US federal government's "plain English" initiative suggests that drafters use the word "must" when a matter is imperative.[38] As one expert has stated, "'Must' is the only word that imposes a legal obligation on your readers to tell them something is mandatory. Also, 'must not' are the only words you can use to say something is prohibited."[39]

But whatever terms are used, they should be defined up front. As noted by one legal scholar, "Courts that have interpreted 'shall' inconsistently would likely interpret 'must' inconsistently."[40] Lee County, Florida, defines "must": "*Must*. The term 'must' shall be construed as being mandatory and will mean 'is required to (be).'"[41]

Box 3.2: State Municipal Planning Statutes – Examples from Florida and Washington
Florida, at the Southeastern tip of the US, contrasts with Washington State, in the far Northwest.
Comprehensive Plans in Florida (US). The Sunshine State (in Chapter 163, Fla. Stat.[42]) requires each local government to create, adopt, and maintain a comprehensive land use plan with legally enforceable guidelines for local planning.[43] Under the statute, a comprehensive plan must "provide the principles, guidelines, standards, and strategies for the orderly and balanced future economic, social, physical, environmental, and fiscal development of the area that reflects community commitments to implement the plan and its elements."[44] In Chapter 163, Section 3177, Florida lists required elements of comprehensive plans, namely: capital improvements, future land use, transportation, water and sewer,[45] conservation, recreation and open space, housing, coastal management, and intergovernmental coordination. (The statute permits inclusion of other "optional" elements but not does list suggestions.)
Comprehensive plans in Washington (US). The Evergreen State, true to its moniker, shows a conservation commitment in its statutory requirements for comprehensive plans. The state has two different standards for cities depending on size and growth rate. The standard law requires that plans address just nine elements: land use, housing, capital facilities, utilities, rural development (for counties), transportation, economic development, parks and recreation, and ports. But it also suggests optional elements such as conservation and solar energy. For high growth cities, the environmental standards are stronger. Under the Growth Management Act (GMA), comprehensive plans for fast-growing cities must address 14 goals,[46] of which nearly half address environmental concerns. GMA-compliant plans aim to reduce sprawl, defined as "the inappropriate conversion of undeveloped land into sprawling, low-density development" (#2). They also foster several aspects of the environment: natural resource industries such as timberlands and farming (#8); open space and recreation, including conservation of fish and wildlife habitat (#9); the environment generally, including air and water quality (#10);

and finally, with its own set of goals, shorelines (#14). The statute calls for economic development as a goal (#5), but it cautions that this should be "within the capacities of the
state's natural resources, public services, and public facilities."

Where: GIS and Other Tools

Pinpointing the exact location of the areas to be covered involves mapping them
in space – and using GIS to produce maps.

Future Land Use Maps

Many land development codes require the publication of a variously called fu-
ture land use map (FLUM). Except for highly urbanized cities where there is no
land left to conserve, categories (typically broken out in numbered subcatego-
ries as in Residential 1, Residential 2) often include the following:
- Residential
- Commercial
- Mixed Use
- Industrial
- Agricultural
- Recreational/Open Space
- Conservation

There may also be zones set apart for educational, public, historic, transportation, and various categories pertaining to water including water wells, beaches
and shores, including estuaries, rivers bays, lakes, floodplains, harbors, and
wetlands. For ocean shores there may be coastal high hazard areas. The 2020
zoning map for the City of Tokyo in Japan has 12 designations ranging from
low-rise residential to industrial.[47] While none of these is deemed conservation
land, four of the categories (pertaining to residential) have as their purpose "to
protect living environment."[48]

GIS

As noted in Chapter 2, environmental or geographic assets can be mapped via a
GIS. Such as system can collect, store, and manage the geographic (spatial) data

in a particular location, such as a city.[49] GIS systems are often capable of machine or deep learning – a kind of learning in which the computer program learns from data without relying on rules-based programming.[50]

The intersection of mapping and planning poses a challenge due to differing terminologies that might be used in a plan or ordinance versus the term used by the mapping system.

In his 2005 PhD dissertation proposing a "A Geographical Ontology of Objects in the Visible Domain," Dr. Barry Bitters developed a system called Visual Objects Taxonomy/Thesaurus (VOTT). To create it, he drew from 167 "heritage taxonomic" structures, including formal ontological domain studies, taxonomies, classification schemes, formal map legends, and geospatial data model. His goal was to create a data structure that would allow improved interoperability between organizations producing and reusing disparate sources of geospatial data.[51]

Virtual Reality

In addition to GIS systems for locating and mapping city areas, there are also virtual reality tools that can help city planners visualize the impact of their plans.[52] In 2021, at least 14 products are available.[53]

Reblocking

In the process of developing plans and land use codes, and in the process of land use mapping, cities have an opportunity to demarcate which blocks lack access to city services. The Santa Fe Institute in the US, working with numerous partners including organizations focused on the urban poor,[54] has developed a technology for reblocking, used currently for informal settlements, also called slums.

The Santa Fe reblocking project "analyzes the spatial structure of informal city blocks, and uses an algorithm to suggest reblocking solutions that provide access to all structures within the block in a minimally disruptive way." Case studies so far include Harare Zimbabwe and Cape Town, South Africa.[55]

When: Timeframe for Planning – Balancing the Needs of Today and Tomorrow

Sustainability, according to the well-known definition of the Brundtlands Report sponsored by the United Nation's World Commission on Environment and

Development, is "development that meets the needs of the present without compromising the ability of future generations to meet their own needs." This dual time frame – considering both present and the past – defines the "when" of planning, especially for new cities.

According to research by the group Next City, half of the world's some 10,000 cities are younger than 40 years old.[56] As an example, the study cites Shenzhen, which was a fishing village in the 1970s, but today is a megacity with over 12 million people.[57]

At the other extreme are cities that are thousands of years old, with an historic heritage to protect – for example Jericho, which has existed for 12,000 years.[58] Sustainability in such locations means balancing past, present, and future.

But whether a city is developing a new plan or revising an existing one, it is important to plan for the long term. Every city plan should consider long-term trends such as climate change and pandemic risk. In addition to dealing with immediate threats such as the next hurricane or the next rise in COVID-19, city planners can consider likely scenarios.

According to the World Bank, today some 55 percent of the world's population – 4.2 billion inhabitants – live in cities – a trend expected to continue.[59] By 2050, with the urban population more than doubling its current size, nearly 7 of 10 people in the world will live in cities. This rate of growth can create problems if planners are too rigid in their approach. The World Bank notes, "Once a city is built, its physical form and land use patterns can be locked in for generations, leading to unsustainable sprawl." And further, "the expansion of urban land consumption outpaces population growth by as much as 50%, which is expected to add 1.2 million km^2 of new urban built up area to the world in the three decades. Such sprawl puts pressure on land and natural resources."[60]

Why: Some Ethical Issues

Why plan? The answer may seem obvious. A municipality must prepare for the future and planning can help it do so. But as with any complex activity, there can be ethical challenges and dilemmas when it comes to the relationship between city hall and the people.

The AICP ethics code says that planners shall:
- Always be conscious of the rights of others.
- Have special concern for the long-range consequences of present actions.
- Pay special attention to the interrelatedness of decisions.
- Provide timely, adequate, clear, and accurate information on planning issues to all affected persons and to governmental decision-makers.

- Give people the opportunity to have a meaningful impact on the development of plans and programs that may affect them.
- Seek social justice by working to expand choice and opportunity for all persons.
- Promote excellence of design and endeavor to conserve and preserve the integrity and heritage of the natural and built environment.
- Deal fairly with all participants in the planning process.

The ethics code of the American Institute of Certified Planners states that planners must above all "serve the public interest."[61] This is no mere catch phrase; the AICP makes it real by saying that planners therefore owe their allegiance to "a conscientiously attained concept of the public interest that is formulated through debate." In other words, planners do not work in isolation from their communities, but should pay attention to and contribute to meaningful dialogue on matters of interest and even controversy.

Concluding Reflections

"Plan in the real world."
Wheeler L. Baker, *Crisis Management: A Model for Managers* (1993)

Planning deals with the unknown – the future – so city plans need continual revision as circumstances change. Yet if planners base themselves in the real world – based on the best possible data and information – their work can move cities toward a more sustainable future. The next three chapters of this book address the main tools needed to build that future – in the natural and built environment, in the economic (as well as social) domain, and in a city's infrastructure.

Notes

1 https://www.archives.gov/federal-register/write/legal-docs/clear-writing.html; https://plainlanguage.gov/guidelines/conversational/shall-and-must/
2 What's Next for the World's Chief Resiliency Officers? – Next City, https://nextcity.org/daily/entry/whats-next-for-the-worlds-chief-resiliency-officers
3 "Chief Resilience Officer: New Key Figure for Cities in the Making," *The Agility Effect,* March 13, 2020. https://www.theagilityeffect.com/en/article/chief-resilience-officer-new-key-figure-for-cities-in-the-making/
4 http://apps2.coj.net/City_Council_Public_Notices_Repository/Final%20Report%20-%20Special%20Committee%20on%20Resiliency.pdf

5 The website Platetizen, which maintains a list of urban planning programs, has identified 45 areas of study that fall under urban planning.
6 Urban and Regional Planners: Occupational Outlook Handbook: US Bureau of Labor Statistics (bls.gov), https://www.bls.gov/ooh/
7 See https://www.ckdr.net/classifieds/planning-coordinator/
8 https://www.vibrantcitieslab.com/wordpress/wp-content/uploads/2020/05/New-York-City-STEW-MAP.pdf
9 Public trust is one of the citizen concerns in the City of Fernandina Beach, Florida, according to the volunteer group we call the Amelia Island Working Group. We are recommending that the revised version of the City's comprehensive plan (for 2045) include a goal titled Public Trust.
10 For a plan by the City of Ann Arbor, Michigan, to reduce carbon emissions, see A2Zero Climate Action Plan _3.0.pdf, https://www.a2gov.org/departments/sustainability/Documents/A2Zero%20Climate%20Action%20Plan%20_3.0.pdf
11 Jamaal Green, "Institutional Readings on Zoning. A Review of Zoning: A Guide for 21st-Century Planning," *Metropolitics*, 20 November 2020. URL: https://metropolitics.org/Institutio nalReadings-on-Zoning.html
12 https://ufmptoolkit.net/wp-content/uploads/2016/03/SF_Urban_Forest_Plan_Final-051414.pdf
13 Example Plans | Urban Forest Management Plan Toolkit, ufmptoolkit.net
14 Brazil Inputs for a Strategy for Cities A Contribution with a Focus on Cities and Municipalities (In Two Volumes) Volume II: Background Papers (2006), http://documents1.worldbank.org/curated/en/810791468005449718/pdf/357490BR.pdf p. 277.
15 R. Simoes, M.C.A. Picoli, G. Camara, G. et al. "Land use and cover maps for Mato Grosso State in Brazil from 2001 to 2017," *Sci Data* 7(4), 2020. https://doi.org/10.1038/s41597-020-0371-4
16 R. Simoes, M.C.A. Picoli, G. Camara, G. et al. "Land use and cover maps for Mato Grosso State in Brazil from 2001 to 2017," *Sci Data* 7(34), 2020. https://doi.org/10.1038/s41597-020-0371-4
17 (16) (PDF) The Right to the City: Theory and Practice in Brazil (researchgate.net) (Abigail Friendly, *Planning Theory and Practice 14*(2), May 2013).
18 Constitution of the Federative Republic of Brazil; the law in Portuguese: http://www.planalto.gov.br/ccivil_03/leis/LEIS_2001/L10257.htm
19 Statute of the City (in English) https://www.wiego.org/sites/default/files/resources/files/Brazil-The-Statute-of-the-City-Law-No-10.257-of%20-2001.pdf; Estatudo da Cidade (in Portuguese) L10257 (planalto.gov.br) or http://www.planalto.gov.br/ccivil_03/leis/LEIS_2001/L10257.htm
20 https://www.researchgate.net/publication/259953398_The_RighBr_to_the_City_Theory_and_Practice_in_Brazil
21 http://www.planalto.gov.br/ccivil_03/leis/LEIS_2001/L10257.htm https://www.research gate.net/publication/259953398_The_Right_to_the_City_Theory_and_Practice_in_Brazil
22 Abigail Friendly, The Right to the City: Theory and Practice in Brazil, *Planning Theory and Practice 14*(2), May 2013: 158–179. https://www.researchgate.net/publication/259953398_The_Right_to_the_City_Theory_and_Practice_in_Brazil
23 453_11832_commitment_GPS – SCP.pdf (un.org).
24 Land use – European Environment Agency (europa.eu).

25 CLC 2018 – Copernicus Land Monitoring Service. To see a map, visit CLC 2018 – Copernicus Land Monitoring Service, https://land.copernicus.eu/pan-european/corine-land-cover/clc2018

26 Handbook of Sustainable Urban Development Strategies | EU Science Hub (europa.eu).

27 Handbook of Sustainable Urban Development Strategies | EU Science Hub (europa.eu).

28 https://ec.europa.eu/regional_policy/sources/docgener/factsheet/new_cp/simplification_handbook_en.pdf

29 EUR-Lex - 52019DC0640 - EN - EUR-Lex (europa.eu) See also: A European Green Deal | European Commission (europa.eu).

30 Article 7 of EU Regulation No 1301/2013 - EUR-Lex - 02013R1301-20200424 - EN - EUR-Lex (europa.eu).

31 EUR-Lex - 32017R2056 - EN - EUR-Lex (europa.eu). For more details see What is Urban Innovative Actions? | UIA – Urban Innovative Actions (uia-initiative.eu).

32 ec_rtd_mission-board-report-climate-neutral-and-smart-cities.pdf (europa.eu) hubs.

33 ec_rtd_mission-board-report-climate-neutral-and-smart-cities.pdf (europa.eu).

34 Alia, "Perpetual Affordability Covenants," Ibid.

35 https://www.planning.org/growingsmart/enablingacts/

36 "The vast majority of state enabling legislation is based on the Standard State Zoning Enabling Legislation," says Elizabeth Alia, "Perpetual Affordability Covenants: Can These Land Use Tenants: Can These Land Use Tools Solve the Affordable Housing Crisis?" *Penn State Law Review, 124* (2019): Issue 1, Article 2. Available at: https://elibrary.law.psu.edu/pslr/vol124/iss1/2 https://elibrary.law.psu.edu/cgi/viewcontent.cgi?article=1001&context=pslrx

37 PEOPLE v. GEILER | FindLaw, https://caselaw.findlaw.com/il-supreme-court/1741661.html

38 https://www.archives.gov/federal-register/write/legal-docs/clear-writing.htmlhttps://plainlanguage.gov/guidelines/conversational/shall-and-must/

39 What's the only word that means mandatory? Here's what law and policy say about "shall, will, may, and must" (faa.gov).

40 Deborah Cupples, University of Florida, UF Law. State Supreme Court Fuels Debate over "Shall"; Possible Solutions to the "Shall Problem" – Faculty Blogs – UF Levin College of Law.

41 Chapter 1 – GENERAL PROVISIONS | Land Development Code | Lee County, FL | Municode Library, https://library.municode.com/fl/lee_county/codes/land_development_code?nodeId=LADECO_CH1GEPR

42 https://www.flsenate.gov/Laws/Statutes/2019/Chapter163/All

43 https://floridadep.gov/sites/default/files/CRI_AAA_Planning_Guidebook_for_Florida%27s_Local_Government.pdf

44 Fla. Stat. 163.3177 http://www.leg.state.fl.us/statutes/index.cfm?App_mode=Display_Statute&URL=0100-0199/0163/0163.html

45 This is spelled out as "general sanitary sewer, solid waste, drainage, potable water, and natural groundwater aquifer recharge element correlated to principles and guidelines for future land use."

46 MRSC – Growth Management Act, https://mrsc.org/Home/Explore-Topics/Planning/General-Planning-and-Growth-Management/Comprehensive-Planning-Growth-Management.aspx

47 令和2年3月_港区用途地域等図 (city.minato.tokyo.jp).

48 Urban Land Use Planning System in Japan (jica.go.jp) Figure 3.2, p. 23.

49 https://researchguides.library.wisc.edu/GIS

50 Rohit Singh. *Where Deep Learning Meets GIS.* https://www.esri.com/about/newsroom/arcwatch/where-deep-learning-meets-gis/. For an example in Brazil, see Land use and cover maps for Mato Grosso State in Brazil from 2001 to 2017 | Scientific Data (nature.com). For a discussion of the definition of machine learning see Daniel Faggella, *What Is Machine Learning?*, February 26, 2020. What Is Machine Learning? | Emerj, https://emerj.com/ai-glossary-terms/what-is-machine-learning/

51 B. Bitters, *A Geographical Ontology of Objects in the Visible Domain*. PhD thesis, Florida State University, 2005.

52 Virtual Reality for Planners | Planetizen Courses, https://courses.planetizen.com/track/virtual-reality-for-urban-planning

53 https://www.g2.com/categories/urban-planning-and-design

54 One of the partners in developing reblocking is SDI "a network of community-based organisations of the urban poor in 32 countries and hundreds of cities and towns across Africa, Asia and Latin America." https://sdinet.org/who-is-sdi/about-us/

55 http://openreblock.org/about.html

56 There are 10,000 Cities on Planet Earth. Half Didn't Exist 40 Years Ago – Next City, https://nextcity.org/daily/entry/there-are-10000-cities-on-planet-earth-half-didnt-exist-40-years-ago

57 Ibid.

58 https://www.worldatlas.com/articles/the-oldest-cities-in-the-world.html

59 Urban Development Overview (worldbank.org).

60 Ibid.

61 https://planning-org-uploaded-media.s3.amazonaws.com/document/AICP-Ethics-Revised-AICP-Code-Professional-Conduct-2016-04-01.pdf

PART II: **Using Environmental, Economic, and Engineering Tools to Advance Sustainability**

Chapter 4
Tools for the Natural and Built Environment: Ordinances for Zoning and Preservation

Although it may be last in alphabetical listings, zoning is often first in the toolbox of city leaders and activists balancing environmental, economic, and environmental goals. Zoning ordinances are a type of law enacted by a municipality to classify a specific geographic area (or zone) so that only certain types of properties can be constructed within its boundaries. While zones are traditionally defined by use (e.g., commercial, residential, and so forth), cities that practice "form-based planning" (or a "hybrid" approach) may define them by form (e.g., frontage types, building types, or landscaping).[1]

Zoning, whether by use or form, plays an important role in defining and preserving a town or city's identity. As explained in the previous section of this book, in chapters 2 and 3, forward-looking cities strive to identify the most important what assets they own and manage, and they create long-term plans to steward them. From these plans come land development codes and ultimately zoning ordinances.

Unfortunately, however, zoning can be determined by planning staff who may have a view of "growth" that differs from the citizenry. Planning staff members often report to a city manager focused on maximization of tax revenues. While this is a valid goal to have, it must be balanced with other goals, such as maintaining the character of certain neighborhoods that help to define a city's identity. Although city governments do appoint volunteer boards or committees for planning and/or zoning, the composition of those bodies may be biased toward developers interested in obtaining contracts. Unless citizens attend these meetings and express their views on development, they can be blindsided by their town's zoning decisions and variances.

In some cities subject to heavy growth, building projects arise on the landscape replacing trees and vistas or endangering wetlands and wildlife. And when environmental activists protest them, they learn all too late that the developers acted lawfully under zoning ordinances or approved variances. Another problem is gentrification – a process by which longtime residents with low income get replaced by wealthier newcomers.[2]

Therefore, to avoid such bad surprises, environmental and social activists must familiarize themselves with local zoning ordinances and learn how to anticipate and prevent variances from them.

https://doi.org/10.1515/9783110689860-004

Zoning Basics

Zoning ordinances are local laws enabled by state, provincial, or national law permitting such local authority. A state statute for example may require municipalities to have a comprehensive plan setting forth goals, and a land development code applying those goals to land use, including zoning provisions.[3] Some cities put all these documents into a single document called a unified development code, also called unified development ordinance.[4]

Within a municipality, staff will propose the zone or a zoning change, and the city council will approve or deny it, often relying on a volunteer citizen advisory board for planning and/or zoning. During the public hearing process, views can vary. Some see zoning as a violation of their property rights; others see it as a protection. As one zoning veteran has stated, "So long as landowners' unrestrained freedom to exercise their own interests is not threated by others, they tend to view zoning as a limitation. On the flip side, when landowners' interests are threatened by the unrestricted actions of others, they tend to view zoning as a protection."[5] The notion of zoning as a limitation has merit, as even proponents of it will admit. Indeed, one definition of sustainability itself turns around limits: Dr. Liu Jianfeng et al. define it as "a probability of a particular system being able to restrict its degree of development, coordination, and continuity within the threshold of sustainable development during the specified target and preset stages of its development, namely, an ability a specific system has to successfully achieve the goals of sustainable development."[6]

Jurisdictions within the same country may vary greatly in how many restrictions they place on land use.[7] As long as zoning is not unreasonable, it is well within the powers of a municipality under most legal systems, including the US.[8] A zoning ordinance will often set requirements for *density*, *height*, and *setback*, and may include provisions for *easements*.

Density is the amount of development per acre permitted on a parcel under applicable zoning policy. It is typically measured as dwelling units per acre (DU/AC). Average density in the world went from 24 people per km to 59 people per km in just the past half century.[9]

Height is measured as the vertical distance at any point from the average natural grade[10] within the building pad area to the highest level of the structure, including roofing elements. In a typical height ordinance, any decorative roof elements such as railings or elevator shafts are included in the maximum building height.[11] Height is a common point of controversy in zoning, with developers and pro-growth city officials championing increased height, and neighborhood residents often resisting it (see Box 4.1).

Setback is the distance between a property line and the building next to it. The setback provisions in zoning ordinances are intended to ensure space between buildings, and between a building and the road. They are needed not only for aesthetic reasons, but also for drainage and utilities. Setback requirements can be a double-edged sword for tree preservation. While they tend to promote conservation, because they protect trees in the setback, they can work the opposite way if the trees are located behind a building subject to the setback. In such a case, the builder of a house with a large footprint will say that due to the setback in front of the planned the trees in the back of the planned property must be cut down, as they are too near the structure. City planners writing setback provisions should word them with care to avoid this result.

Easements are interests in land granted by a landowner to an interested party who wishes to use the land in certain ways. A *common area easement* is an area set aside via easement for common use in a particular community such as a homeowner's association or a planned community.[12] A *conservation easement* is one dedicated to conservation.[13] A *utility easement* is granted to allow a utility company access to the land.

A model conservation easement will identify the grantor and grantee of the easement (e.g., the private owners and the city or nonprofit caretakes) to which they are granting access. The easement will have sections for purpose, rights of the grantee, prohibited uses, reserved rights, requirements for advance notice of certain actions, grantee remedies, access, costs and liabilities, extinguishment, assignment, and subsequent transfers, as well as provisions for an estoppel certificate to verify statements, and due notice.[14]

Box 4.1: Zoning Battles in Richmond, VA

On December 8, 2020, the Richmond Virginia City Council saved some city sky. They voted to shelve plans to permit buildings of 20 stories or more in residential areas with much shorter buildings.[15] The move would have hurt the neighborhood's character. "Most of the corridor backs up to historic neighborhoods, three of which are historically Black neighborhoods that are constantly in battle for the preservation of their character and housing stock," said Councilmember Kim Gray, citing "eight distinct civic associations" opposing the plans.

Soon thereafter, however, Gray and other members Council voted to approve a master Plan called Richmond 300, for an "equitable, sustainable, and beautiful future for all Richmonders" in time for Richmond's 300th anniversary in 2037. The plan involves city-wide rezoning – "developing new zoning category descriptions for the entire city and then mapping the new zoning categories to every parcel in the city."[16] Opponents have complained that the master plan does not do enough for historic preservation, environmental conservation, or affordable housing,[17] but councilmembers have promised to address these issues in coming years as the plan is implemented.

Zoning Categories

Zoning, like politics, is local. Categories and symbols vary widely among communities when creating designations for land use.[18] Zoning ordinances can also limit what types of buildings can be near each other – such as proximity of a gun shop or gambling arcade to a school or church.

Most cities use the letters of the alphabet (followed by numbers) to set zones – typically the following:

A is for agricultural. This category allows raising of crops and animals. In many states in the US, agricultural zoning can qualify for special subsidy and tax abatement programs.

C for commercial. This is a broad category for land hosting nonindustrial businesses that can include hotels, restaurants, shopping malls, and some kinds of (nonindustrial) warehouses. For one fairly typical city C1 designates a neighborhood commercial zone, C2 a downtown zone, and C3 a general commercial zone, with C1 having the most restrictions and C3 the fewest.[19]

C/R for conservation/recreation. The purpose of a conservation/recreation zone is to protect lands for uses associated with natural area preservation or activities dependent on the use or enjoyment of nature, such as agriculture, ranching, gardening, forestry, or public recreation.[20]

H for historic. Buildings 50 years and older are eligible to be considered historic zoning. In historic districts cities impose restrictions on changing structures from the original conditions but make allowances for restoration and repair. The designation can extend to artifacts, structures, sites, buildings, or entire districts. For more on historic preservation, see the next section of this chapter.

I for industrial. The kinds of enterprises considered to be industrial rather than commercial are those that involve machinery, warehousing, transportation fleets, and the like. A key indicator for industrial zoning is the floor area ratio. There may be subcategories for certain types of industrial use, such as airports.

O–S for open space. The purpose of this zoning is to prevent building on a space intended to be left open for public use.[21]

R for residential. This category can have special designations for single family versus multifamily residences as well as for duplexes, trailer parks, cooperatives, and condominiums. R1 is typically single family residential, R2 is for a duplex, and R3 is for multifamily. Again, the higher the number the least restrictive.

M or MU is for mixed use. Common mixed uses under this category include commercial, industrial, and/or residential. It may be horizontal (with differing uses in proximity), vertical (with uses stacked), or both. Consistent with other uses of numbers from lowest to highest impact, M1 can mean low intensity while M2 can mean moderate intensity.[22]

Another type of zoning that is similar and goes by various letters is *aesthetic zoning*. Such zoning seeks to protect the visual character of an area through restrictions on architectural style, building materials, paint colors, and other features. Cities using such zoning will have a board for design review, much like a homeowners association but on a broader scale, applying to commercial and/or mixed-use areas as well.[23]

Aesthetic zoning, which operates like historic district zoning but is less restrictive, can align itself with other important goals such as historic preservation. Still, this type of zoning has its critics. In 2010, a lawsuit invoking property rights and challenging aesthetic zoning made it all the way to the Supreme Court, where it failed – but not without establishing precedent that could support a future challenge.[24] In 2015, North Carolina passed a law restricting aesthetic zoning.[25]

Aesthetic zoning aligns with form-based planning. As mentioned at the outset of this chapter, form-based planning zones by form rather than use. Cities that practice "form-based planning" (or a "hybrid" approach) may define them by frontage types, building types, or landscaping).[26] (For more on form-based planning, see Box 4.2.)

Box 4.2: Two Award-Winning Zoning Codes
Hartford, CT and Rancho Cucamonga, CA are the winners of the 2020 Richard H. Driehaus Form-Based Codes Award, presented by the Form-Based Codes Institute at Smart Growth America. Each year, the Driehaus Award recognizes communities that have adopted and implemented exemplary form-based zoning codes.

Hartford, CT
Rewriting the zoning for an entire city is a huge challenge, but that is exactly what the City of Hartford did in 2016. Hartford threw out its 50-year-old zoning code and replaced it with a new form-based code that recognizes and reinforces the distinct character of each neighborhood. The comprehensive code will make future development more predictable and streamline the project approval process. Whereas the old code had 63 pages of complex "use tables" that made development costly and time consuming, the new form-based code has just three pages of use tables with much more general categories. And easy-to-read graphics guide the reader through the standards that apply to their project, helping to facilitate, rather than hinder development.

As Hartford Mayor Luke Bronin noted, "Our citywide form-based code breathes new life into the walkable, historic neighborhoods our community has cherished for decades. It's a forward-looking roadmap that positions Hartford to attract investment in vibrant, sustainable development for years to come."

With the adoption of this new zoning code, Hartford also became the first city (with a population over ~100,000) that completely eliminated parking requirements. This will improve housing affordability and support the growth of walking and biking in the long term, but also has important implications during a pandemic. Combined with new flexibility to set up "outdoor shop displays (with four feet of sidewalk clearance), farmer's markets, and outdoor cafes," Hartford's new zoning code will help the city's businesses rebound in the open air.

The Hartford Zoning Code is politically smart and offers an excellent example of a citywide solution for enhancing diverse neighborhoods while decreasing auto-dependence.

Rancho Cucamonga, CA

When land outside Rancho Cucamonga was no longer needed by the county and was labeled "excess property," the city saw an opportunity to create a unique, walkable neighborhood while dramatically expanding the size of its existing nature preserve. The resulting collaboration between the county and city led to the annexation of previously unincorporated land and the creation of the Etiwanda Heights neighborhood plan and code.

The plan contains two main sections: a "rural/conservation area" and a "neighborhood area." About 75 percent of the area covered by the new zoning is classified as rural/conservation, which includes three new nature preserves and a network of trails for recreation and education. The remaining quarter of land – adjacent to existing residential development – makes up the "neighborhood area" and with a connected, multimodal street network, a flexible menu of housing types, a mixed-use neighborhood center.

"The City of Rancho Cucamonga greatly appreciates this recognition of the new Etiwanda Heights Neighborhood and Conservation Plan – an innovative form-based development code, which provides the ideal balance between high-quality development and permanent conservation of the natural habitat. With its clear and market-based vision, Etiwanda Heights will offer environmentally friendly, walkable neighborhoods to a wide diversity of residents," said L. Dennis Michael, Mayor of Rancho Cucamonga.

The code is easy to follow and includes ample visuals that make the document clear and approachable. It also satisfies stringent California environmental requirements and avoids possible litigation with an innovative policy for transfer of development rights from the rural/conservation area to the neighborhood area.

Excerpted from Sean Doyle, "Progress and Preservation in Award-Winning Zoning Codes," June 1, 2020. https://smartgrowthamerica.org/progress-preservation-in-award-winning-zoning-codes/

Tree Ordinances

Towns and cities that want to protect their trees need to devote the necessary tome to crafting tree ordinances, which can have the force of law within municipal boundaries. Ordinances define what trees are protected and the extent of protection, and conditions for alteration or removal.

Tree protection regulations are often incorporated within other ordinances – such as the landscaping or buffer sections of land development codes. A landscape ordinance typically establishes required landscaping provisions, such as number, placement, and types of suitable plants or trees. It may require landscaping or trees in parking lots or buffer zones, which may fall under a separate buffer ordinance as well. A buffer ordinance may protect views of adjacent property owners in commercial and/or residential developments, and may protect water quality in ponds, streams, and other water bodies. It may also establish specifications for acceptable buffers for noise, sightlines, and the vegetation next to water bodies, known as riparian buffers.[27] The riparian zone is the ecosystem where water meets land. While riparian zones comprise under 10 percent of the land mass in the US, they provide nearly all the instream nutrients to the aquatic food chain.[28]

Fortunately, many model ordinances have developed.[29] A standard approach might follow an outline[30] like this:

Purpose and Definitions – setting forth the intent of the ordinance and sets for definitions for key terms such as arborist, heritage trees, or tree canopy. Terms such as "street tree," "small tree," "medium tree," and "large tree" may also be defined as well as "private tree," and "public hazard."

Authorities – describing the authority of the ordinance and any decision-making body, such as a department, board, or commission that may have responsibility for maintaining and/or enforcing the ordinance.

Applicability – describing the areas covered by the ordinance such as public land, parks, medians, rights of way, easements, and cemeteries.

City Arborist – describing qualifications, duties, and authority of the arborist position.

Certification of Arborists – listing conditions for certification of arborists, including fees for certification, frequency of renewal, and need for surety bonds.

Insurance – describing an insurance that must be carried by private arborists (may also be part of the permits section).

Landscaping – explaining the procedure to approve landscaping on public property – for example review by the director of the City's parks and recreation director.

Tree planting, maintenance, and removal – detailing who has authority to plant, maintain, and remove trees; any criteria for species and spacing; distance from sidewalks and public buildings; restrictions on topping (the controversial practice of pruning trees by removing their highest branches). This section may have separate clauses for public versus private trees, or these may become their own sections in the ordinance. Adjacent landowner responsibilities may also be included.

Permits – covering permits needed for planting, maintenance, removal, and replacement.

Enforcement – covering the mechanisms for enforcement of the tree ordinance.
Penalties, Claims, and Appeals – describing the consequences for violating the tree ordinance and the process for litigating and appealing violations.
Other – covering any areas not described in other sections.

Tree ordinances need not follow any particular format; they can be customized to fit different situations such as streets, parks, public areas, commercial buildings, and residential neighborhoods. However, a tree ordinance is structured, it should be reviewed by expert environmentalists and attorneys to ensure that it offers the maximum protection permitted under law.

Heritage Preservation

Zoning for conservation and for historic districts is clearly an indispensable tool for conserving a locality's character. So too are strong tree ordinances. In addition to such local tools, there can be additional protections through "heritage preservation" initiatives.

The World Heritage Convention

A key document for environmental conservation and historic preservation is the report on the World Heritage Convention held in 1972 that formed the basis for much conservation since that time. A website maintained by the United Nations Educational, Scientific, and Cultural Organization (UNESCO)[31] identifies the kind of natural or cultural sites that can be considered for inscription on the World Heritage List.[32] The list includes some 150 cities and towns deemed worthy of protection in their entirety.

Towns and cities faced with the destruction of their key assets can ask their national governments (typically via a legislative representative) to apply for recognition as a World Heritage site. The benefits include increased tourism and often financial assistance for preservation.[33]

Categories for "cultural heritage" are the following (citing verbatim from the UNESCO website[34]):

Monuments: architectural works, works of monumental sculpture and painting, elements or structures of an archaeological nature, inscriptions, cave dwellings, and combinations of features, which are of outstanding universal value form the point of view of history, art, or science.

Groups of buildings: groups of separate or connected buildings that, because of their architecture, their homogeneity, or their place in the landscape, are of outstanding universal value from the point of view of history, art, or science.

Sites: works of man or the combined works of nature and man, and areas including archaeological sites that are of outstanding universal value from the historical, aesthetic, ethnological, or anthropological point of view.

Categories for "natural heritage" are as follows:

Natural features consisting of physical and biological formations or groups of such formations, which are of outstanding universal value from the aesthetic or scientific point of view.

Geological and physiographical formations and precisely delineated areas that constitute the habitat of threatened species of animals and plants of outstanding universal value from the point of view of science or conservation.

Natural sites or precisely delineated natural areas of outstanding universal value from the point of view of science, conservation, or natural beauty.

National and Regional Registers

Many countries and regions maintain registries of historic properties.

China has inventoried and protected its "immovable cultural relics" and has identified certain cities as having "cultural value." According to a law passed in 1982 and most recently revised in 2002, it is illegal to harm cultural relics or to alter the nature of heritage.[35] There are also consequences for altering the nature of a city.

> Where the layout, environment, historical features, etc. of a famous city of historical and cultural value are seriously undermined, the State Council shall revoke its title of famous city of historical and cultural value; where the layout, environment, historical features, etc. of a town, neighborhood or village of historical and cultural value are seriously undermined, the peoples government of the relevant province, autonomous region or municipality directly under the Central Government shall revoke its title of neighborhood, town or village of historical and cultural value; and the persons directly in charge and the other persons directly responsible shall be given administrative sanctions according to law.[36]

The European Union offers a European Heritage label to heritage sites. This relatively new program has identified 48 sites to date, with so far 25 member nations participating.[37] These are defined as "monuments; natural, underwater, archaeological, industrial, or urban sites; cultural landscapes, places of remembrance, cultural goods and objects and intangible heritage associated with a place, including contemporary heritage."[38]

In the US, the National Register, administered by the National Park Service under the US Department of the Interior, accepts applications for buildings that meet certain criteria for historical value. The National Register supports a nation-wide program to link public and private efforts for identification, evaluation, and preservation of historic and archeological resources. The process begins when a national, state, or tribal preservation officer; a scholar; or a property owner nominates a structure for preservation.[39] Property owners in the Register may qualify for federal grants, and/or for a 20 percent investment tax credit for the certified rehabilitation of income-producing structures, including commercial buildings, industrial buildings, and multifamily rental properties.[40] Federal tax deductions may also be available for cities or citizens making charitable contributions to historically important land areas or structures.

Concluding Reflections

"When it's gone – it's gone."

The character Scotty, in
Star Trek, The Next Generation, 1992

A city's zoning ordinance makes a critical difference in defining and preserving a city's character and – ultimately – sustainability. Citizen involvement in the planning and zoning process can help ensure positive results for the current and future generations. This is not to say that cities and their residents can ignore the economic impact of their zoning decisions. The next chapter of this book will explore the economic implications of varying zoning policies, offering guidance on how to achieve an optimal approach.

Notes

1 Part 3: Typical Elements of a Form-Based Code – PlannersWeb. See also https://mrsc.org/Home/Explore-Topics/Planning/Development-Types-and-Land-Uses/Form-Based-Codes.aspx and see https://planning-org-uploaded-media.s3.amazonaws.com/document/Zoning-Practice-2008-05.pdf
2 Gentrification is pricing out longtime Salt Lake City residents from their neighborhoods (sltrib.com).
3 See, for example, 163.3202, Fla. Stat. https://m.flsenate.gov/Statutes/163.3202 and https://www.fbfl.us/80/Land-Development-Code
4 https://www.epa.gov/smartgrowth/codes-support-smart-growth-development
5 Cook County Farm Bureau | Illinois Zoning and Agriculture (cookcfb.org).

6 Microsoft Word – 147-Urban Sustainable Development. Measuring Capacity Outweighs Measuring Development Level_rev (un.org), p. 1.

7 See this graphic from the Cato Institute: https://www.freedominthe50states.org/land

8 The first court case affirming this was Village of Euclid v. Ambler Realty Co., 272 US 365 (1926). Justia summarized it here: If they are not arbitrary or unreasonable, zoning ordinances are constitutional under the police power of local governments as long as they have some relation to public health, safety, morals, or general welfare. https://supreme.justia.com/cases/fed eral/us/272/365/#tab-opinion-1931541

9 1961–2018 – link lost.

10 Natural grade typically means the original condition of the ground surface as it existed prior to mechanical grading or disturbance.

11 Atherton Municipal Code, https://www.codepublishing.com/CA/Atherton/html/Athe rton17/Atherton1742.html

12 For "common area easement" language, see https://casedocs.omniagentsolutions.com/ cmsvol2/pub_47370/827657_825.pdf

13 A sample conservation easement, https://www.law.uh.edu/faculty/thester/courses/Envi ronmental-Practicum-2020/sample_easement_deed.pdfSmap

14 See this Model Conservation Easement from the Natural Lands Trust, https://www.epa. gov/sites/production/files/2015-12/documents/nps-ordinanceuments-a2e-model-land.pdf

15 https://richmondbizsense.com/2020/12/10/city-withdraws-pulse-zoning-changes-plans-to-revisit-proposal-next-year/

16 http://www.richmond300.com/

17 https://richmondbizsense.com/2020/12/15/city-council-adopts-richmond-300-plan-with-promise-to-amend-it/

18 For more on this topic, see the real estate category at Findlaw, https://realestate.findlaw. com/land-use-laws/types-of-zoning.html

19 See the code for Hermosa Beach, https://www.codepublishing.com/CA/HermosaBeach/ html/HermosaBeach17/HermosaBeach1726.html#17.26.030

20 For a sample code, Article 5, page 16, on the Park County code for Colorado. https:// parkco.us/DocumentCenter/View/264/Article-V?bidId%26%23x003D

21 https://www.codepublishing.com/CA/HermosaBeach/html/HermosaBeach17/Hermosa Beach1732.html#17.32

22 In St. Anthony Idaho, "The low intensity mixed-use district (MU1) has an allowable housing unit density of up to 8 units per acre and is intended to have a more residential style rather than commercial.[18] The moderate intensity mixed-use district (MU2) has a permitted housing unit density of 16 units per acre with a special use permit and is more commercial in style." https://sustainablecitycode.org/brief/mixed-use-zoning-3/

23 See for example, the Richmond, California, Design Review Board. Design Review Board | Richmond, CA – Official Website. See also RLCMappingMtgFLyer (richmond.ca.us).

24 Equal Protection and Aesthetic Zoning: A Possible Crack and a Preemptive Repair (ufl.edu).

25 https://lrs.sog.unc.edu/bill/zoningdesign-aesthetic-controls-1

26 Part 3: Typical Elements of a Form-Based Code – PlannersWeb. See also https://mrsc.org/ Home/Explore-Topics/Planning/Development-Types-and-Land-Uses/Form-Based-Codes.aspx and see https://planning-org-uploaded-media.s3.amazonaws.com/document/Zoning-Practice -2008-05.pdf

27 https://conservationtools-production.s3.amazonaws.com/library_item_files/1486/1594/de veloping-successful-tree-ordinances.pdf?AWSAccessKeyId=AKIAIQFJLILYGVDR4AMQ&Ex pires=1603673785&Signature=cuivJLUpPiTHV2el%2FxPcy62Q3mU%3D

28 https://www.ripariantours.com/what-is-riparian

29 For links to many tree ordinances, see https://www.asca-consultants.org/page/ TreeOrdinances

30 This outline is based on samples from the Urban Forestry Network Model Tree Ordinance (urbanforestrynetwork.org) and the Arbor Day Foundation Print ED356962.TIF (9 pages), https:// files.eric.ed.gov/fulltext/ED356962.pdf, The sample text is from a variety of ordinances.

31 World Heritage Convention 1972, https://whc.unesco.org/en/convention/

32 https://whc.unesco.org/en/list/

33 For an explanation of benefits, see https://whc.unesco.org/en/faq/20. For a link to finan cial assistance see https://whc.unesco.org/en/intassistance/

34 https://whc.unesco.org/en/compendium/

35 https://web.archive.org/web/20120501152230/http://www.sach.gov.cn/tabid/311/InfoID/ 383/Default.aspx

36 Ibid.

37 https://ec.europa.eu/programmes/creative-europe/actions/heritage-label_en

38 https://ec.europa.eu/programmes/creative-europe/actions/heritage-label_en

39 https://www.nps.gov/subjects/nationalhistoriclandmarks/nomination-process.htm

40 "This credit can be combined with a straight-line depreciation period of 27.5 years for resi dential property (31.5 years for nonresidential property) for the depreciable basis of the rehabil itated building, reduced by the amount of the tax credit claimed." https://www.nps.gov/ subjects/nationalregister/faqs.htm

Chapter 5
Tools for a Sustainable Economy: Budgeting, Accounting, and Taxes

Few if any communities can sustain themselves without taxing their citizens. While some local governments can survive without a tax on income and/or sales, most find it necessary to levy a tax on property.[1] Communities by nature share a natural, social, and physical infrastructure, and they need funds to support it. While national, state, and county governments may provide such support, for many localities, the seats of these governments are neither close nor committed enough to serve them well. Such communities opt for a more local government – hence, the array of towns, townships, boroughs, and cities that dot our maps.

These local governments have their work cut out for them. The yearly expenditures of local governments in the US alone (including state-level expenditures) amount to some $3 trillion, or nearly 14 percent of the US gross domestic product (GDP) of $21 trillion.[2] In Europe, local government expenditures amount to less than $1 trillion euros, or about 6 percent of the bloc's €14.8 trillion GDP[3] – although there are great differences by country. For example, in Scandinavia, most government spending is done by local rather than national governments, while in Eastern Europe, the relationship is reversed.[4]

While payments from the federal or central government finance some of these expenditures, the local citizenry makes up the difference. Municipal revenue comes from a variety of sources, including issuances of bonds and receipt of grants from land trusts or other nonprofit institutions (discussed in chapters 7 through 9), but a significant portion of municipal revenue comes from local taxes, the focus of this chapter. The following pages will explain the basics of three interrelated topics – municipal budgeting, municipal accounting, and municipal taxation – with guidance on how to achieve environmental conservation without an undue tax burden on citizens.

How Budgeting, Accounting, and Taxation Interrelate

Municipal budgeting does not occur in a vacuum. It is part of a planning continuum that includes planning, periodic financial reporting (accounting), and periodic taxation – typically on an annual basis (see Figure 5.1).

https://doi.org/10.1515/9783110689860-005

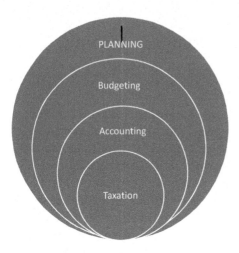

Figure 5.1: Budgeting, Accounting, and Taxation as Interdependent Aspects of Planning.

Figure 5.1 shows a sequence from planning to budgeting to accounting to taxes to emphasize the political importance of taxes. In setting their budgets, city leaders always have taxes in mind because they do not want to raise the tax rate if they can help it. (Nothing makes a politician less popular.) Similarly, when accounting for how the city is spending money, reports must answer the fundamental question that citizens may have: what am I getting for my tax dollars?

The citizens' tax burden is a function of two things – property values and the millage rate.

– Property values are determined by a designated property appraiser (typically an employee of the municipality or its county); millage rate is set by the municipality (typically recommended by staff and approved by the governing body).
– The millage rate may be based on budgetary needs, but cities must have due process.

When property values go up, the millage rate is supposed to go down to match the previous year's taxes – as the so-called rollback (or "rolled back") rate. Municipalities are expected to use the rollback rate, unless there is a good budgetary reason to exceed it. Meanwhile, the published financials of a municipality should explain the budget and the tax rate. In some jurisdictions, there is a requirement, called Truth in Millage, or TRIM. Such a requirement mandates that municipalities must clearly identify any millage that produces a tax over the rollback rate as a tax increase.[5] This is required even for millage rates that have gone down, if they did not go down far enough to offset increases in property values. For cities concerned about the public perception of tax rates, budgeting and taxation are interconnected; planning budgets include consideration of tax rates (as shown in Figure 5.1).

Municipal Budgeting: Importance of Citizen Participation

Every year (or in some cases every other year[6]) cities plan for what they will spend and what income they will receive. The budget cycle may follow the calendar year or another cycle, following national governments. Many local governments (like their states and/or countries) use the calendar year, that is January through December. Other common choices are April through March, July through June, and October through September. When referring to fiscal years, it is common to refer to the year that ends the cycle; so, the 2021–2022 fiscal year is referred to as FY 2022.[7]

A public budget is a plan of expected incomes and expenditures for the upcoming fiscal period – generally a twelve-month period that may or may not correspond to the calendar year.[8] A common budget format shows an *operating budget*, showing income and expenditures for the current period, and a *capital budget*, which shows income and expenditures related to long-term capital investments and improvements. Many jurisdictions are legally required to balance their budgets. While they may carry debt, they may not run at a deficit; they are required to have a reserve fund.[9] This balanced budget requirement forces localities to raise taxes and/or reduce expenditures, difficult choices that each jurisdiction experiences in its own way.

How expenses get categorized must of course follow the accounting rules that govern the jurisdiction (typically set by a national body). Sometimes accounting rules require one way of classifying expenses but permit the use of notes or supplemental information that shows the same information in a different way. Municipal governments are wise to report as fully as possible, including in the drafting stage. Draft budgets can draw public attention and (ideally) inspire public commentary when it comes time for the municipal government to approve the budget.

Government accounting standards typically classify municipal expenditures by nature, distinguishing between wages and supplies, for example. But they can also be classified by function, distinguishing between wages and supplies for police versus wages and supplies parks.

The International Public Sector Accounting Standards Board® (IPSASB®), which publishes accounting standards for government bodies,[10] lists categories of government expenditures by economic nature, such as:

- Wages, salaries, and employee benefits. In a typical US municipality, about 60 percent of compensation will be awarded in wages and salaries, and about 40 percent in benefits. (In the business world, the balance is 70 to 30.[11])
- Supplies used.
- Depreciation and amortization expense. These required entries for "expenses" do not actually represent cash expenditures but conform to an accounting convention that recognizes the diminution of value of physical assets over time. (Ironically, when it comes to heritage assets such as historic buildings that attract tourists, true economic value may actually increase, so this is an example of a disconnect between accounting conventions and economic reality.)
- Finance costs. Many municipalities carry debt, so financial reports organized by nature would disclose the cost of interest payments made on loans. For major cities in the US (with populations exceeding 500,000), the average percentage of municipal budgets spent in paying off debt is about 20 percent.[12] That figure is lower for smaller cities – with 5 percent as a reasonable estimate.[13]

But for those who went to get a real sense of how city spends money, the IP-SASB offers a different template, which it says can also be used for financial reports, or at least for budgeting (where standards are more flexible).[14] Here are some categories of expenses by function:
- General public services
- Public order and safety
- Recreation, culture, and religion
- Economic affairs
- Environmental protection

The inclusion of environmental protection as a category is a reasonable practice, particularly for municipalities in states or countries that require environmental protection by their constitutions.[15]

Budgets in the public sector, as in the corporate world, go through preparation, approval, implementation, and evaluation (including an independent audit to ensure proper accounting).[16] A municipality's planning and financial departments will be involved in all phases, but arguably the most important of these phases are the preparation and approval phases, because the citizenry and their elected representatives are involved.

Budgets should be prepared and approved in a manner consistent with the official goals of a municipality as expressed in documents such as a comprehensive plan (as discussed in Chapter 3: Creating a Sustainability Plan). Many jurisdictions require citizen involvement in such plans. Furthermore, as an additional safeguard for democracy, in the approval phase, town or city councils consider budgets and the citizenry (or should be) is invited to comment. During periods of budget tightening, when popular social services are being eliminated, citizens can appear and speak out in favor of the programs. Conversely, if a city plans to spend money on projects that citizens do not support, the residents of a city can appear and speak out against the expenditures – whether because of their high cost, their negative environmental impact, or their adverse impact on the local culture.

Municipal Accounting: Valuing Assets

Most local governments follow the accounting standards of their countries. In the US, these are called government accounting standards (GAS) and are set by the Government Accounting Standards Board (GASB). Other countries around the world have their own standards. Countries that are part of the European Union follow the International Financial Reporting Standards (IFRS) set by the International Accounting Standards Board in the private sector, but what of local governments? Their standards vary from country to country. The European Commission has launched an initiative to develop European Public Sector Accounting Standards.[17]

Furthermore, at a more global level, the International Public Sector Accounting Standards Board® (IPSASB®) strives to improve public sector financial reporting worldwide through the development of IPSAS®, which are international accrual-based accounting standards intended for use by governments and other public sector entities around the globe.[18] While these standards do not have the force of law unless they are adopted, they represent what will likely be the wave of the future for many local governments.

For example, consider asset valuation. One of the problems of accounting in the private sector also appears in the public sector, and that is the gap between the historical cost of an asset (sometimes not even known in the case of an older city) and the book value of the asset. The Parthenon of Athens, the Bois de Boulogne in Paris, and the Brandenburg Gate in Berlin have value far beyond how they are carried on the cities' books. At the same time, they may not generate cash in any direct way, and in fact may cost the city money to maintain and protect (and rightly so). In this sense they are like city streets, which, while of indispensable value, also have the effect of a liability – another proof that government accounting may work at cross purposes with economic reality.[19]

Global accounting standards via the IPSASB (in paragraphs 88–90) has tried to tackle this problem with respect to disclosures of property, plant, and equipment values.[20] The IPSAS standards cover the topic of heritage assets.

As noted by IPSASB, "Public sector entities may have large holdings of heritage assets that have been acquired over many years and by various means, including purchase, donation, bequest, and sequestration. These assets are rarely held for their ability to generate cash inflows, and there may be legal or social obstacles for their being used for such purposes" (see Box 5.1). Such assets lie well outside the reach of traditional accounting. For this reason, the standards give cities great flexibility in accounting treatment.

Box 5.1: Heritage Assets – Discussion from the International Public Sector Accounting Standards Board
Some assets may be described as heritage assets because of their cultural, environmental, or historical significance. Examples of heritage assets include historical buildings and monuments, archeological sites, conservation areas and nature reserves, and works of art. Certain characteristics, including the following, are often displayed by heritage assets (although these characteristics are not exclusive to such assets):
-Their value in cultural, environmental, educational, and historical terms is unlikely to be fully reflected in a financial value based purely on a market price.
-Legal and/or statutory prohibitions may impose prohibitions or severe restrictions on disposal by sale.
-They are often irreplaceable, and their value may increase over time, even if their physical condition deteriorates.
-It may be difficult to estimate their useful lives, which in some cases could be several hundred years.
Source: *IPSASB Handbook 1* (2020): 527–528.

Municipal Taxation

When it comes to taxes, the question, of course, is *how* to tax local citizens, and *how much* to tax them. Municipalities may levy property tax, income tax, sales tax, and/or various special fees to generate the income they need to pay for public needs.

The tax rate is a function of two things – the millage rate and the assessment of property values.
- The assessment of property values is done by an appraiser in a separate process. Growth can increase the market value of homes.
- The millage rate is set by the municipality. It may be based on budgetary needs, but cities must have due process. When property values go up, *the*

millage rate is supposed to go down unless there is a good budgetary reason not to use the roll back rate.

Every year a municipality (hereinafter referred to as city) sets its ad valorem (property) tax rate. It sets a millage rate expressed as dollars per $1,000 in assessed value (hence the term "millage").

The city either increases it, decreases it, or leaves it the same as the previous year through the millage "rollback" rate. The rollback strategy of keeping the millage rate the same is relatively common.[21]

The rollback rate is the number that, when multiplied by the assessed value, would give you the same dollar amount as the previous year.

- Assuming property values are flat (equal to what they were the previous year, the "rollback rate" would be the same as in that year.
- If property values decline (unlikely) the rollback rate would be a higher millage.
- But if property values increase, then the rollback rate would need to be set at lower millage.

Some municipalities have capped property tax assessments[22] – an idea made real in California nearly half a century ago (in 1978) through Proposition 13. which required that residential, commercial, and industrial properties be taxed based on their purchase price. The tax is limited to no more than 1 percent of the purchase price (at the time of purchase), with an annual adjustment equal to the rate of inflation or 2 percent, whichever is lower. Thus, the taxable value of property in California is often less than its market value, keeping property taxes low. In 2020, voters narrowly defeated Proposition 15, which would have created a split roll in which commercial properties would be taxed at their full market value.[23]

Concluding Reflections

> Our new Constitution is now established, and has an appearance that promises permanency; but in this world nothing can be said to be certain, except death and taxes.
> Benjamin Franklin, Letter to Jean-Baptiste Le Roy (November 13, 1789)

Benjamin Franklin's wisdom still holds after nearly a quarter century. The US Constitution has endured, and so too has human mortality as well as that necessary evil we call taxation. Fortunately, as mentioned earlier, taxes are not the only source of revenue for cities. Cities can also raise money by bonds, defray expenses by working with land trusts, or seek funding from grants – the subjects of the next three chapters.

Notes

1 The Rise and Fall of the 'Freest Little City in Texas', https://www.texasobserver.org

2 Josh Bivens, "How to make federal aid to state and local governments more transparent and effective," *Economic Policy Institute,* December 18, 2019, Bivens | How to make federal aid to state and local governments more transparent and effective: Boost direct grants and make them respond more automatically to downturns | Economic Policy Institute, https://www.epi.org

3 Archive: Government finance statistics – revenue and expenditure by subsector of general government – Statistics Explained, https://www.europa.eu. "In 2016 in the EU, total revenue at general government level was equal to 44.7% of GDP. In 2016, central government total revenue accounted for 51.9 % of general government total revenue, state government for 7.1%, local government for 13.3% and social security funds for 27.7%."

4 Archive: Government finance statistics – revenue and expenditure by subsector of general government – Statistics Explained, https://www.europa.eu

5 In Florida, for example, "The resolution or ordinance adopting the millage rate must include the percentage increase over the rolled-back rate. When the percent change of rolled-back rate is greater than 0.00, publish a Notice of Proposed Tax Increase advertisement with an adjacent Budget Summary advertisement," MEMORANDUM, https://www.floridarevenue.com

6 "Most state governments use an annual budget cycle, just under half of the states use a biennial budget cycle which spans two years, and 2 states employ a combination of annual and biennial cycles," https://www.nlc.org/resource/cities-101-budgets/

7 For a chart of fiscal years, see Fiscal year – Wikipedia, https://www.epi.org Archive: Government finance statistics – revenue and expenditure by subsector of general government – Statistics Explained, https://www.europa.eu. "In 2016 in the EU, total revenue at general government level was equal to 44.7% of GDP. In 2016, central government total revenue accounted for 51.9 % of general government total revenue, state government for 7.1%, local government for 13.3% and social security funds for 27.7%."

8 The observations in this section are based on the author's own experience and research as well as the following source: https://www.nlc.org/resource/cities-101-budgets/

9 See for example https://www.newportbeachca.gov/home/showdocument?id=20838

10 See 2020 Handbook of International Public Sector Accounting Pronouncements | IFAC, https://www.ipsasb.org/publications/2020-handbook-international-public-sector-accounting-pronouncements

11 Employer Costs for Employee Compensation – December 2020, https://www.bls.gov/news.release/pdf/ecec.pdf

12 What Are Cities Spending Big On? Increasingly, It's Debt, https://www.governing.com/archive/gov-legacy-cities-bills-debt.html

13 This estimate is based on 2017 data that includes state governments, https://www.urban.org/policy-centers/cross-center-initiatives/state-and-local-finance-initiative/state-and-local-backgrounders/state-and-local-expenditures#Question2

14 2020 Handbook of International Public Sector Accounting Pronouncements | IFAC, https://www.ipsasb.org/publications/2020-handbook-international-public-sector-accounting-pronouncements, p. 2001.
15 Conservation-Funding-at-a-Glance-updated-Nov-2019.pdf (conservationalmanac.org)
16 https://www.nlc.org/resource/cities-101-budgets/
17 "Information on income and expenses, and assets and liabilities is important for accountability and informed decision-making. In contrast to the private sector, no common accounting standards for financial reporting are in place for the public sector in the EU." https://ec.europa.eu/eurostat/web/epsas
18 IPSASB-HandBook-2020_Volume-1_W_0.pdf, https://www.ifac.org/system/files/publications/files/IPSASB-HandBook-2020_Volume-1_W_0.pdf
19 Is a street an asset?, https://www.strongtowns.org/journal/2014/8/19/is-a-street-an-asset.html
20 IPSASB-HandBook-2020_Volume-1_W_0.pdf, https://www.ipsasb.org/publications/2020-handbook-international-public-sector-accounting-pronouncements, pp. 544–545.
21 For example, in Florida, some 80 percent of cities followed rollback from 2015 through 2019 (roughly 10 percent increased the millage rate and roughly 10 percent lowered it). State of the Cities (Florida League of Cities, 2019) https://www.floridaleagueofcities.com/docs/default-source/default-document-library/2019-state-of-the-cities.pdf?sfvrsn=c405dad5_6
22 https://www.lincolninst.edu/publications/policy-focus-reports/property-tax-assessment-limits
23 California Proposition 15, Tax on Commercial and Industrial Properties for Education and Local Government Funding Initiative (2020), https://ballotpedia.org/California_Proposition_15,_Tax_on_Commercial_and_Industrial_Properties_for_Education_and_Local_Government_Funding_Initiative_(2020). See also Just so you know, there's no loophole in Proposition 13 – Orange County Register, https://www.ocregister.com/2020/07/26/just-so-you-know-theres-no-loophole-in-proposition-13/

Chapter 6
Tools for Sustainable Engineering

A road trip through small towns in any country will reveal the varied physical backdrop for civic life: street signs, sidewalks, and bridges; stop signs, traffic lights, and utility poles; post offices and city buildings; ball parks and public parking lots; reservoirs and recycling centers. Unseen will be the workings of water and sewer systems serving these public facilities as well as homes and commercial buildings. These elements exist within an even wider infrastructure that includes the electronic communication networks operating and connecting all these systems.

Thus, even as the world economy moves toward the digital and virtual, our collective reality still includes the three-dimensional and tangible. We live among structures that are not only natural and societal but also "man-made" – engineered by men and women past and present. And much of this physical infrastructure is constructed according to local building codes.[1]

Such codes exist within an even broader infrastructure and include the socioeconomic situation and the environment itself (see Figure 6.1).[2]

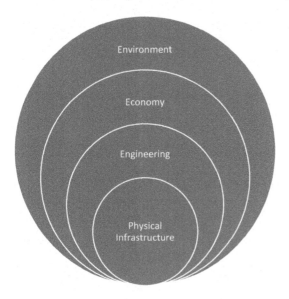

Figure 6.1: How Physical Infrastructure Fits into a Larger System.

https://doi.org/10.1515/9783110689860-006

City governments play a major role in the creation of local physical infrastructure and in ensuring its connection to higher values. While national, state, and county authorities bear some responsibility for the construction and maintenance of facilities located within the boundaries of a town or city, in many cases these facilities are planned, built, and maintained locally on behalf of local citizens. Therefore, no guide to municipal sustainability would be complete without a careful look at local civil engineering.

The first part of this chapter aims to capture the principles that govern local "hard infrastructure" by presenting the key issues that city leaders and activists are now monitoring for the common good. After some basic definitions, the chapter continues with discussions on roadways, water systems, and building codes as a kind of primer for nonengineers serving as city leaders and advocates. The chapter concludes with some emerging paradigms for a truly integrated approach. In the words of one expert, civil engineering today must "holistically consider the environmental, economic, and social impacts of its work on local, regional, and global systems."[3]

Some Key Definitions

Because terms like engineering and infrastructure can be used very broadly, this chapter begins with a discussion of terminology.

Definition of Civil Engineering

The quality of life for people all over the world, particularly in developed economies, is determined in part by civil engineers. After all, engineering, by definition, uses scientific principles to "design and build machines, structures, and other things, including bridges, roads, vehicles, and buildings,"[4] and a civil engineer is one who builds these structures for public use.[5] A civil engineer who works for a local government may get involved in the city's infrastructure at every phase – including not only design itself but also planning, review, and budgeting.[6] Most municipalities employ at least one engineer who is dedicated to infrastructure. Among other roles, such engineers ensure that public buildings and structures meet a variety of standards, including safety codes.

Definition of Infrastructure

Municipalities striving to strengthen their infrastructure can consider the following checklist of engineering issues from the Conference Board's Center for Economic Development:

> A reasonable definition of infrastructure projects includes those relating to surface transportation; aviation; ports; water resources projects; energy production, generation, storage, transmission, and distribution; pipelines; stormwater and sewerage; drinking water; broadband internet communication; and cybersecurity. This long list of vital items illustrates the reach of infrastructure throughout US economic life.[7]

For a longer (and more specific) list of infrastructure items, readers can consult the 2021 guide by the American Society of Civil Engineers (ASCE).[8] ASCE publishes the *Journal of Infrastructure Systems* featuring articles exploring interconnections of infrastructure elements in larger systems.[9]

Funding for City Roads and Water

Many infrastructure initiatives concentrate on roads and water,[10] with the state and local governments bearing most of the burden – rather than the federal government or public-private partnerships.

In its study of average annual expenditures on transportation (e.g., highways, mass transit, aviation, water transportation, and rail) and water (e.g., dams, levees, water distribution system, and wastewater treatment), the Congressional Budget Office (CBO) found that state and local governments shouldered three-quarters of the burden for financing these – not only for the most recent period studied but also for the previous 60 years.[11] Meanwhile, a separate CBO study found that public-private partnerships for financing transportation or water have been extremely rare.[12] With little federal or private money available, state, and municipal governments are often on their own when it comes to funding infrastructure.[13]

Of course, this balance can vary from one country to another and from one administration to another within a given country. Federal infrastructure spending rose in the Great Depression of the 1930s and is likely to rise over the next several years as governments around the world cope with the effects of the global pandemic. In such eras, cities may prevail upon higher government authorities to assist them in the construction and maintenance of infrastructure. Conversely, there may be times and political climates in which the private sector becomes trusted enough to pay a major role in the physical infrastructure of a municipality.

Green Engineering: A Global Trend

Many of the items traditionally associated with engineering involve hard materials such as concrete and steel. These are referred to as "gray engineering." But there is a trend in the engineering community to work more adaptively with nature, giving rise to "green engineering." The US Environmental Protection Agency has defined this as "the design, commercialization, and use of processes and products in a way that reduces pollution, promotes sustainability, and minimizes risk to human health and the environment without sacrificing economic viability and efficiency."[14] It has published a municipal guide that covers funding options (fees, loans, grants); retrofitting (adaptation of existing built environment); green streets (green infrastructure in public right of way); rainwater harvesting (why and how to capture rainwater); and incentives (what a local government can offer private landowners to motivate collaboration).[15]

The US is not the only country promoting green engineering. In fact, this value has been embraced by the International Federation of Consulting Engineers based in Geneva, Switzerland (known as the Fédération Internationale des Ingénieurs-Conseils, or FIDIC, its founding name in the French language).[16] FIDIC has produced a manifesto on Consulting Engineers and the Environment that sets principles for green engineering.[17] FIDIC, which has a membership of more than one million engineers in more than 100 countries, has had an influence on engineering in cities around the world through its publications and programs on urban engineering.[18]

Green Engineering for Roads

Roadways, ranging from city streets to the highways passing through cities, have a major impact on the quality of life for local citizens. With much of the economic burden for streets falling on cities, leaders and activists are rightly interested in ensuring that their roads are built to last. The traditional approach to roads placed them squarely in the realm of a "gray" infrastructure – known for its use of highly impermeable concrete. But a new and promising approach is arising that may be even more sustainable in the long run. The nickname for this is "green streets."

Green streets enable a biofriendly stormwater management approach, using vegetation and permeable surfaces to the greatest extent possible. As defined by the US Environmental Protection Agency, such streets may incorporate vegetation (perennials, shrubs, trees), soil, and engineered systems (including permeable pavements) to slow, filter, and cleanse stormwater runoff from impervious surfaces (e.g., streets, sidewalks). Green streets are designed to capture and absorb rainwater rather than move it along into storm sewer systems (gutters, drains, pipes) that move the water into surface waters, rivers, and streams.[19] Unlike traditional streets, green streets retain runoff at the source rather than discharging to a runoff off-site. Green streets offer many other potential benefits that include improving water quality, absorbing carbon (sequestration), and reducing urban heat island effects – an issue that can have unfairly disparate social impact.[20]

Street Safety

Another important goal in the engineering of streets and sidewalks is safety. As described by the Complete Streets initiative techniques include sidewalks, bike lanes (or wide-paved shoulders), bus lanes, comfortable and accessible public transportation stops, frequent and safe crossing opportunities, median islands, accessible pedestrian signals, curb extensions, narrower travel lanes, and roundabouts.[21] All these engineering feats serve to enhance the quality of life in towns and cities. In fact, roadways can even be a matter of life and death – the reason that many cities have joined formal initiatives to reduce traffic accidents by lowering speed limits and redesigning areas that have a history of crashes.[22]

Parking

Another hot topic for the engineering concerns of cities is parking. Since much of the sustainability movement supports walkability, bicycling, and public transit,[23] it is not surprising that parking lots – which accommodate cars and trucks – are not a high priority for municipal sustainability initiatives. Many municipalities have ordinances setting parking minimums that require builders to provide a minimum number of off-street parking spaces. Such ordinances obviously cause the proliferation of parking lots and parking garages. This trend poses two problems for sustainability. First, the lots and garages tend to be created with impermeable materials, contributing to stormwater runoff, and hence flooding. Second, and more gravely, these structures often cause the destruction of existing buildings. This was the case in Detroit, where a city council voted to demolish the historic Saturday Night Building[24] to create more parking in a city that already has ample parking spaces.[25]

When citizens get involved in the design of their streets, whether for environmental, safety, or other reasons, this involvement can motivate cities to spend more on infrastructure.[26] In the short term, this can have a negative impact on city budgets. But infrastructure investments made with environmental principles in mind can pay off financially in the long run.[27]

Green Engineering for Water Systems

There are some 3.5 million miles of storm sewers, 270 million storm drains, and 2.5 million stormwater treatment assets across the US alone.[28] Under a program of the US Environmental Protection Agency (EPA), municipalities are required to map their stormwater systems. The program establishes a national pollutant discharge elimination system (NPDES),[29] and notes that polluted stormwater runoff is commonly transported by municipal separate storm sewer systems (MS4s).[30] As of 2018, nearly 40 percent of stormwater utilities had taken this step.[31] The standard for municipal stormwater systems has evolved over many years and has been subject to court challenges. The final rule as of 2021 ensures public participation and regulatory accountability.[32]

In the US, the EPA has compiled guidance for MS4s,[33] including a series of municipal notices.[34] Globally, the Water Environment Federation, has also produced useful resources for environmentally sound MS4s.[35]

Green Engineering for Building Codes

In addition to addressing issues of transportation and water, cities also play a role in controlling the design and construction of buildings. Most cities have a code of ordinances that includes a chapter on building, and the standards they impose can make a major difference in a city's resiliency.

A leading standard for building codes is the International Green Construction Code most recently updated in 2018 by the International Code Council (ICC) and the American Society of Heating, Refrigerating and Air-Conditioning Engineers (ASHRAE).[36] While there are many green building standards,[37] this one is dominant globally (ASHRAE, despite its legacy name, has global membership).

At the time of the 2018 code's release, many municipalities (at least one in each of 14 US states), plus the District of Columbia, had adopted this code in their building codes.[38] The building code for Washington, DC, not only cites the ICC but also includes a LEED standard for energy.[39] The DC code aims to reduce building energy demand by using "passive design," by improving envelope performance, by installing high-efficiency systems for hot water, lighting, and power; and by supplying remaining energy needs from renewable sources of energy.[40] In 2021, the nation's capital released a new guide identifying the District's primary climate vulnerabilities (extreme heat and flooding), detailing a risk assessment methodology for particular project sites, and sharing building and landscape strategies to enhance resilience.[41]

The International Green Construction Code, which is still current as of mid-2021, sets forth model requirements for selecting a site, planning water and energy, controlling the environment of the interior of buildings, and standards for selecting materials and for construction – all this to "support the goal of development that meets the needs of the present without compromising the ability of future generations to meet their own needs."[42] The voluntary, professional code is guided in part by ASHRAE's vision of a "healthy and sustainable built environment for all."[43]

Accordingly, the introduction to the code states that its purpose is to provide minimum requirements for the siting, design, construction, and plans for operation of high-performance green buildings to: reduce emissions from buildings and building systems; enhance building occupant health and comfort; conserve water resources; protect local biodiversity and ecosystem services; promote sustainable and regenerative materials cycles; enhance building quality; enhance resilience to natural, technological, and human-caused hazards; and support the goal of development that meets the needs of the present without compromising the ability of future code Green Construction Code covers six main topics, ranging from site sustainability to construction. These six topics form a useful organizing structure to discuss green engineering.

Site Sustainability

In selecting a site for a city project, it is important to consider such issues as light pollution, mitigation of heat island effect, and the impact of the site on transportation, such as increase in traffic volume. Furthermore, site selection should adapt to the needs of the site if it is a brownfield, greyfield, or greenfield (see Box 6.1).

Box 6.1: Special Considerations for Construction Site Selection
When considering a site for a city project, it is important to consider whether it falls into any of the special "field" categories that bring unique sets of risks and opportunities.

A *brownfield*, according to the Environmental Protection Agency (EPA) a brownfield is "real property, the expansion, redevelopment, or reuse or which may be complicated by the presence or potential presence of a hazardous substance, pollutant, or contaminant."[44] The EPA estimates that there are more than 450,000 brownfields in the US. While it may seem unfortunate that they have this label, there is hope. The EPA notes that "Cleaning up and reinvesting in these properties increases local tax bases, facilitates job growth, utilizes existing infrastructure, takes development pressures off of undeveloped, open land, and both improves and protects the environment."[45] The EPA maintains a data base of success stories for grant recipients.[46] For two of those stories, see Chapter 9, Box 9.4.

A *greyfield* site has no authoritative definition but it generally describes a commercial site that is underused or abandoned.[47] They have been aptly described as "economically obsolescent, outdated, or underutilized lands such as older retail malls or strip centers that no longer attract adequate investment or tenants." Greyfields (unlike brownfields) are not usually contaminated; however, they may be older types of materials or design that may need to be replaced.[48]

A greenfield site is one that unlike a brownfield or greyfield has never been developed.[49]

Water Use Efficiency

A key green construction goal is to conserve water, both potable and nonpotable. This is a key goal of FIDIC, the international engineering group mentioned earlier.[50] Landscape and irrigation design can meet this goal by limiting flow rates, and setting requirements related to specific equipment and/or appliances. New York City, for example, sets a maximum for flow rate and flow pressure.[51]

Energy Efficiency

Energy efficiency addresses the use of energy in buildings, in appliances, and in energy systems. The concept of a "building envelope" is helpful here. A building envelope comprises all the material on the exterior of the building, including roofing, wall systems, exterior materials (known as cladding), windows, and foundations.[52]

Indoor Environmental Quality

Many building codes contain provisions on the environmental quality of the interior of buildings. Areas covered might include indoor air quality, thermal environmental conditions, and control of acoustics, lighting (including daylighting vs. glare), and moisture. Regarding indoor air quality, some building codes address problems of volatile organic compounds (VOCs) that can cause so-called soil gas (in affect, unhealthy air). The health effects of these indoors are much higher than when inhaled outdoors – and they can lead to so-called sick building syndrome.[53] (VOCs are gases that are emitted from various commonly used materials, numbering in the thousands[54] but mostly based on a few toxic chemicals.[55]) As an example of indoor environmental concerns in a municipal code, consider the code of Stratford, Connecticut, which has a chapter that has as an aim to "prevent soil gas potentially contaminated with volatile organic compounds (VOCs) from migrating into homes and commercial buildings within the Vapor Intrusion Zone."[56]

Materials and Resources

Some building codes contain provisions about treatment of materials, most of them with applications to construction and industry, but also related to recycling in general.

Construction and Plans for Operation

Another typical code provision might cover the construction process, including waste management and erosion and sedimentation control during construction.

Emerging Topics

Climate change is another topic that can be covered in a building code. The Global Resiliency Dialogue, an initiative endorsed by more than a dozen leading professional groups as well as a variety of stakeholders, wants cities to update their building codes with references to the risk of climate change.[57] In a recent report titled *Findings on Changing Risk and Building Codes*, asserts that "Building code developers and representatives from across the building industry must work with climate scientists and regulators to establish reliable, authoritative and appropriate models and methodologies that allow development of forward-looking strategies to address changing risks." This is not yet the case, however, as they state in a January 2021 report on the topic.[58]

Another topic that may appear in a building code is the architecture that gives rise to buildings. Most building codes do not address this subject but at least one architectural firm believes they should. HGAA, writing out of Vietnam, has written:

> In the future, we need to have further and better long-term vision for environmental issues such as the enactment of regulations, legislation and policies for planning ... specific architectural solutions. Each individual in society should have specific thoughts and

actions which protect the environment and soon bring the living environment back to a state of balance in order to ensure the sustainable development of humanity.[59]

Design and codes can go together. This is the view of the US Green Building Council, a sponsor of the ICC,[60] is also the developer of the standard known as LEED, for Leadership in Energy and Environmental Design. This is another voluntary standard developed by professionals and used in some municipal codes. More than 200 cities around the globe follow LEED standards.[61] The US Green Building Council rewards cities that adopt the International Green Construction Code by giving those cities credits toward LEED certification.[62]

A global organization called the Global Resiliency Dialogue, endorsed by more than a dozen leading professional groups as well as a variety of stakeholders, has a mission of ensuring that future city codes address the risk of climate change.[63] In a recent report titled *Findings on Changing Risk and Building Codes*, asserts that "Building code developers and representatives from across the building industry must work with climate scientists and regulators to establish reliable, authoritative and appropriate models and methodologies that allow development of forward-looking strategies to address changing risks." This is not yet the case, however, as they state in a January 2021 report on the topic.[64]

A Search for Holism

So far, this chapter has discussed green principles for roads, water systems, and building codes. City leaders and advocates who have not studied civil engineering can benefit from understanding accepted principles for all these discreet working parts of a city's infrastructure. This chapter has been organized accordingly. But are subsets of the larger issue of green infrastructure, which takes a more holistic approach.

It is common now for universities to have a "Department of Civil and Environmental Engineering" that looks at both the built and natural environment.[65] The University of Illinois at Urbana offers such a program as a "broad, systems – level perspective on the complex civil and environmental challenges facing the world today." While the school still teaches some engineering fundamentals, it presents them in a larger context.

Box 6.2: Profile in Activism – San Diego's Green Infrastructure Consortium
Citizens active in the City of San Diego in California have launched an initiative called the Green Infrastructure Consortium. The group defines green infrastructure as a system including living things; other natural elements such as water, air, and soil; and man-made

infrastructure to support these elements. The group has published what it views as the principal requirements for green infrastructure integration.

Vegetation: Plant trees and other vegetation, using appropriate species in locations to reduce runoff, erosion, greenhouse gas (GhG), and heat, while ensuring proper maintenance and biodiversity.

Animals: Re-balance appropriate species for the location, ranging from insects to fish, amphibians, reptiles, birds, and mammals.

Surfaces: Remove unneeded impervious surfaces and replace needed impervious surfaces with permeable materials where feasible, such as for parking lots, driveways, and sidewalks. Improve soil quality as needed, including nutrients, moisture, and compaction levels. Coat existing surfaces with materials that reflect heat rather than absorb it.

Diversions: Install appropriate features such as bioswales, berms, and other devices that allow water to infiltrate in place, reducing erosion, increasing soil moisture, and replenishing water tables.

Fire prevention techniques: Remove fire-prone vegetation from high-risk areas; add fire-resistant plants as needed.

Maps and eco-benefit calculations: Using GIS and other aerial sensors, map trees and plants, heat islands, impervious surfaces, and other elements to identify locations for improvement or existing green infrastructure elements. Apply contemporary computational techniques to these data and existing data to calculate and track human and environmental benefits.

Waste reduction: Conserve natural resources such as water, oxygen, and energy. Examplesinclude state-of-the-art irrigation, renewable energy devices powered by the sun, and wind.

Waste repurposing: Divert both green and gray waste from our waterways and landfills and re-use It as effectively as possible.

Energy efficiency: Install or replace items such as lighting that create safe and usable spaces while using minimal energy.

Source: The Green Infrastructure Consortium. https://www.greeninfrastructureconsor tium.org/ Reprinted with permission.

The Green Infrastructure Consortium (see Box 6.2) represents a new way of thinking about green infrastructure. Another organization working in this direction is the American Institute of Architecture (AIA). The 2020 AIA Framework for Design Excellence (which can be applied to engineering as well as design) lists the following design elements that can leverage engineering to capture environmental and economic or social elements.[66]

- *Design for integration* – for example, "What design strategies can provide multiple benefits across the triple bottom line of social, economic, and environmental value?"
- *Design for equitable communities* – for example, "How can the design process and outcome remove barriers and promote inclusion and social equity, particularly with respect to vulnerable communities."

- *Design for ecosystems* – for example, "How is the project supporting regional habitat restoration?"
- *Design for water* – for example, "How does the project contribute to a healthy regional watershed?"
- *Design for economy* – for example, "How will the design choices balance first cost with long-term value?"
- *Design for energy* – for example, "How can the project exceed building code efficiency standards to approach net zero energy and net zero carbon?"
- *Design for well-being* – for example, "How can the project connect people with place and nature?"

For communities seeking ways to implement the concepts and values of green infrastructure, the US EPA a program called Vision to Action that has several tools, such as how to develop green streets, green jobs, and green towns – nick-named G3.[67] Such programs may or may not describe themselves as being about "infrastructure systems," yet they are precisely that.

Concluding Reflections

Engineering is the art of directing the great sources of power in nature for the use and convenience of man.

Royal Charter of the Institution of Civil Engineers, 1828

Two centuries after Thomas Tredgold wrote these eloquent words in definition of his trade, we can reflect on how far civil engineering has come. For not only do today's civil engineers harness the power of nature to serve man, but they also harness the power of humankind to serve nature. The FIDIC's publication on *Consulting Engineers and the Environment* notes that engineers have contributed to the quality of life through better water supplies and sanitation, and by the development of various resources and systems. But the paper it also laments the fact these advancements have contributed to "rapid population growth and environmental problems" – hence the group's green mandate:

Consulting Engineers accept the challenge of the endangered environment. Because of their professional training and background, they have a particular role and obligation towards the protection of the environment. Engineers should provide leadership in achieving sustainable development – development that will meet the long-term needs of future generations of all nations without causing major modification to the earth's ecosystems.

Engineers who are professionally attuned to sustainable development strive to work with a larger system. As one source[68] has noted, it is useful to think in terms of "infrastructure systems." Such systems encompass both built infrastructure (e.g., roads, water systems, and buildings, as discussed in this chapter), and natural systems (the environment), and the infrastructure services that rely on both to provide for the fundamental needs of society. To be sustainable and resilient, these infrastructure systems, including their interconnected ecosystems and social systems, must be able to absorb disturbance while retaining their basic function and structural capacity.

Safety comes first, as tragic building collapse in Surfside, Florida, and Mexico City, Mexico, have reminded us all.[69] To a cash-strapped town just wanting to fix or replace what is broken in its infrastructure, the notion of system integration may seem a bridge too far, but it is a bridge that must be built to make cities safer and more livable – not only for their citizens but for the living ecosystems that surround them. The next section of this book provides guidance on how to fund such initiatives without raising taxes.

Notes

1 See, for example, this city checklist: Civil Permit Checklist (cityofmlt.com); https://www.cit yofmlt.com/DocumentCenter/View/1306/Civil-Permit-Submittal-Checklist
2 InfraCSOen (laohamutuk.org); https://www.laohamutuk.org/econ/14TLDPM/InfraCSOen.pdf
3 Chapter reviewer commentary reported by Rene Smith April 20, 2021, via email.
4 ENGINEERING | meaning in the Cambridge English Dictionary; https://dictionary.cam bridge.org/dictionary/english/engineering
5 CIVIL ENGINEER | meaning in the Cambridge English Dictionary; https://dictionary.cam bridge.org/dictionary/english/civil-engineer?topic=civil-engineering-in-generalv
6 What Does a Municipal Engineer Do? – WSB (wsbeng.com); https://www.wsbeng.com/ what-does-a-municipal-engineer-do/
7 Committee for Economic Development (2020) A US Infrastructure Plan: Building for the Long Haul | Committee for Economic Development of The Conference Board (ced.org), https:// www.conference-board.org/research/sustaining-capitalism/infrastructure-building-for-the-long-haul
8 The ASCE lists the following: aviation, bridges, dams, drinking water, energy, hazardous waste, inland waterways, levees, parks and recreation, ports, rail, roads, schools, solid waste, stormwater, transit, and wastewater. It also has a section on broadband. https://infrastructurer eportcard.org/wp-content/uploads/2020/12/National_IRC_2021-report.pdf
9 See, for example, "Infrastructure Interdependencies: Opportunities from Complexity," by Darren R. Grafius, et al., *Journal of Infrastructure Systems*, 26(4), 2020, presenting a typology for considerations of both risks and opportunities, as well as case studies. Along these lines, see also Neil Carhart and Ges Rosenberg, *International Journal of Complexity in Applied Science and Technology 1*(1), 2016, cited in Grafius.

10 These topics are the leading items in US President Biden's March 2021 American Jobs Plan, for example, FACT SHEET: The American Jobs Plan | The White House; https://www.white house.gov/briefing-room/statements-releases/2021/03/31/fact-sheet-the-american-jobs-plan/

11 Public Spending on Transportation and Water Infrastructure, 1956 to 2017 | Congressional Budget Office (cbo.gov); https://www.cbo.gov/publication/54539

12 Public-Private Partnerships for Transportation and Water Infrastructure | Congressional Budget Office (cbo.gov); https://www.cbo.gov/publication/56003

13 Most studies combine state and local spending numbers, but it is fair to assume that the burden is shared. For spending on roads, for example, the Urban Institute found that 8 percent of a state budget is spent on roads, compared to 4 percent of a municipal government. Highway and Road Expenditures | Urban Institute; https://www.urban.org/policy-centers/cross-center-initiatives/state-and-local-finance-initiative/state-and-local-backgrounders/highway-and-road-expenditures#Question2Highway

14 About Green Engineering | Green Engineering | US EPA; https://www.epa.gov/green-engineering/about-green-engineering

15 Policy Guides | Green Infrastructure | US EPA; https://www.epa.gov/green-infrastructure/policy-guides#Municipal%20Handbook

16 FIDIC | Federation | International Federation of Consulting Engineers; https://fidic.org/about-fidic/federation

17 "Consulting Engineers and the Environment," https://fidic.org/node/756

18 See, for example, FIDIC | Rethink Cities – White Paper 2013 | International Federation of Consulting Engineers; https://fidic.org/books/rethink-cities-white-paper-2013 or FIDIC | Join FIDIC in supporting World Cities Day | International Federation of Consulting Engineers; https://fidic.org/membership

19 Benefits of a Green Street | Green Streets, Green Jobs, Green Towns (G3) Program | US EPA; https://greeninfrastructurefoundation.org/news-unlinked/2020/5/27/green-infrastructure-projects-can-have-shorter-payback-and-greater-value-for-climate-adaptation-new-report-finds

20 Disproportionate exposure to urban heat island intensity across major US cities | Nature Communications, https://www.nature.com/articles/s41467-021-22799-5

21 What are Complete Streets? | Smart Growth America; https://smartgrowthamerica.org/pro gram/national-complete-streets-coalition/publications/what-are-complete-streets/

22 https://infrastructurereportcard.org/wp-content/uploads/2020/12/National_IRC_2021-report.pdf, pp. 110–111.

23 SUM-tools-leaflet-2-april-2019.pdf (sustainableurbanmobility.org); https://sustainableur banmobility.org/wp-content/uploads/2016/05/SUM-tools-leaflet-2-april-2019.pdf

24 A closer look at the Detroit Saturday Night building – Preservation Detroit; https://preser vationdetroit.org/what-we-care-about/2018/12/5/a-closer-look-at-the-detroit-saturday-night-building

25 Detroiters Push for Parking Reform in the Heart of Motown (strongtowns.org); https://greeninfrastructurefoundation.org/news-unlinked/2020/5/27/green-infrastructure-projects-can-have-shorter-payback-and-greater-value-for-climate-adaptation-new-report-finds

26 Infrastructure Costs by Leah Brooks and Zachary Liskow, Hutchins Center Working Paper #54, August 2019. https://www.brookings.edu/wp-content/uploads/2019/08/WP54_Brooks-Liscow_updated.pdf

27 Green Infrastructure – Environment – European Commission (europa.eu); Green Infrastructure Projects Can Have Shorter Payback and Greater Value for Climate Adaptation, New Report Finds – Green Infrastructure Foundation; https://greeninfrastructurefoundation.org/

news-unlinked/2020/5/27/green-infrastructure-projects-can-have-shorter-payback-and-greater
-value-for-climate-adaptation-new-report-finds
28 American Society of Civil Engineers, A Comprehensive Assessment of America's Infrastructure: 2021 Report Card (2020). https://infrastructurereportcard.org/wp-content/uploads/2020/
12/National_IRC_2021-report.pdf
29 The US Clean Water Act of 1972, as amended, prohibits any discharge of "pollutants"
through a "point source" into a "water of the United States" unless they have an NPDES permit. https://www.epa.gov/npdes/npdes-permit-basics
30 Stormwater Discharges from Municipal Sources | National Pollutant Discharge Elimination
System (NPDES) | US EPA; https://www.epa.gov/sites/production/files/2018-11/documents/
final_compendium_intro_document_rev-11-15-18.pdf
31 American Society of Civil Engineers, A Comprehensive Assessment of America's Infrastructure: 2021 Report Card (2020). https://infrastructurereportcard.org/wp-content/uploads/2020/
12/National_IRC_2021-report.pdf
32 NPDES Stormwater Final MS4 General Permit Remand Rule | National Pollutant Discharge
Elimination System (NPDES) | US EPA; https://www.epa.gov/npdes/npdes-stormwater-final-
ms4-general-permit-remand-rule
33 MS4 Permits: Compendium of Clean, Specific & Measurable Permitting Examples (epa.gov)
34 Stormwater Rules and Notices-Municipal Notices | National Pollutant Discharge Elimina-
tion System (NPDES) | US EPA; https://www.epa.gov/npdes/stormwater-rules-and-notices-
municipal-notices
35 About Stormwater Report – Stormwater Report (wef.org); https://stormwater.wef.org/
about/
36 2018 International Green Construction Code by the international Code Council, Inc., and ASH-
RAE, p. 1. Section 101.2.1 https://www.ashrae.org/File%20Library/Technical%20Resources/Book
store/2018-IgCC_preview_1102.pdf
    In May 2021, ASHRAE released a User's Guide. See also 2018 INTERNATIONAL GREEN CON-
STRUCTION CODE (IGCC) – EFFECTIVE USE (iccsafe.org) 2018 IgCC User's Manual with Technical
provisions from ANSI/ASHRAE/ICC/USGBC/IES Standard 189.1-2017, Standard for the Design of
High-Performance Green Buildings Except Low-Rise Residential Buildings (iccsafe.org); https://
shop.iccsafe.org/codes/2018-international-codes-and-references/2018-international-green-
construction-code/2018-igcc-user-s-manual-with-technical-provisions-from-ansi-ashrae-icc-usgbc-
ies-standard-189-1-2017-standard-for-the-design-of-high-performance-green-buildings-excep
37 For a partial list of green building standards, see "Green Certification Standards," TL;DR of
green certification standards – SPOT – Blog (ul.com); https://spot.ul.com/blog/tldr-of-green-
certification-standards/
38 ICC releases collaborative 2018 green building; https://www.constructiondive.com/news/
icc-releases-collaborative-2018-green-building-code/541969/g code | Construction Dive.
39 Washington, DC's energy conservation code includes LEED Zero pathways | US Green
Building Council (usgbc.org); https://www.usgbc.org/articles/washington-dcs-energy-
conservation-code-includes-leed-zero-pathways
40 Washington, DC's energy conservation code includes LEED Zero pathways | US Green
Building Council (usgbc.org), https://www.usgbc.org/articles/washington-dcs-energy-
conservation-code-includes-leed-zero-pathways – summarizing the code's Appendix Z.
41 https://www.buildinggreen.com/newsbrief/washington-dc-releases-resilient-design-
guidelines

42 2018 International Green Construction Code by the international Code Council, Inc., and ASHRAE, p. 1. Section 101.2.1 https://www.ashrae.org/File%20Library/Technical%20Resources/Bookstore/2018-IgCC_preview_1102.pdf

43 https://www.ashrae.org/

44 Overview of EPA's Brownfields Program | Brownfields | US EPA; https://www.epa.gov/environmentaljustice/environmental-justice-small-grants-program#tab-2

45 Overview of EPA's Brownfields Program | Brownfields | US EPA; https://www.epa.gov/environmentaljustice/environmental-justice-small-grants-program#tab-2

46 Brownfield Grant Recipient Success Stories | Brownfields | US EPA; https://www.epa.gov/brownfields/brownfield-grant-recipient-success-stories

47 Sustainability | Free Full-Text | Characteristics and Retrofit Constraints of Grayfield in Korean Cities | HTML (mdpi.com); https://www.epa.gov/brownfields/brownfield-grant-recipient-success-stories

48 Planning Toolbox: Brownfield and Greyfield Redevelopment (chescoplanning.org); https://www.epa.gov/brownfields/brownfield-grant-recipient-success-stories

49 What Is Greenfield And Brownfield Engineering? (planacademy.com); https://www.epa.gov/brownfields/brownfield-grant-recipient-success-stories

50 SOTW_2021_report02_design_FINAL_complete.pdf (fidic.org); https://www.epa.gov/environmentaljustice/environmental-justice-small-grants-program#tab-2

51 https://codelibrary.amlegal.com/codes/newyorkcity/latest/NYCadmin/0-0-0-67664 – See Table 6.04

52 For more on building envelopes, see https://www.buildingenclosureonline.com/topics/2663-building-envelope

53 Indoor Air Facts No. 4 Sick Building Syndrome | Indoor Air Quality (IAQ) | US EPA; https://www.epa.gov/environmentaljustice/environmental-justice-small-grants-program#tab-2

54 Volatile Organic Compounds' Impact on Indoor Air Quality | Indoor Air Quality (IAQ) | US EPA; https://www.epa.gov/indoor-air-quality-iaq/volatile-organic-compounds-impact-indoor-air-quality

55 These chemicals include benzene, ethylene glycol, formaldehyde, methylene chloride, tetrachloroethylene, toluene, and xylene Volatile Organic Compounds (VOCs) in Your Home – EH: Minnesota Department of Health (state.mn.us); https://www.health.state.mn.us/communities/environment/air/toxins/voc.htm

56 Town of Stratford, CT Groundwater and Vapor Intrusion Zones (ecode360.com); https://ecode360.com/32942272

57 Findings_ChangingRisk_BldgCodes.pdf (iccsafe.org); https://cdn-web.iccsafe.org/wp-content/uploads/Findings_ChangingRisk_BldgCodes.pdf

58 *The Use of Climate Data and Assessment of Extreme Weather Event Risks in Building Codes Around the World: Survey Findings from the Global Resiliency Dialogue* 21-19612_CORP_CAN-ZUS_Survey_Whitepaper_RPT_FINAL_HIRES.pdf (iccsafe.org); https://cdn-web.iccsafe.org/wp-content/uploads/21-19612_CORP_CANZUS_Survey_Whitepaper_RPT_FINAL_HIRES.pdf

59 From Past to Future: The Urgency of "Green" in Architecture, by Victor Delaqua, *Arch Daily*, March 10, 2021. The website of HGAA is HGAA: Hon Gai Architecture | ArchiDiaries; https://www.archidiaries.com/hgaa-hon-gai-architecture/ or From Past to Future: The Urgency of "Green" in Architecture | ArchDaily; https://www.archdaily.com/958188/from-past-to-future-the-urgency-of-green-in-architecture

60 2018 International Green Construction Code Released | US Green Building Council (usgbc.org); https://www.usgbc.org/articles/2018-international-green-construction-code-released

61 Engaging with state and local governments on LEED | US Green Building Council (usgbc.org); https://www.usgbc.org/articles/engaging-state-and-local-governments-leed

62 Green codes | US Green Building Council (usgbc.org); https://www.usgbc.org/about/pro grams/green-codes

63 Findings_ChangingRisk_BldgCodes.pdf (iccsafe.org); https://cdn-web.iccsafe.org/wp-content/uploads/Findings_ChangingRisk_BldgCodes.pdf

64 *The Use of Climate Data and Assessment of Extreme Weather Event Risks in Building Codes Around the World: Survey Findings from the Global Resiliency Dialogue* 21-19612_CORP_CAN-ZUS_Survey_Whitepaper_RPT_FINAL_HIRES.pdf (iccsafe.org); https://cdn-web.iccsafe.org/wp-content/uploads/21-19612_CORP_CANZUS_Survey_Whitepaper_RPT_FINAL_HIRES.pdf

65 Universities include: In the US, Auburn, Cal Poly, Cornell. MIT, Princeton, Rice, Rutgers, Stanford – to name just a few examples.

66 https://content.aia.org/sites/default/files/2020-08/Framework_for_design_excellence_v3.pdf

67 Develop Your Green Streets, Green Jobs, Green Towns (G3) Vision | Green Streets, Green Jobs, Green Towns (G3) Program | US EPA; https://www.epa.gov/G3/develop-your-green-streets-green-jobs-green-towns-g3-vision

68 Chapter reviewer commentary reported by Rene Smith April 20, 2021.

69 Two recent and notable examples of construction failure of concern to local governments were the collapse of a metro overpass in Mexico City, Mexico, on May 3, 2021, and the collapse of a condominium in the town of Surfside in Miami-Dade County, Florida, June 24, 2021. For engineering details, see "Report Finds Six Construction Faults Led to Deadly Collapse of Mexico City Metro Bridge," https://www.globalconstructionreview.com/news/report-finds-six-con struction-faults-led-deadly-co/ and see "Federal Response to Surfside Building Collapse in Florida," Federal Emergency Management Agency, July 17, 2021. https://www.fema.gov/fact-sheet/federal-response-surfside-building-collapse-florida

PART III: Beyond Taxes: Green Financing

Chapter 7
Municipal Green Bonds

In the best of circumstances, cities can finance their operations and maintain a prudent reserve by taxing property and/or income, and by charging for services such as water and sewer. But such funding may fall short when it comes to major initiatives such as building a public transportation system or buying conservation lands. In such a circumstance, a municipality may decide to issue bonds, and back them by either future tax revenue (general obligation [GO] bonds) or project revenue (revenue bonds).

By selling debt securities to institutions and individuals, a city promises to pay them interest on the bond at certain intervals (such as twice a year) and to repay principal at a maturity date. The duration of municipal bonds (aka muni bonds) can range from 1 to 30 years.[1]

The exchange of muni bonds has created a growing market, particularly in the US, where there are now some 1.2 million of them now outstanding; by contrast, outside the US, where private markets are less dynamic and government support is stronger, there are fewer than 6,000 municipal bonds on record.[2]

In the US, muni bonds are a way of life for governments. Some 50,000 state and local governments are qualified to raise money through muni bonds,[3] and one in three US infrastructure projects is funded by a bond offering.[4] Currently, the total US muni bond market is worth some $3.9 trillion, which is the amount of municipal debt outstanding.[5] In 2020, US cities issued $252 billion in new bonds, both taxable and nontaxable.[6] Green municipal bonds were almost unheard of a decade ago but today in the US they account for nearly 5 percent of bonds and they are growing in prevalence.[7]

Worldwide, the muni bond market may be approaching $4.5 trillion, including now an estimated $500 billion in new green bonds.[8] From 2013 to 2019, cities issued more than $23 billion in green bonds to fund environmental projects.[9] The Climate Bonds Initiative estimates that the total value of green bonds outstanding is $1 trillion.[10]

There is some evidence that investors are willing to pay a premium for bonds that have a positive environmental impact. Amundi SA in Paris recently calculated that companies and cities issuing green bonds received an average premium of 11 percent for the green label,[11] although one recent study casts doubt on the existence of such a "greenium" in the municipal bond market.[12]

https://doi.org/10.1515/9783110689860-007

Green Bonds

Cities as well as other bond issuers can have their green bonds certified by the Green Bond Initiative, which certifies bond issuances as green according to a standard that incorporates the Green Bond Principles and Green Loan Principles and is aligned with the proposed EU Green Bond Standard as well as guidelines and rules in China, ASEAN, Japan, India, and other countries and regions.[13] A review of Green Building Initiative (GBI) certified municipal bonds in 2020 includes bond issuances for agriculture, energy (solar, wind, renewable), forestry, low-carbon buildings, low-carbon transportation, and water infrastructure.[14]

Any municipal bond can be marketed as a green bond if the purpose of the bond pertains to environmental causes. A common example is a transit system that markets itself as a green bond. Green bonds can be described as debt obligations tied to investment activities targeting new and existing projects with environmental benefits.[15] If they are financed through taxes, they are GO bonds.

A leading source of information and guidance is the Climate Bonds Initiative, a charity based in London.[16] This source covers both corporate and government bonds. With respect to government bonds, most issuers are states (in the US) or provinces (in the Americas), but city governments have also issued them – notably Gothenburg in Sweden and Johannesburg in South Africa.

The first green muni bond was issued by Massachusetts in June 2013, followed by Gothenburg in October of that same year.

US states are major green bond issuers, but issuers also include Province of Ontario, City of Johannesburg, and Province of la Rioja (Argentina). Local government green bonds continue to grow.

As an example of a green bond financed as a GO bond, consider one issued in August 2020 by the Bay Area Rapid Transit System, which has so far issued five green bonds to fund its transportation initiatives.[17] To understand how green bonds work, it is important to understand the basic mechanics of municipal bonds, starting with GO bonds.

Types of Bonds

Various types of bonds may be issued by municipalities:
- *GO bonds* are issued by states, cities or counties and not secured by any assets. They are backed by the government's taxing power.
- *Revenue bonds* are backed by revenues from a specific project or source, such as (in order of prevalence) transportation, water and sewer, special tax, hospitals, hospitals, education, leasing, and other (such as green bonds).

- *Conduit bonds* offer a third model. Here, the government borrows on behalf of a private entity. As in the case of revenue bonds, the income stream from the project provides the funds for repayment of investors. These bonds form a distinct minority in the world of bonds.

There are also *special purpose bonds* that combine features of the three bond types listed here, as discussed below. Most discussions of bonds focus on what they mean for the investor. By contrast, this chapter will explain bonds from the point of view of the town or city that will issue it, starting with an overview of the steps involved.

GO Bonds

GO bonds, which comprise less than one-third of all investment-quality muni bonds issued in the US are backed by the government itself, much like a US Treasury bond.[18] The term used is "full faith and credit." These kinds of bonds are often used for projects that do not have a revenue stream, such as the purchase of conservation lands. Importantly, voter approval (through a referendum) is required for a GO bond. Sometimes the power of a GO bond is also bolstered by a revenue stream from a project. These are called "double barrel" bonds.[19]

Revenue Bonds

Revenue bonds make up about two-thirds of the investment grade US bond market.[20] Unlike GO bonds, these instruments have no government backing. Their ability to repay bondholders interest and to repay principal is based on projected revenues from a specific project or source, such as highway tolls or lease fees. Some revenue bonds guarantee repayment while others do not give the buyer any recourse if the project fails. Some revenue bonds are nonrecourse; the municipality is not required to pay the bondholders. With these "nonrecourse" bonds, in case of default, the bondholders have no claim on the underlying revenue source. Voter approval is not required for a revenue bond.[4]

Not surprisingly, a revenue bond must come with certain assurances. The term for these is trust indentures, also called trust agreement. These are legally binding contracts between bond issuers and trustees that make certain guarantees to represent bondholder interests to be respected by the trustee.

Conduit Bonds

These types of bonds, which are issued by hospitals, schools, or charities in concert with municipal taxpayers, are rare, constituting only about 5 percent of US muni bonds.[21] Common types of conduit bonds[22] include:
- Industrial development revenue bonds (IDRBs)
- Private activity bonds (PABs)
- Affordable housing bonds

Beyond these three basic bond types, there are some bonds that defy easy labels.

Special Tax Revenue and Other Special Purpose Bonds

Some bonds do not fit neatly into either a GO bond or a revenue bond.

For example, a *pension obligation bond* enables state and local governments to pay off pension liabilities by borrowing against future tax revenue, then investing the proceeds in higher-yield investments. The justification for the bond is that the investments will produce a higher return than the interest rate on the bond, earning money for the pension fund.[23] The Government Finance Officers Association advises against the issuance of such bonds by state and local governments.[24]

There is also a hybrid type of bond that is a revenue bond financed through a tax on a separate activity. A *special tax revenue bond* repaid by taxing an activity or asset that is tangentially related to the project being financed. For example, as noted by the Build America Transportation Center (BATIC) Institute, Limited and special tax bonds are payable from a pledge of the proceeds against a specific tax. This tax could be a gasoline tax, a special assessment, an incremental sales tax, or a property levied at a fixed price. Unlike GO bonds and their unlimited ability to raise taxes, with these bonds, the issuer is limited by the specific source for the revenue to pay the bonds.

Sales tax revenue bonds are a good example of this. As noted by BATIC, sales tax bonds differ from most transportation financings because the debt is paid from sales taxes rather than from transportation revenues. BATIC notes that this kind of financing may require special enabling legislation, so the municipality or other government authority can give tax revenues to the bond issue trustee.

Lease Revenue Bonds

When cities raise money via bonds, they pledge collateral. For GO bonds, the collateral is the power of the city to tax its citizens. For revenue bonds, the collateral is income from a project. But in some cases, the collateral can be an asset of the city that is structured like a lease. For example, the West Covina Public Financing Authority in West Covina, California, priced $205 million in lease revenue bonds in July 2020 to pay off nearly $200 million in unfunded accrued pension liabilities.[25] The bond issue also provided $1 million in working capital that would be paid back in four years. The bonds, rated A-plus by S&P Global Ratings and carrying a 10-year par call, priced to yield between 1.747 percent for a 2021 maturity and 3.892 percent for 2044.

How to Issue a Municipal Bond

Municipal bonds are not only for big cities with sophisticated financial advisors. Any municipality willing to take certain steps can qualify. The following steps are based on a "playbook" developed by the Green Bond Pledge, an initiative of city and sustainability leaders committed to green financing.[26]

1. *Identify qualifying green projects or assets.* Green projects and assets can be found in several domains, including energy, green buildings, land use, industry, waste, water, and transportation.

2. *Arrange independent review.* this can be from an environmental group such as the Climate Bonds Standard Board or from an audit firm such as KPMG or EY.

3. *Set up tracking and reporting.* To ensure that green projects or assets receive all proceeds, the total of amounts invested in the green projects or assets, plus any cash accounts, must not be less than the amount of the bond.

4. *Obtain a credit rating for the bond.* The standard credit rating agencies have services in this regard (see section on Credit Rating Agencies later in this chapter).

5. *Structure, market, and price the bond.* Working with an investment banker, a city can decide what kind of bond will be issued, how much it will cost, and who will buy it.

6. *Monitor use of proceeds and report annually.* The municipality's annual financial report should include a section explaining the status of each of the city's bonds.

The Costs of Municipal Bonds

Bonds, particularly revenue bonds, the distinct advantage of bringing in money without having to use taxpayer money for the project at hand. But unless the bond is a revenue bond that pays for itself out of project cashflow, it can put pressure on city finances as the city strives to make the interest payments to the bondholders, and then at maturity repay principal. But bonds have costs beyond those repayment. A town or city may need to pay some or all the following at some point.

Rating Agency Fees. To issue bonds, towns need to obtain credit ratings from a credit rating agency. These agencies charge fees for giving their rating.

Underwriter's Commission, Fees, and Expenses. A likely customer for the city's bond offering will be one or more municipal securities dealers – also known as underwriters – who will purchase newly issued securities from the city and sell the securities via brokers to investors at a markup, which must be disclosed to investor. In some cases, the underwriter may hire its own law firm to prepare and certify the official statement, and then pass along its fees to the issuer.

Advisory Fees and Expenses. The municipality may hire a financial advisor such as a consulting firm, an investment banking firm, or a commercial bank to help with the bond.

Bond Counsel Fees and Expenses. An attorney is needed to write a legal opinion that confirms are "valid and binding obligations of the issuer," and, when applicable, that interest on the bonds is exempt from federal and state income taxes. The same attorney or sometimes a separate attorney will prepare the 10-b-5 statement that declares that the bond offering is free of material misstatements.

Bond Insurance Premiums. About one in ten new bonds issued come with insurance.[27] While the premium costs money, it can "pay for itself" through a higher credit rating. "Bond insurance allows an issuer to borrow at lower rates than their credit ratings might allow by giving assurance to investors that they get paid no matter what. The insurer guarantees repayment of principal and interest over the life of the debt in return for a one-time premium," *Insurance Journal* explains.[28]

Verification Agent. A verification agent checks various calculations in bond documents. For example, when a local government issues a new bond to pay off a previous bond issue (a refunding bond), a verification agent checks to see whether there are enough proceeds from the new bond issuance in escrow to fully pay the interest and principal on the original bonds.

Paying Agent, Fiscal Agent, and/or Trustee. The paying agent ensures payment of principal and interest to bondholders. The fiscal agent maintains records and ensures compliance with financial provisions of contracts. The trustee ensures compliance with the contract and pursues remedies if there is a default.[29] In some cases, all roles are combined in the trustee, a financial institution that performs specific financial functions including the acceptance and disbursement of (bond) funds, the maintenance of reserve funds, and the custody of investments.[30] This institution may also play the role of registrar, paying agent, and/or transfer agent, maintaining a registry of bond holders and collecting debt service payments from the issuer and paying it to the bondholders.

Printing. Every bond must have a prospectus. This requires not only the advisor and/or attorney guiding the content, but also a printer to produce and distribute a physical and/or electronic copy of the prospectus and other final official statements for distribution to the marketplace.

CUSIP Fees. Just as retail items have bar codes, securities have a CUSIP number as determined by the Committee on Uniform Security Identification Procedures. A bond offering may include dozens of individual securities, each requiring a CUSIP identifier. The CUSIP numbering system is administered by CUSIP Global Services, a unit of Standard & Poor's (S&P). The fees are relatively minor.

Contingency funds. A bond issuer typically sets aside about 1 percent of the bond's offering amount as a contingency against loss.

Other Costs. These include any fees paid to local authorities, any appraisal work that may be necessary, and the opportunity cost represented by the lost hours of the municipal employees working on the bond issue.

All in all, the total for these costs average between 1 and 2 percent of the principal, but they can run as high as 8 percent.[31]

Credit Rating Agencies

An important step in qualifying to issue a bond is to obtain a credit rating for the town or city in need of issuing the security. As in the case of individuals or companies, credit ratings express a judgment about the issuer's ability to pay back the debt it is taking on – fully and on time.

In the US, the government recognizes nine credit rating agencies (CRAs), including some not based in the US.[32] Of these, four are notable in the bond arena: Moody's, S&P Global Ratings, Fitch, and Kroll Bond Rating Agency. They all rank municipal bonds based on credit ratings from high to low, but they use different lettering (see Box 7.1).

Box 7.1: The Language of Municipal Bond Ratings

Moody's	S&P Global	Fitch	Kroll
Aaa	AAA	AAA	AAA
Aa1, Aa2,Aa3	AA-, AA, or AA+	AA	AA
A1, A2,A3	A, A+	A	A
Baa1, Baa2,Baa3	BBB	BBB	BBB
Ba1,Ba2,Ba3	BB	BB	BB
B1, B2, B3	B	B	B
Caa1, Caa2, Caa3	CCC	CCC	CCC
Ca	CC	CC	CC
C	C	C	C

Key: Gray shading means investment grade. Other levels are considered speculative.

In addition to using different lettering, the bond rating agencies use different descriptions of their rating. The follow looks at each level, on a descending scale, with descriptions from the two most dominant bond raters, Moody's and S&P Global (S&P).

Aaa or AAA. Moody's calls this the "highest rating, representing minimum credit risk," noting that default ratings for such debt is "negligible across all horizons."[33] S&P describes this investment grade level has "extremely strong capacity to meet financial commitments."[34] Fitch states "lowest expectation of default risk. They are assigned only in cases of exceptionally strong capacity for payment of financial commitments. This capacity is highly unlikely to be adversely affected by foreseeable events."[35]

Aa or AA comes next. Moody's labels these bonds "high grade."[36] S&P says that these have "Very strong capacity to meet financial commitments."[37]

A means "upper medium grade" for Moody's.[38] For S&P these have "Strong capacity to meet financial commitments, but somewhat susceptible to economic conditions and changes in circumstances."[39] *Baa or BBB* bonds come next. Moody's calls them "medium grade."[40] S&P judges these bonds as having "adequate capacity to meet financial commitments," but sates that they are "more subject to adverse economic conditions."[41]

All the above are considered "investment grade." Below this level, the bonds are considered speculative.

Ba or BB. Moody's says this bond grade has "speculative elements."[42] For S&P such a bond is "less vulnerable in the near-term but faces major ongoing uncertainties to adverse business, financial and economic conditions."[43]

B. Moody's finds that this grade is "subject to high credit risk."[44] S&P states that a such a bond is (and its issuer) is "more vulnerable to adverse business, financial and economic conditions but currently has the capacity to meet financial commitments."[45]

Caa or CCC. Moody's calls these "bonds of poor standing."[46] S&P calls them "currently vulnerable and dependent on favorable business, financial and economic conditions to meet financial commitments."[47]

Ca or CC. Moody's calls these "highly speculative or near default."[48] S&P says that there are "highly vulnerable; default has not yet occurred, but is expected to be a virtual certainty."[49]

C. Moody's describes these lowest-rated bonds as "bonds typically in default," warning that they offer "little prospect for recovery of principal or interest."[50] S&P says these are "currently highly vulnerable to non-payment, and ultimate recovery is expected to be lower than that of higher rated obligations."[51]

The Muni Bond Credit Rating Process

The credit rating process involves several steps. Here is the timeline given by S&P Global:[52]

1. The issuer requests a rating and signs an engagement letter.
2. The rating agency assembles a team of analysts to review pertinent information.
3. Analysts meet with city management.
4. Analysts propose rating to a rating committee.
5. The rating committee votes on the rating.
6. The issuer receives the rationale for the rating.
7. The CRA publishes a press release on the rating.
8. The CRA continues to monitor the city's performance on the bond, adjusting the rating up or down as needed.

Sample Municipal Credit Ratings

Moody's Rates GO Bond of Plattsburg, New York

Moody's has given the mediocre Baa1 rating to the Town of Plattsburgh, NY (population 19,534),[53] but it gave a higher rating (Aa3) to the town's most recent

$10 million GO bonds – Public Improvement Serial Bonds, Series 2020. This was the first new bond that the town had issued in 20 years.[54] As a rating's rationale, Moody's says, "The Aa3 rating reflects the Town of Plattsburgh's moderately sized tax base and strong local economy, strong reserves and liquidity grown through successive years of positive operations and manageable fixed costs. The rating also reflects the high proportion of operating revenues derived from sales tax and sales tax revenue shortfalls anticipated due to Coronavirus-driven economic downturn. The town's long-term liabilities are somewhat elevated, driven by recent issuances to improve its water and wastewater systems but are expected to remain stable."[55]

S&P Rates Revenue Bonds of Bella Vista, Arkansas

S&P Gives Bella Vista, AR, AA-rating for $24 million in bonds. The revenue for the bond funds is to come from a 1 percent city sales tax that will cover a new public safety building to include the police department, dispatch office and court facility: a fire training facility off Chelsea Road and the razing and rebuilding of Fire Station 3. These projects were approved by voters during the March 3, 2020, primary election.[56]

Fitch Rates GO Bonds of Suffolk, VA

On August 24, 2020, Fitch Ratings put out a press release announcing that it had given a Triple A ("AAA") rating to two Suffolk, VA, GO bonds:[57]
 – $28 million GO and refunding bonds series 2020A (tax exempt).
 – $104 million GO refunding bonds, series 2020B (taxable).

Bond proceeds will finance various public improvement capital projects and refund certain GO bonds previously issued by the city. Fitch also affirmed its past "AAA" rating for approximately $586 million in outstanding GO bonds, as well as the issuer default rating (IDR), considered unlikely.

A Deeper Look at a Triple A Bond

Regarding bond security, the Suffolk, VA, press release on GO bonds states that the bonds are "The bonds are general obligations of the city, secured by its full faith and credit and unlimited taxing power." (This language is significant because in some states municipalities have limits on their power to tax. In California, Proposition 13 passed in 1978, amending the state's constitution to set a limit on property tax increase.[58])

In its "analytical conclusion," Fitch stated that the ratings reflect not only an "unlimited legal ability to raise revenues" but also a "solid expenditure flexibility that support a superior level of inherent budget flexibility." The report notes that the city's reserves are high relative to expected revenue volatility and that debt and net pension liabilities are at the "low end of the moderate range."

The report also looks at the city's economic resource base, noting size and growth of the population and its industrial growth in the defense, healthcare, and distribution sectors; revenue framework, noting trends in city revenues; expenditure framework, and reference to "flexibility to manage labor-related costs." Virginia is a right to work state with low levels of unionization; the City of Suffolk is not unionized.[59] For "long-term liability burden," Fitch makes a proprietary estimate of debt and net pension liabilities over personal income, calculating this at 11 percent and finding that to be sustainable. (In other words, if citizens had to repay all the city's debt, it would cost them $11 out of every $100 in income.) Fitch's "operating performance" is a combine metric of several indicators, including reserves.

The Fitch release on its AAA rating for Suffolk, Virginia, includes a disclosure of factors that could lead to a downgrade. These include significant and sustained decline in revenues and/or reserves, and/or a risk that the long-term liability metric mentioned above rises about 20 percent. Also included in the rating is a description of current developments, including coronavirus risks; a general credit profile for the area; and ESG considerations. Regarding this last item, Fitch notes that ESG risks "generally have a minimal direct effect on credit ratings," but ESG topics are relevant for credit rating analysis. Fitch Ratings scores each ESG risk element against its rated public finance/infrastructure coverage for its relevance to the ultimate rating decision.[60]

Bond Paperwork

Typically, a town or city must put in a good deal of paperwork. In the US, standards are set by Municipal Securities Rulemaking Board (MSRB),[61] which is overseen by the Securities and Exchange Commission (SEC). The bond paperwork must include the following disclosures:

- Type (e.g., GO vs. revenue).
- Yield (if the bond goes to maturity, how much will it return to the investors, based on the price in comparison to the interest rate it pays, also called the

"coupon," based on an old practice of having physical, cashable coupons attached to a paper bond).
- Maturity (date when the bond issuer will repay the principal).
- Credit quality (rating by a recognized rating agency).
- Call features (potential for an issuer to repay a bond before its maturity date).
- Risk factors (listing everything that can go wrong, often written in boilerplate). In early 2020, the US municipal debt market went through turmoil, as investors began selling their bonds, which caused a decline in bond prices.[62] Risks like that need to be flagged for investors.
- Audited financial statements (from the municipality issuing the bond).
- Material event notices (letting investors know of risk events in real time).
- Other continuing disclosures (e.g., ratings changes, payment delinquencies, and defaults).

For an example of effective disclosure, see Box 7.2.

Box 7.2: Exemplary Municipal Disclosures by Cities
Most cities include information about their bonds in their audited financial reports each year, but some go further. The City of West Linn in Oregon devotes part of its website to facts and figures about its outstanding bonds.[63] For each bond, there is a succinct paragraph in a similar format.
Here is one example:
Series: 2018 (issued in August 2018 at a competitive sale and receiving an overall 20-year interest rate of 3.22%)
Purpose: To improve roads, parks, and city facilities
Original Issuance Amount: $20,000,000
Maturity Date: 06/30/2036[64]

An Alternative to a Public Offering: Selling Directly to Banks

Raising money by a public bond is expensive and involves extensive paperwork. In recent years, local governments have begun to borrow directly from banks, including through private placements – essentially bonds purchased by banks directly from local governments. This movement has pros and cons.[65] In some cases, cities take out a loan instead of issuing a bond.[66] Such private-sector innovations will help to sustain the market for municipal bonds for years to come.

Concluding Reflections

> Neither a borrower nor a lender be.
> Polonius in William Shakespeare's Hamlet Act 1, Scene 3 (circa 1600)

While muni bond issuers and buyers would disagree with Shakespeare's Polonius, both parties to a bond purchase should be careful. A century and a half ago, US President Rutherford B. Hayes who urged "every village, town, and city" to "get out of debt and keep out of debt," rightly observing that "It is the debtor that is ruined by hard times."[67] Bond issuers would be wise to heed this wisdom, bearing in mind that a bond is nothing more or less than a public debt that must be repaid to the purchaser. Fortunately, bonds and their close allies tax revenues, are not the only source of revenue for municipalities. Cities may also turn to the nonprofit sector, including land trusts, the subject of the next chapter.

Notes

1 http://www.msrb.org/msrb1/pdfs/Facts-About-Municipal-Bonds.pdf
2 Source: The data company EDI, which has identified 1,201,856 municipal bonds to track in the US, but only 5,381 non-US municipal bonds. https://www.exchange-data.com/wp-content/up loads/2020/07/EDI-North-American-Services-V-2.7.pdf. The number of bonds outstanding changes from year to year as bonds come to the end of their term, and as new bonds are issued. Another interesting data point is that between 2000 and 2014, nearly two million bonds were issued.
3 "SIFMA Statement on the Municipal Bonds Emergency Relief Act," March 20, 2020. https:// www.sifma.org/resources/news/sifma-statement-on-the-municipal-bonds-emergency-relief-act/ The bill itself appears here: https://www.congress.gov/bill/116th-congress/senate-bill/ 3550/text?r=5&s=1
4 See the US government website, https://www.investor.gov/introduction-investing/inves ting-basics/investment-products/bonds-or-fixed-income-products-0
5 http://www.msrb.org/msrb1/pdfs/MSRB-Muni-Facts.pdf
6 Source Refinitiv, cited in Heather Jillers, "Covid-19 Pandemic Drives Municipal Borrowing to 10-Year High," *Wall Street Journal*, January 13, 2021.https://www.wsj.com/articles/covid-19-pandemic-drives-municipal-borrowing-to-10-year-high-11610447402?mod=newsviewer_click For discussion of taxable vs. nontaxable bonds, see Why Investors Should Consider Taxable Municipal Bonds | Charles Schwab; https://www.schwab.com/resource-center/insights/con tent/why-investors-should-consider-taxable-municipal-bonds
7 US Municipal Green-Labeled Debt to Soar by 4.1 percent in 2021 (environmentalleader.com); https://www.environmentalleader.com/2021/02/municipal-market-embraces-esg-boosts-green-labeled-debt/
8 The 500 billion estimate is a forward-looking estimate made in January 2021. "Analysts expect as much as $500bn of green bonds in bumper 2021," by Bill Nauman, *Financial Times*, January 4, 2021. https://www.ft.com/content/021329aa-b0bd-4183-8559-0f3260b73d62

9 Mijat Kusudic, "In Search of Greenium," April 19, 2021. https://cyanreef.com/in-search-of-greenium/

10 https://www.climatebonds.net/

11 "Why Going Green Saves Bond Borrowers Money," by Matt Witz, *Wall Street Journal*, December 17, 2020. Why Going Green Saves Bond Borrowers Money – WSJ; https://www.wsj.com/articles/why-going-green-saves-bond-borrowers-money-11608201002?mod=searchre sults_pos1&page=1.

12 David F. Larcker and David M. Watts, Stanford University Graduate School of Business, February 22, 2019, Working Paper No. 3766, Where's the Greenium? | Stanford Graduate School of Business; https://www.gsb.stanford.edu/faculty-research/working-papers/wheres-greenium

13 https://www.climatebonds.net/certification

14 https://www.climatebonds.net/certification/certified-bonds

15 See "Green Bond Guidelines for the Real Estate Sector" (GRESB, 2016). GRESB, formerly the "Global Real Estate Sustainability Benchmark." https://www.icmagroup.org/assets/documents/ Regulatory/Green-Bonds/Green-Bond-Guidelines-for-the-Real-Estate-Sector.pdf The main website of GRESB is https://gresb.com/

16 https://www.climatebonds.net/

17 https://www.bart.gov/news/articles/2019/news20190603

18 https://www.schwab.com/resource-center/insights/content/understanding-revenue-bonds

19 See "Municipal Bond Tips for the Series 7 Exam," January 30, 2020. https://www.investope dia.com/articles/professionaleducation/07/series_7_municipal.asp

20 Sources vary on this percentage, but the two-third figure is corroborated by two sources: Understanding Municipal Revenue Bonds by Cooper Howard of Schwab, December 10, 2020; https://www.schwab.com/resource-center/insights/content/understanding-revenue-bonds and Municipal Bonds Aren't Out of Peril – WSJ; https://www.wsj.com/articles/municipal-bonds-arent-out-of-peril-11608892206?mod=searchresults_pos2&page=1. The following source states that special revenue bonds comprise only one-third of the bond market; https://scholar ship.law.unc.edu/cgi/viewcontent.cgi?article=1506&context=ncbi

21 https://www.schwab.com/resource-center/insights/content/understanding-revenue-bonds

22 https://www.municipalbonds.com/education/introduction-to-a-conduit-bond/

23 Pension obligation bonds are often discussed in the context of GO bonds but at least one municipal bond analyst believes that they are closer to being like lease bonds. "I would argue that city is indifferent from financial flexibility standpoint whether . . .. statutory pension bonds or lease revenue bonds are issued. Both are not voted GOs and debt service and ad valorem taxes cannot be used to pay the bonds. I assume the bonds will be taxable because tax exemption is based on use of proceeds and not security . . .. At the end of the day, both lease revenue bond and POBs are paid from the same limited revenue source, despite the legal security coming from a different statute." See the comment by analyst Jamie Lyon here: https:// www.forbes.com/sites/ebauer/2020/09/02/forget-pension-obligation-bonds-two-cities-areno-jokeleasing-their-streets-to-fund-pensions/#7b1f995a2233

24 https://www.gfoa.org/materials/pension-obligation-bonds

25 https://www.bondbuyer.com/news/city-streets-back-new-bonds-california-cities-issue-to-fund-pensions

26 https://www.greenbondpledge.com/files/files/Green-City-Playbook_2018.pdf

27 https://www.insurancejournal.com/news/national/2020/06/26/573599.htm

28 https://www.insurancejournal.com/news/national/2020/06/26/573599.htm

29 https://www.treasurer.ca.gov/Cdiac/seminars/2013/20131022/day3/1.pdf, slide 17.
30 https://www.treasurer.ca.gov/Cdiac/seminars/2013/20131022/day3/1.pdf
31 https://haasinstitute.berkeley.edu/sites/default/files/haasinstituterefundamerica_doubly bound_cost_of_issuingbonds_publish.pdf
32 https://www.sec.gov/ocr/ocr-current-nrsros.html
33 https://www.moodys.com/sites/products/productattachments/moody%27s%20rating%20system.pdf
34 https://www.spglobal.com/ratings/en/about/intro-to-credit-ratings
35 https://www.fitchratings.com/products/rating-definitions#about-rating-definitions
36 https://www.moodys.com/sites/products/productattachments/moody%27s%20rating%20system.pdf
37 https://www.spglobal.com/ratings/en/about/intro-to-credit-ratings
38 https://www.moodys.com/sites/products/productattachments/moody%27s%20rating%20system.pdf
39 https://www.spglobal.com/ratings/en/about/intro-to-credit-ratings
40 https://www.moodys.com/sites/products/productattachments/moody%27s%20rating%20system.pdf
41 https://www.spglobal.com/ratings/en/about/intro-to-credit-ratings
42 https://www.moodys.com/sites/products/productattachments/moody%27s%20rating%20system.pdf
43 https://www.spglobal.com/ratings/en/about/intro-to-credit-ratings
44 https://www.moodys.com/sites/products/productattachments/moody%27s%20rating%20system.pdf
45 https://www.spglobal.com/ratings/en/about/intro-to-credit-ratings
46 https://www.moodys.com/sites/products/productattachments/moody%27s%20rating%20system.pdf
47 https://www.spglobal.com/ratings/en/about/intro-to-credit-ratings
48 https://www.moodys.com/sites/products/productattachments/moody%27s%20rating%20system.pdf
49 https://www.spglobal.com/ratings/en/about/intro-to-credit-ratings
50 https://www.moodys.com/sites/products/productattachments/moody%27s%20rating%20system.pdf
51 https://www.spglobal.com/ratings/en/about/intro-to-credit-ratings
52 https://www.spglobal.com/ratings/en/about/intro-to-credit-ratings
53 https://www.pressrepublican.com/news/local_news/citys-bond-rating-unmoved/article_30c83503-d52f-5871-841d-379061d630df.html
54 https://www.pressrepublican.com/news/local_news/town-gets-first-bond-rating-in-20-years/article_3559b197-c7f0-5e31-bf4d-018a676421be.html
55 https://www.moodys.com/research/Moodys-assigns-initial-Aa3-rating-to-Town-of-Platts burgh-NYs–PR_906591653
56 https://bvwv.nwaonline.com/news/2020/aug/26/city-receives-s38p-rating-for-bond-out look-stable/
57 https://www.fitchratings.com/research/us-public-finance/fitch-rates-suffolk-va-132mm-se ries-2020a-b-go-bonds-aaa-outlook-stable-24-08-2020
58 For an early critique of this proposition, see Property Tax Assessment Limits.
59 https://www.ipma-hr.org/docs/default-source/default-document-library/suffolk.pdf?sfvrsn=6ad5dd7f_0

60 https://www.fitchratings.com/research/corporate-finance/public-finance-infrastructure-esg-relevance-map-02-10-2019

61 http://www.msrb.org/

62 Clarence E. Anthony, CEO and Executive Director of the National League of Cities, quoted in "Menendez Introduces Bill to Ease Borrowing Costs for State and Local Governments Fighting COVID-19," March 20, 2020. https://www.menendez.senate.gov/news-and-events/press/menendez-introduces-bill-to-ease-borrowing-costs-for-state-and-local-governments-fighting-covid-19. See also Cooper Howard, "2020 Mid-Year Outlook: Municipal Bonds," July 9, 2020.

63 https://westlinnoregon.gov/finance/municipal-bond-issues

64 https://westlinnoregon.gov/finance/municipal-bond-issues

65 For a favorable view, see https://tax.unc.edu/wp-content/uploads/2019/03/22-The-Impact-of-Bank-Financing-on-Municipalities-Bond-Issuance-and-the-Real-Economy.pdf. For a cautionary view see https://www.brookings.edu/research/the-privatization-of-municipal-debt/

66 https://www.governing.com/topics/finance/gov-muni-bonds-replaced-direct-bank-loans.html

Chapter 8
Land Trusts

Conservation land trusts play a vital role in environmental protection for many towns and cities around the world. As their name implies, land trusts hold land on behalf of others. The purpose of land trusts varies, as does their relationship to local communities and their governments. Some "land trusts" are anonymous trusts used for land development for private purposes. Other "land trusts" are nonprofit corporations that play a role in the conservation of land for public purposes.

This brief chapter delves into the legal, financial, and political character of land trusts in the US (and to a lesser extent, globally), with emphasis on conservation land trusts operating as nonprofits for the public good while cooperating with local governments.

Land Trusts as an Example of Collaboration

Land trusts require a high degree of collaboration, whether they are formed via a simple trust agreement, or operate as a charity under a national tax code (e.g., 501 (c) 3 in the US). When they are organized via a legal agreement as a trust, in most cases the trustee and trustor are two different parties. The trustee acts in a fiduciary capacity on behalf of another party – the beneficial owners.

For example, a land trust may protect and restore land, and then transfer it to a local government for future stewardship – in the so-called protect, restore, transfer model starting with the trust in the protection role and ending with local government stewardship.[1] This model can work in the opposite direction, when a local government provides the initial capital for a land trust, and develops the trust until it can exist on its own as a separate nonprofit (see Figure 8.1).

LT protects ➝ LT restores ➝ LT transfers to City

City protects ➝ City restores ➝ City transfers to LT

Figure 8.1: Protect, Restore, Transfer Approach for Land Trusts.

https://doi.org/10.1515/9783110689860-008

Types of Land Trusts in the US

A land trust in its generic technical sense is an entity created by a legal contract in which the owner of real estate transfers the title of the property to a trustee. At the national level, the US holds lands in trust for Native Americans, and some of these are recognized as reservations.[2] For the most part, however, land trusts are creations of state law.

Land trusts can take various forms in the US, depending on the state where they are formed. Although a designated *conservation land trust* is the only type of trust dedicated to environmental causes, other forms of land trusts may play a role – for better or worse – in municipal sustainability.

All states except Louisiana permit land trusts, but very few US states have land trust laws.[3] These include Florida,[4] Hawaii,[5] and Illinois.[6] In states that do not have land trust laws, guidance comes from generic trust law, and from court decisions. Some jurisdictions prohibit the use of the term "land trust" except by charities that have land conservation as their stated purpose.

When dealing with land trusts it is important to ascertain the nature and purpose of the trust, as some land trusts do not operate for the public good. The land trust law of Illinois has been known for its use of anonymous control by beneficial owners, although recent reforms have removed the option of absolute anonymity.[7]

The presence or absence of a state land trust law does not affect prevalence of land trusts. For example, conservation land trusts may thrive in states where there is no developed land trust law. California has no land trust statute, but it has some 150 land trusts formed for environmental preservation, protecting 2.5 million acres in the state. This is partly due to a new tax break available to California-based land trusts that conserve timberlands in exchange for carbon emission tax credits.[8] (In a similar fashion, the IRS gives tax breaks to owners of conservation land, although the application of the tax break has been narrowing in recent years.[9])

The "Illinois" Land Trust

As mentioned earlier, a land trust in its generic technical sense is an entity created by a private legal contract in which the owner of real estate transfers the title of the property to a trustee. The most well-known type of land trust contract is called the Illinois land trust, due to its state of origin.

The Illinois land trust (also called a title holding trust) is different from a conventional trust, in which the trustee holds legal title, and the beneficial owner holds equitable title. In Illinois land trusts, by contrast, real property is conveyed to a trustee, but the beneficiary retains full management and control of the property – for example, to build, rent, sell, and/or transfer it.[10] Another unique twist in Illinois land trusts is that the identity of the beneficial owner may be anonymous – although recent amendments to the law in Illinois do require disclosures in some cases – for example, if the land trust applies for a grant.[11] Illinois-type land trusts can work against community sustainability, because they can be a vehicle to purchase sensitive environmental assets or historic properties under the cover of anonymity and develop them in ways that the community may not support (see Box 8.1).

Box 8.1: Land Trusts in Florida: The Good, the Bad, and the Ugly

Florida is a living paradox for land trusts. The Florida state government and the state's charitable sector have a given rise to strong environmental trusts. Yet Florida is one of the few states in the country that condones anonymous land trusts used for nonpublic purposes.

The Good Story

Florida's Division of State Lands has established a Florida Communities Trust for land preservation.[12] Local governments and nonprofit environmental organizations may apply for grants from the Trust, which is at least partially funded by green bonds. The Trust has been instrumental in the protection of more than 1.25 million acres of land. Also, Florida is the birthplace of at least 22 conservation land trusts, which have aligned their goals through the Alliance of Florida Land Trusts.[13]

Another Story

Yet another story runs parallel with this commendable progress in sustainability – and that is the use of anonymous land trusts to accomplish private goals.

In the 1960s, Walt Disney used an anonymous land trust in Florida to purchase thousands of acres in swampland trusts to conceal his plans for Disney World. He used land trusts to hide his identity so that the price would remain low.

In February 2020, in the midst of Black History month, citizens in the beach town of American Beach suffered the partial demolishment of an historic landmark: the first home built by Abraham Lincoln Lewis on American Beach in Florida. Known as America's first Black millionaire, Abraham Lewis founded American Beach in the 1930s as a respite from American racism, and the area has enormous significance in the Black community. The demolition was traced to Land Trust # 4022. Uproar followed. In response to calls for stop work orders, the trust's beneficial owner revealed his identity publicly, and explained that he did the demolition because restoration was impossible; he vowed replication. The development put a bad light on anonymous land trusts in Florida.[14]

Happy Ending

Overall, the Florida record on conservation is strong, thanks to its conservation land trusts. On December 15, 2020, the North Florida Land Trust, a member of the Alliance mentioned earlier, purchased land containing Little Nana Dune, a sand dune in Florida that had tremendous environmental and cultural value.[15]

Community Land Trusts

A *community land trust,* by contrast, is a private, nonprofit corporation that acquires, manages, and develops land for a social purpose, such as affordable housing.[16] In the US today there are approximately 300 of these organizations.[17] The goal of these organizations is social, rather than environmental, sustainability. As one source noted "Keeping open land available for gardens can . . . be a difficult pitch for CLTs that focus primarily on housing."[18] Although this same source (a study by MIT Community Innovation Lab) featured pictures of community gardens.

In Irvine, California, the city of Irvine provided a grant of $250,000 as the startup capital plus initial staffing for a community land trust, devoted to affordable housing with sustainable features.[19] Once the CLT was operating successfully, it approved the decision to let the CLT convert to an independent nonprofit.[20] The city's inclusionary zoning rules require that developments over 50 units dedicate 15 percent of the units as affordable housing. Developers may convey their affordable units to the CLT portfolio.

Conservation Land Trusts

Finally, and most importantly for the purposes of this chapter, a *conservation land trust* is a nonprofit organization set up to acquire and/or steward land or easements in a particular area for conservation purposes. Acquisition of land may be accomplished by buying the land, often at bargain rates, or by receiving the land as a donation.

A land trust may have the legal form of a trust – with trustees and beneficial owners. Or it may be formed as a standard charity, which has no owners but is under direction of a board of trustees.[21]

Today conservation land trusts hold some $2.2 billion in funding.[22] A conservation land trust, which may also be called a conservancy, typically takes the legal form of a trust, but some organizations that have land trust in their title may be organized as nonprofit charities, not as trusts. Conservation land trusts or nonprofit conservancies often carry the name of the geographic area that is being conserved.

In the US, the Land Trust Alliance connects conservation land trusts and conservancies from all over the country.[23] One of the goals of the Land Trust Alliance is to "increase the rate of land conservation, not only in rural and suburban areas but also in urban communities that have not been the traditional focus of the land trust community."[24] There are well over 1,000 land trusts in the US today. The Land Trust Alliance counted 1,363 land trusts in its most recent survey. One in five land trusts surveyed ranked urban parks as "very important" or "important" as a priority.[25]

The Open Space Institute, a conservancy based in New York, has also helped Florida, New Jersey, and South Carolina, through large land purchases. Through its loans and grants the program has distributed over $122.8 million to partner land trusts around the country to protect more than 2 million acres valued at $700 million.

How Conservation Land Trusts Operate

Conservation land trusts raise awareness of the value of conserving land in particular areas. They raise funds from people who share their concerns and want to see land protected. They also ask for donations of land, or at least the opportunity buy land preferably at below-market dates. If landowners do not wish to donate the land, they can put it under easement.

Easements are an important strategy for land trusts as well as for municipalities. A conservation easement is a piece of land and/or body of water protected by a legal agreement between a landowner and a land trust or government entity. The easement contract (also called "easement") limits the use of the land to protect its natural resources. For example, the easement contract may ban clearcutting of trees on the property. Such a contract allows landowners to continue to own and use their land, and they can also sell it or pass it on to heirs. The conditions of the contract run with the land; even if the land is sold or passed on via inheritance, the restrictions stay in place. Alternatives to easements include bargain sale to the land trust or outright donation to the land trust.[26]

Some Examples of Conservation Land Trusts

The oldest conservation land trust in the US is Trustees of Reservations, founded in Massachusetts in 1891.[27] This trust seeks donations of land and funds, uses the funds to acquire land and historic properties, and then serves as steward to the properties. The trust not only preserves natural lands but also some key city resources such as the Boston waterfront, through a recent park initiative.[28]

In any given jurisdiction, there may be multiple land trusts. Here are a few examples:

- California has 250 land trusts dedicated to conservation.
- Connecticut has 115 land trusts protecting over 62,000 acres of valuable open space.[29] The Connecticut Land Conservation Council helps these organizations access grants, among other activities.[30] Some are based in urban areas. For example, Gather New Haven, a merger of the New Haven Land Trust, and New Haven Farms, sponsors several programs in the city of new Haven.[31]
- In Illinois, there are 40 conservation land trusts, according to the Prairie State Conservation Coalition.[32]
- North Carolina is home to a federation of 20 land trusts, each of which makes a variety of contributions to municipal sustainability.[33] For example, one of the federation members, the Triangle Land Conservancy, supported a successful municipal bond vote for the town of Cary Parks.[34] The general obligation bond, approved by 77 percent of voters,[35] delivered $112,00 in funding for parks, open spaces, and the purchase of land, among other goals.[36] (For more on bonds, see Chapter 5.)
- New York is home is home base for many environmental groups, including the Open Space Institute and the Land Trust Alliance, mentioned earlier. These two organizations are part of a 175-member coalition called New Yorkers for Clean Water & Jobs, formed in December 2020 for environmental advocacy.[37]

Global Developments

The US is not the only country to develop land trusts. The International Land Conservation Network, founded in Berlin, Germany, in 2015 and modeled after the Land Trust Alliance in the US,[38] plays an educational and connective role in support of land trusts around the world.[39]

The International Land Conservation Network has a mission to "connect organizations and people around the world that are accelerating voluntary private sector action that protects and stewards land and later resources."[40] It focuses on conservation finance, conservation law and policy, stewardship and land management, large landscape conservation, and organization and governance. As part of its service to the conservation community, it has conducted a census of major global land trusts and conservancies, finding significant organized conservation efforts on every continent (see Figure 8.2).

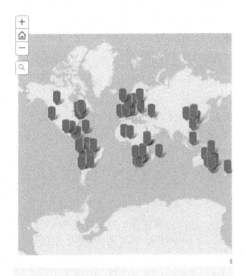

Figure 8.2: Map Showing Location of Major Conservation Groups Including Land Trusts.
Note: Each of the arrows on this figure indicates an organization that has many institutional members. Available at https://landconservationnetwork.org/locationsasaninteractive map.
Source: International Land Conservation Network (2021).

The World Land Trust, established in 1989 in the UK, has purchased over 2.2 million acres and has been instrumental in the protection of a total of more than 4 million acres worldwide.[41] This organization has 35 nonprofit partners around the world, including in South America, Africa, Asia (including India), and the Middle East.[42] While its mission does not extend to small parcels in cities, much can be learned from its approach to partnering. The Word Land Trust helps communities all over the globe but does not take ownership of land outside the United Kingdom, to avoid what it calls "green colonialism." This term, also called "green grabbing" among other unflattering terms, refers to the conservation of land by nonlocal interests without local agreement.[43] Instead, the World Land Trust works with local organizations, including indigenous tribes.

Indigenous Tribes Using Land Trusts

Indigenous tribes around the world have had a strong impact on the protection of land through land trusts, including the passage of national laws protecting indigenous lands. As mentioned earlier, the US protects Native American lands with a trust. However, the US has no dedicated land trust law. Countries with longstanding land trust statutes include:

- Australia – Natural Heritage Trust of Australia Act[44]
- Guam – Chamorro Land Trust Act[45]
- Fiji – Itaukei Land Trust Act[46]

All these land trust laws are focused on the rights of indigenous people to continue conservation of their lands. For more about indigenous rights to land, see Appendix 7: Notable Accomplishments of Tribal Governments.

Concluding Reflections

The English poet John Donne channeled a profound truth when he wrote the following words in 1624:

> *No man is an Iland, intire of itselfe; every man*
> *is a peece of the Continent, a part of the maine;*
> *if a Clod bee washed away by the Sea, Europe*
> *is the lesse, as well as if a Promontorie were, as*
> *well as if a Manor of thy friends or of thine*
> *owne were; any mans death diminishes me,*
> *because I am involved in Mankinde;*
> *And therefore never send to know for whom*
> *the bell tolls; It tolls for thee.*

As the world faces the tolling bell of global warming, communities need to help each other and learn from each other. The conservation land trust community provides proof that we can learn from and help one another. The next chapter of this book will explore how a city can get grants – from conservation land trusts or other grantmaking bodies.

Notes

1 https://www.prairiestateconservation.org/pscc/resources/stewardship-study-and-tools/.
2 https://www.fns.usda.gov/distinction-between-reservations-and-land-held-trust
3 Some states have trust law that can be interpreted for land trust purposes, but the states cited here have explicit "land trust" sections in their legal codes.
4 Title XL, 689.071, Florida Land Trust Act.Statutes & Constitution: View Statutes: Online Sunshine (state.fl.us); http://www.leg.state.fl.us/Statutes/index.cfm?App_mode=Display_Statute&URL=0600-0699/0689/Sections/0689.071.html

5 Trusts and Fiduciaries (760 ILCS 3/) Illinois Trust Code. Hawaii Revised Statutes > Chapter 558 – Land Trusts–Beneficiary Controlled » LawServer; https://www.lawserver.com/law/state/hawaii/hi-statutes/hawaii_statutes_chapter_558

6 Illinois' Land Trust Beneficial Interest Disclosure Act. (Source: P.A. 86-1324), effective in 2013, now requires disclosure of the beneficial owner under certain circumstances. https://www.ilga.gov/legislation/ilcs/ilcs3.asp?actID=2185 Previously, beneficial owners could remain anonymous. For the entire section, see https://www.ilga.gov/legislation/ilcs/ilcs2.asp?ChapterID=62

7 Note that there is a new Illinois trust law that explicitly does not apply to land trusts. https://www.ilga.gov/legislation/ilcs/ilcs5.asp?DocName=&ActID=4001&ChapterID=61&SeqStart=&SeqEnd=&Print=True

8 California has a "cap-and-trade" that rewards owners of untouched forestland with carbon-offset credits Preserving Trees Becomes Big Business, Driven by Emissions Rules – WSJ; https://www.wsj.com/articles/preserving-trees-becomes-big-business-driven-by-emissions-rules-11598202541?mod=searchresults_pos2&page=1

9 Trump Golf Course Tax-Break Deal Appears Vulnerable to IRS Challenge – WSJ; https://www.wsj.com/articles/trump-golf-course-tax-break-deal-appears-vulnerable-to-irs-challenge-11599039002?mod=searchresults_pos1&page=1

10 Alward v. Jacob Holding of Ontario LLC, 2019 IL App (5th) 180332 (illinois.gov); https://courts.illinois.gov/Opinions/AppellateCourt/2019/5thDistrict/5180332.pdf

11 Land Trust Beneficial Interest Disclosure Act, Section 2.1. https://www.ilga.gov/legislation/ilcs/ilcs3.asp?ActID=2185

12 Florida Communities Trust (FCT) | Florida Department of Environmental Protection; https://floridadep.gov/lands/land-and-recreation-grants/content/florida-communities-trust-fct

13 Alliance of Florida Land Trusts; https://www.allianceoffloridalandtrusts.com/

14 In this case, the beneficial owner, following public outcry, identified himself and assured the community of his good intentions.

15 North Florida Land Trust Signs $1.3M Contract to Buy 3 American Beach Parcels | WJCT NEWS; https://news.wjct.org/post/north-florida-land-trust-signs-13m-contract-buy-3-american-beach-parcels

16 http://commonstransition.org/community-land-trusts-urban-land-reform-and-the-commons/

17 *A Guide to Transformative Land Strategies: Lessons from the Field* (MIT Community Innovation Lab, June 2020). https://static1.squarespace.com/static/59e749467131a5e036c15d82/t/5f06708154b02120ab2c8ef0/1594257540711/Community+Land+Trusts_CoLab.pdf

18 *A Guide to Transformative Land Strategies: Lessons from the Field* (MIT Community Innovation Lab, June 2020). https://static1.squarespace.com/static/59e749467131a5e036c15d82/t/5f06708154b02120ab2c8ef0/1594257540711/Community+Land+Trusts_CoLab.pdf

19 Case Study: Irvine Community Land Trust – Irvine, California | Adaptation Clearinghouse; https://www.adaptationclearinghouse.org/resources/case-study-irvine-community-land-trust-irvine-california.html

20 Case Study: Irvine Community Land Trust – Irvine, California | Adaptation Clearinghouse; https://www.adaptationclearinghouse.org/resources/case-study-irvine-community-land-trust-irvine-california.html

21 Greg McRay, "Who Really Owns a Nonprofit?" The Foundation Group, May 2019.https://www.501c3.org/who-really-owns-a-nonprofit/

22 Source: Land Trust Alliance56 Million Acres Voluntarily Conserved in America, National Land Trust Census Reveals | Land Trust Alliance.

23 What We Do | Land Trust Alliance; https://www.landtrustalliance.org/what-we-do

24 Rate | Land Trust Alliance; https://www.landtrustalliance.org/what-we-do/our-strategy/rate

25 http://s3.amazonaws.com/landtrustalliance.org/2015NationalLandTrustCensusReport.pdf

26 See Land Trust Alliance, Conservation Options, undated. Conservation Options | Land Trust Alliance; https://www.landtrustalliance.org/what-you-can-do/conserve-your-land/conservation-options

27 Land Conservation & Stewardship – The Trustees of Reservations; https://thetrustees.org/content/land-conservation-stewardship/

28 The Trustees of Reservations – GuideStar Profile; https://www.guidestar.org/profile/04-2105780

29 Land Trusts (ct.gov); https://portal.ct.gov/DEEP/Open-Space/Land-Trusts

30 About Us | Connecticut Land Conservation Council (ctconservation.org); https://gatherne whaven.org/

31 l Gather New Haven Farms | Health & Wellness | CT Farm Stands; https://gathernewhaven.org/

32 https://www.prairiestateconservation.org/pscc/directory-land-trusts-illinois/#:~:text=In%20Illinois%2C%20there%20are%20more,PSCC%20Conservation%20Land%20Trust%20Directory

33 Triangle Land Conservancy joins forces with 19 other land trusts – Triangle Land Conservancy; https://www.triangleland.org/blog/triangle-land-conservancy-joins-forces-with-19-other-land-trusts

34 https://www.triangleland.org/blog/cary-parks-bond

35 https://www.townofcary.org/Home/Components/News/News/15038/715

36 Parks Bond Offering, Town of Cary, North Carolina (2021). Cary Bonds; https://carybonds.org/parks/

37 Open Space Institute Joins Broad Coalition Calling for Full Funding of State Environmental Programs – Open Space Institute (en-US); https://www.openspaceinstitute.org/news/open-space-institute-joins-broad-coalition-calling-for-full-funding-of-state-environmental-programs

38 International Land Conservation Network to Launch in Berlin (prnewswire.com); https://www.prnewswire.com/news-releases/international-land-conservation-network-to-launch-in-berlin-300159224.html

39 International Land Conservation Network; https://landconservationnetwork.org/who-we-are

40 Who We Are | International Land Conservation Network; https://landconservationnetwork.org/who-we-are

41 https://www.worldlandtrust.org/who-we-are-2/our-impact/

42 Partner Organisations – World Land Trust; https://www.worldlandtrust.org/who-we-are-2/partners/

43 Other terms include green greed, greenshit, carbon cowboys, and fortress conservation. See Frank Vanclay, "Principles to gain a social licence to operate for green initiatives and biodiversity projects," *Current Opinion in Environmental Sustainability 29* (2017): 48–56.
Source: (16) Principles to gain a social licence to operate for green initiatives and biodiversity projects | Request PDF (researchgate.net); https://www.researchgate.net/publication/321693182_Principles_to_gain_a_social_licence_to_operate_for_green_initiatives_and_biodiversity_projects

44 https://www.legislation.gov.au/Details/C2016C00641

45 Chamorro Land Trust Act amendments up for vote | Guam News | postguam.com; https:// www.postguam.com/news/local/chamorro-land-trust-act-amendments-up-for-vote/article_ a2e0bcbc-2d25-11eb-aec0-130c0131244e.html

46 ITAUKEI LAND TRUST ACT 1940 – Laws of Fiji; https://news.wjct.org/post/north-florida- land-trust-signs-13m-contract-buy-3-american-beach-parcels

Chapter 9
Federal, State, and Nonprofit Grants

Grants play a unique role in the financing of municipal sustainability. They can supplement the usual source of revenue for towns and cities, which comes from either municipal tax (levied on income, property, and/or sales) or from municipal bonds (either general obligation or revenue).

These two ordinary revenue sources offer significant support for municipal operations, but as discussed in chapters 7 and 8, they come with financial consequences. Every tax dollar a municipality raises reduces the real income of the citizens and businesses that pay that dollar; and every bond dollar collected by the city increases city debt until it is repaid.

The only source of money that does not have such financial strings attached is grant money – whether from government sources or from nonprofits. There is no such thing as free money, but grants come close to being just that. Grants are given by governments or charities for social purposes, with no absolute obligation for repayment. Although grant money may be earmarked for specific uses and may have to be returned if unspent, it does not create obligations in the way that taxes and bonds do. As such, grants offer opportunities that should not be overlooked by communities striving to become more sustainable. As mentioned in Chapter 4, some cities collect as much money from grants as they do from ad valorem (property) taxes.

The Grant Universe

The website grantwatch.com, an online directory of funding opportunities, has curated links to more than 25,000 funding sources for grants of all types, with more than 5,000 of these offering a current grant at any given time.[1]

To fully appreciate the power of grants, it is important to understand the relationships among the entities that give and receive them. For municipalities, grants are a two-way street. As shown in Box 9.1 and Figure 9.1, local governments can both give and receive grants, which can come from a variety of sources.

– Cities may be grantors. All towns and cities want their social needs to be met. In many cases, local nonprofits meet those needs for the city, so those local nonprofits need support. If a town or city has discretionary funds, the city leaders may decide to give grants to its own local nonprofits.

https://doi.org/10.1515/9783110689860-009

–   Conversely, cities may be grantees. A city may seek grants for its own operations from nonprofits (which may or may not be located within the city), as well as from federal, state, and corporate sources, rather than spending taxpayer money (see Box 9.1).

Box 9.1: Eight Types of Grants to Empower Municipal Sustainability in the US.

Municipality is Grant Recipient	Local Nonprofit is Grant Recipient
Federal Grants to Municipalities	Federal Grants to Nonprofits
State Grants to Municipalities	State Grants to Nonprofits
Corporate Grants to Municipalities	Corporate Grants to Nonprofits
Nonprofit Grants to Municipalities	Municipal Grants to Nonprofits

Note: Combinations also occur, for example, a federal or national nonprofit grant to a state that in turn goes to towns or cities within the state.

This chapter will discuss federal, state, and nonprofit grants available to municipalities and their local nonprofits, as well as grants or other payments that a municipality may make to its local nonprofits. The discussion should make it clear that the flow from giving to receiving moves along several lines. For example, as noted by the US Congressional Research Service, federal grants may go first to a state capital, in one congressional district, then get distributed to one or more city or county governments (in additional congressional districts), which then may pass the funds to an organization that spends the money in yet other locations.[2] To see how a particular town or city is affected, it is best to focus on the place of performance rather than the recipient only (see Figure 9.1).

Federal Grants to Municipalities

The US federal government provides significant funding to the nation's towns and cities The US Office of Management (OMB) reported a planned $810 billion in funding for state and local governments in FY 2021, up 2.4 percent from FY2020.[3] By 2025, the OMB predicts that states and local governments will be receiving an annual amount of some $848 billion in federal grants,[4] an average of approximately $270 million per county (although of course grant values will vary greatly by location).[5] These projected federal grants, based on past trends,

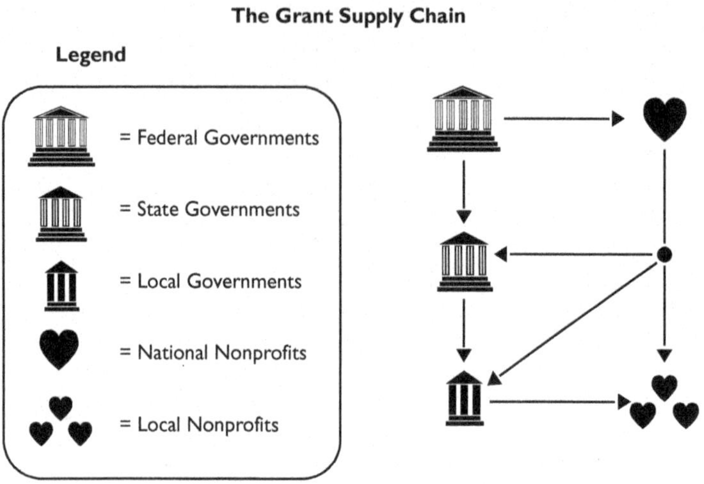

The Grant Supply Chain

Legend

Figure 9.1: The Flow from Abundance to Need: A Conceptual Diagram.
Source: Concept by Alexandra R. Lajoux. Art by Chris Smith, quarternative.com

will include nearly $6 billion for the environment – comprised of $5.1 billion in federal funds, plus $781 million in trust funds projected for 2025.[6]

Grants are distinguished from other forms of government payment. Under US law, to be classified as a federal "grant," a payment cannot be on the form of a tax break, a loan, or a contract for services.[7]

Grants from the federal government can be general "block" grants that give the recipients a set amount of money, but with flexibility on how to spend it; or they can be "categorical" grants that restrict the funding to specific purposes. According to a 2019 GAO report, categorical grants, including grants for "environmental protection," have strong bipartisan support.[8]

Some federal funding to local governments comes in response to major crises such as the global financial crisis of 2007–2008 (American Recovery and Reinvestment Act of 2009), or the COVID-19 pandemic (the Coronavirus Aid, Relief, and Economic Security Act of 2019), or natural disasters (Additional Supplemental Appropriations for Disaster Relief Act of 2019).

A lesser-known source of federal money – used to support about a fifth of all spending from state and local governments[9] – comes from more than 1,000 grants, cooperative agreements, or procurement contracts available to cities.[10] Approximately 10 percent of these are earmarked specifically to support a variety of environmental causes, including disaster prevention, land conservation, river cleanup, and stormwater management. The agencies responsible for the grants include the Department of Agriculture, the Department of Commerce, the Environmental Protection Agency, and the Department of the Interior, as well as the Army Corps of Engineers for shoreline stabilization.[11] Cities looking for federal grants can either start from the giver (by looking for federal grants at grants.gov) or from the receiver (by looking for federal grants from a city manager association such as National League of Cities (NLC), a coalition of 19,000 US cities, towns, and villages).[12] The NLC has a grant tracker to find federal grants.[13]

The Environmental Protection Agency (EPA) has a grant page with links to more than a dozen programs run by the EPA,[14] and the "green Infrastructure funding" page of its website highlights more than 30 programs, including some managed by other organizations.[15] For example, there is a Five Star and Urban Waters Restoration Grant Program, run by the National Fish and Wildlife Foundation, a federally chartered foundation that works in partnership with the EPA and other organizations.[16]

The EPA maintains a data base of success stories featuring recipients of Brownfield Grants, which are awarded so that contaminated properties can be cleaned up and sustainably repurposed. (See Box 9.2 for some profiles.) Many of these success stories show a shift from industrial to residential and/or retail. Such a transition can weaken the sense of identity for a town with an industrial past. The success stories profiled here can be models for towns and cities that wish to maintain their identify as working-class towns.

Box 9.2: EPA Brownfield Grant Success Stories
EPA Grant Recipient: City of Richmond Department of Housing & Community Development
    EPA Grant Type: Brownfields Assessment
    Former Uses: Vacant, Gasworks, Concrete Mixing Plant and Staging Area
    Current Use: Brewery, Distribution Facility, Tasting Room
    Richmond's Fulton Hill neighborhood was severely damaged by flooding in the 1970s and was left untouched by developers for decades. When a California brewery earmarked a section of the neighborhood as an ideal place to use to expand their operations, the city of Richmond used Brownfields funding to assess the area, which was formerly home to a concrete mixing plant and gasworks, and fortified the site for new construction. The brewery, restaurant, and tasting room subsequently built on the site was constructed from repurposed materials, is LEED certified, and created approximately 300 jobs in the neighborhood.
    EPA Grant Recipient: City of Jackson, MI
    EPA Grant Type: Brownfields Assessment
    Former use: Machine shop; assembly of Baker equipment
    Current use: Hi-Tech Flexible Products, LLC

In February 2005, the City of Jackson, Michigan, gained a new neighbor at 2000 Townley Street when Hi-Tech Flexible Products, LLC (HTFP) assumed ownership of an industrial property that had once been a machine tool shop and later a manufacturer of bakery equipment. To accommodate this new business, which creates custom masks for the coating industry, EPA awarded the City of Jackson a $200,000 Brownfields Assessment grant in 2004. Most of the grant was used for purposes other than cleanup, which proved unnecessary. EPA considers this a success: "The City of Jackson suffers from a poverty rate of 19.6 percent, almost double the state poverty rate. The grantee was able to successfully leverage the retention of six jobs, with the possibility of creating one to two new jobs. The $157,000 investment from HTFP for the assessment and redevelopment in this poverty-stricken area has helped to improve economic viability of the area."

Sources: Cheers to a Revitalized Neighborhood (epa.gov), https://www.epa.gov/sites/production/files/2019-09/documents/cheers_to_a_revitalized_neighborhood.pdf; Brownfields Assessment Leads to Jobs (July 2010) (epa.gov), https://www.epa.gov/sites/production/files/2015-09/documents/jackson_mi.pdf

Federal Grants to Nonprofits

The nonprofit sector plays an important part in any national economy. For this reason, most countries provide a tax advantage to nonprofit organizations operating as charities. This stands to reason as charities do the work that might otherwise have to be done by the government. Furthermore, considering the work done by charities, many countries give grants directly to nonprofits rather than following socially or environmentally targeted funds to states and cities.

For example, in the US, the EPA funds a variety of environmental justice grants[17] for nonprofits, including an Environmental Justice Small Grants Program (which funds projects up to $30,000).[18] The EPA has defined environmental justice as "fair treatment and meaningful involvement of all people regardless of race, color, national origin, or income, with respect to the development, implementation, and enforcement of environmental laws, regulations, and policies."[19] Projects must be associated with at least one US environmental statute.

For another example, the US Department of Health and Human Services awards Community Services Block Grants to alleviate the causes and conditions of poverty in communities.[20] These may go to states or nonprofits which in turn might spend the money in towns or cities. One recipient qualified to receive this kind of funding in the US can be a local community action agency (CAA). Funded through a federal "Community Services Block Grant" with roots in 1960s-era antipoverty legislation, a CAA may operate as a nonprofit, or a part of local government.[21]

State Grants to Municipalities and Nonprofits

In the US, the National Conference of State Legislatures publishes resources for municipal governments and citizens in search of grants. For example, it tracks state grants to towns and cities for community gardens.[22] The National League of Cities also maintains a state-by-state list of grants available to cities.[23]

For the most part, however, it is necessary to search for grants state by each state. For example, Florida has several grants for working waterfronts, disbursed through its Department of Environmental Protection.[24] New York State has a Clean Energy Fund for grants to municipalities in New York.[25]

For cities searching for a green energy grant from their state, a good place to start is the National Association of State Energy Officials.[26] In January 2021, the NASEO released a report on Private, State, and Federal Funding and Financing Options to Enable Resilient, Affordable, and Clean Microgrids[27] (see Box 9.3). A microgrid is associated with energy resilience because it is a power source (or group of them) "that can connect or disconnect from the larger electric grid to function independently in case of electrical grid service interruptions."[28]The report reviews costs and benefits of microgrids; identifies barriers to their development; and presents ways to plan, finance, and deploy them.[29]

Box 9.3: Spotlight on Two Microgrid Grants
Spotlight: New Jersey Town Center Microgrid Funding: The New Jersey Board of Public Utilities (NJ BPU) is using grants to help foster the development of Town Center microgrids throughout the state. NJ BPU is currently overseeing the second phase of a three-phase project. The first phase involved the competitive selection of thirteen towns and townships across the state to each receive up to $200,000 to develop feasibility studies for Town Center microgrids. The second phase involves the completion by the participants of detailed designs for each microgrid based on the feasibility studies. NJ BPU plans to award up to $4 million in grants for selected Phase Two applicants to fund the detailed designs. Applicants will be selected based on six criteria: overall project narrative, use of GHG emissions reduction technologies, social considerations, financial cost, technologies used, and design cost estimates. NJ BPU expects to select the winners in 2020 and move on to phase three of its program by the end of the year.

Spotlight: NY Prize Microgrid Competition: The NY Prize Microgrid Competition is an approach to resilience that may spur community-based microgrid development, and was designed by the New York State Energy Research and Development Authority (NYSERDA), the State Energy Office, and the Governor's Office of Storm Recovery (GOSR) in response to the state's disaster recovery after Superstorm Sandy. The competition is organized into three stages: feasibility, design, and construction. In the feasibility stage, the state provided awards to 83 cities, villages, towns, and municipalities, from more than 130 submitted applications, to develop feasibility studies for microgrid systems to serve critical functions at a neighborhood level. In the design stage, $1 million awards were made to 10 proposals . . . based on the design guidelines outlined in the competition structure. These awards are designed to help applicants finalize their technical designs. The final construction stage is designed to select up to five competitors to realize their microgrids, providing up to $7 million in funding to support construction. To support community awareness, emergency response planning and system utilization, communities are expected to secure matching funds for the second and third stages of the competition. The matching fund requirements is also intended to open the door for other financing sources to supplement the funding provided by the state and demonstrate their applicability for microgrid development.

Source: Excerpted from *Private, State, and Federal Funding and Financing Options to Enable Resilient, Affordable, and Clean Microgrids*: v2_NASEO_MicroGrid.pdf, https://www.naseo.org/data/sites/1/documents/publications/v2_NASEO_MicroGrid.pdf, pp. 23 and 25.

Corporate Grants to Municipalities and Nonprofits

The world of corporate grants is broad indeed. From the largest public company to the smallest local firm, most for-profit enterprises give back to the communities where they operate.

CEOs for Corporate Purpose (CECP), a philanthropic coalition composed of the CEOS of 200 large public companies representing $11.2 trillion in revenue has given away more than $23 billion in social investment since its founding in 1999, as well as contributing 30 million hours of employee engagement.[30] Many of the case histories featured on the organization's website feature initiatives with a local emphasis.[31] In January 2021, the organization announced a focus on public-private partnerships, lighting the way for more corporate aid to towns and cities.[32]

Nonprofit Grants to Municipalities

It is quite common for nonprofits to give grants to towns and cities. The website grantwatch.com lists nearly 2,000 such grants in early 2021.[33] Environmentally focused funding available to municipalities includes grants for the following causes:

- Battle ground preservation
- Conservation of longleaf pine ecosystems
- Coral reef protection
- Economic revitalization
- Environmental education
- Green energy for municipal truck fleets
- Open and recreational land preservation
- Shoreline stabilization

Municipal Grants to Nonprofits

While it is not the usual practice to refer to municipal funding for local nonprofits as grants, many municipalities provide discretionary funding for the nonprofits within their jurisdiction. This funding operates very much like a grant. The New York City Council, for example, posts an application form to its website every January.[34] To qualify, organizations must be recognized as charities in New York, or obtain an exemption.[35] It might seem that New York City is using taxpayer money to fund all this support for local nonprofits; however, in many cases, the city may be functioning as a flow-through for grant money coming from outside sources (see Box 9.1 and Figure 9.1).

Community Foundations – A Special Case

Community foundations function like a hybrid of a municipal or state government and a nonprofit because they limit themselves to a particular community or region, and they function as a charity. In the US, a community foundation is defined as a "tax-exempt, nonprofit, autonomous, nonsectarian philanthropic institution . . . supporting the broad-based charitable interests and benefitting the residents of a defined geographic area." Community foundations often carry the name of a town or city.

Global Grants

The United Nations is part of a larger system or family of organizations that includes not only the UN itself but also six funds and programs, and fifteen organizations.[36] The UN has its own Central Emergency Relief Fund (CERF), which gives out grants. In 2020 alone, CERF allocated nearly $827 million.[37] Allocations approved in 2021 so far include funding to address draught in Afghanistan, volcano damage in St. Vincent and the Grenadines, and food insecurity in the Sudan. The UN publishes a guide to grant funding.[38]

Concluding Reflections

Misero datur quodcunque, fortunæ datur.
"Whatever we give to the wretched, we lend to fortune."
Seneca the Younger (4 BC to 65 AD), *Troades*, line 697

Whatever their civic beliefs, humans know by nature that it is good for wealth to share with need – and that what goes around, comes around. So as municipalities set their budgets, they should identify environmental, economic, and engineering needs and try to meet them. Before committing to spend taxpayer money, they can ask: Is this item covered by grants?
– Federal?
– State?
– Nonprofit?
– Corporate?

The search for grant money can be long and arduous, but it is worth the effort.

Grant money can help cities achieve their sustainability goals, and there is no time like the present. Many municipal assets are at risk of degradation and disappearance – ranging from the environment to municipal identity itself. The final section of this book looks at these challenges and the battle to meet them.

Notes

1 See grantwatch.com to search the grants. See also the Society Nonprofits, which has a grant data base of similar size. About Us | Society for Nonprofits (snpo.org); https://www.snpo.org/aboutus/
2 Tracking Federal Awards: USAspending.gov and Other Data Sources (fas.org); https://fas.org/sgp/crs/misc/R44027.pdf
3 OMB, "Chapter 14: Aid to State and Local Governments," Analytical Perspectives: Budget of the US Government, Fiscal Year 2021, at https://www.whitehouse.gov/omb/analytical-perspectives/ cited in https://fas.org/sgp/crs/misc/R44027.pdf "Federal Grants to State and Local Governments: A Historical Perspective on Contemporary Issues," May 22, 2019, p. 24, mentions "more than 29,000 local governments." Federal Grants to State and Local Governments: A Historical Perspective on Contemporary Issues, May 22, 2019. https://fas.org/sgp/crs/misc/R40638.pdf
4 Historical Tables | The White House; https://www.whitehouse.gov/omb/historical-tables/; see Table 12.1.
5 This is based on the Census figure of 3,141 counties referenced in the Introduction to this book. See https://www.usgs.gov/faqs/how-many-counties-are-united-states?qt-news_science_products=0#qt-news_science_products
6 Historical Tables | The White House; https://www.whitehouse.gov/omb/historical-tables/See Table 12.2.
7 [USC02] 31 USC 6501: Definitions (house.gov); https://uscode.house.gov/view.xhtml?req=granuleid:USC-prelim-title31-section6501&num=0&edition=prelim This is important to know because grant money is treated differently from other sources of revenue for accounting and tax purposes.

8 Congressional Research Service, Federal Grants to State and Local Governments: A Historical Perspective on Contemporary Issues, May 22, 2019. https://fas.org/sgp/crs/misc/R40638. pdf The report states: "But, overall, the historical record suggests that for most Members of both political parties, regardless of their personal ideological preferences, federalism principles are often subordinated to other policy goals, such as reducing the federal budget deficit, promoting social values or environmental protection, and guaranteeing equal treatment and opportunity for the disadvantaged. As long at this continues to be the case . . . there is little evidence to suggest that the general historical trends of increasing numbers of federal grants to state and local governments, increasing outlays for those grants, an emphasis on categorical grants, and continued enactment of federal mandates, both funded and unfunded, are likely to change."

9 https://www.grants.gov/web/grants/search-grants.html?keywords=city

10 https://www.grants.gov/web/grants/search-grants.html?keywords=city

11 As of May 25, 2021, the grants.gov website for current (open) federal grants to "city and township governments" showed 101 open grants.

12 National League of Cities – Cities Strong Together (nlc.org); https://www.nlc.org/

13 Federal Budget Tracker – National League of Cities (nlc.org); https://www.epa.gov/green-infrastructure/green-infrastructure-funding-opportunities#Funding%20Sourceshttps://www.nlc.org/resource/federal-budget-tracker/

14 https://www.epa.gov/grants/specific-epa-grant-programs

15 Green Infrastructure Funding Opportunities | Green Infrastructure | US EPA; https://www.epa.gov/green-infrastructure/green-infrastructure-funding-opportunities#Funding%20Sources

16 Five Star and Urban Waters Restoration Grant Program | NFWF; https://www.nfwf.org/programs/five-star-and-urban-waters-restoration-grant-program

17 https://www.epa.gov/environmentaljustice/environmental-justice-grants

18 Environmental Justice Small Grants Program. Environmental Justice Small Grants Program | Environmental Justice | US EPA; https://www.epa.gov/environmentaljustice/environmental-justice-small-grants-program#tab-2

19 Allocations by year | CERF (un.org); https://cerf.un.org/what-we-do/allocations-by-year

20 https://www.acf.hhs.gov/ocs/programs/community-services-block-grant-csbg

21 https://www.ncaf.org/

22 State Statutes and Programs Concerning Community Gardens, National Conference of State Legislatures. https://www.ncsl.org/research/agriculture-and-rural-development/community-gardens-state-statutes-and-programs.aspx

23 National League of Cities – Cities Strong Together (nlc.org); https://cerf.un.org/what-we-do/allocations-by-year

24 Stan Mayfield Working Waterfronts Florida Forever Grant Program | Florida Department of Environmental Protection; https://cerf.un.org/what-we-do/allocations-by-year

25 https://www.nyserda.ny.gov/-/media/Files/About/Clean-Energy-Fund/CEF-Communities-Chapter.pdf

26 State Energy Offices | NASEO; https://cerf.un.org/what-we-do/allocations-by-year

27 v2_NASEO_MicroGrid.pdf; https://cerf.un.org/what-we-do/allocations-by-year

28 Ibid. v2_NASEO_MicroGrid.pdf; https://cerf.un.org/what-we-do/allocations-by-year

29 Ibid. v2_NASEO_MicroGrid.pdf; https://cerf.un.org/what-we-do/allocations-by-year

30 About Chief Executives for Corporate Purpose – CECP; https://cecp.co/about/

31 About Chief Executives for Corporate Purpose – CECP; https://cecp.co/about/

32 CECP-CEO-Roundtable_January_2021_Press_Release_FINAL.pdf; https://cecp.co/wp-content /uploads/2021/01/CECP-CEO-Roundtable_January_2021_Press_Release_FINAL.pdf

33 Municipal Grants – GrantWatch – with "municipalities" and "grantees" as search terms. https://www.grantwatch.com/cat/50/municipalities-grants.html

34 https://council.nyc.gov/budget/fy2021-discretionary-funding-application/ See also The City Budget – Budget (nyc.gov); https://council.nyc.gov/budget/

35 Microsoft Word – charities exemption form.doc (nyc.gov); https://council.nyc.gov/budget/

36 Funds, Programmes, Specialized Agencies and Others | United Nations; https://www.un. org/en/about-us/un-systemThe UN system, also known unofficially as the "UN family," is made up of the UN itself and many programs, funds, and specialized agencies, all with their own leadership and budget. The programs and funds are financed through voluntary rather than assessed contributions. The Specialized Agencies are independent international organizations funded by both voluntary and assessed contributions.

37 Home | CERF (un.org)

38 https://www.un.org/en/sections/about-un/funds-programmes-specialized-agencies-and-others/

PART IV: **Dealing with Conflict Over Sustainability**

Chapter 10
The Rights of Nature

Most national constitutions today make at least some mention of environmental rights or responsibilities[1] – many of them based on a human being's right to a healthy environment.[2] But do natural phenomena such as forests, lakes, or rivers have their own intrinsic natural rights worthy of legal protection, just as humans do? After many years of evolution, this idea is finally becoming a civic reality, as more than two dozen countries, along with a growing number of municipalities, have explicitly asserted the "rights of nature" through a series of unique national and/or local laws.[3] There is even an international movement to deem "ecocide" a crime that should be outlawed under international law as set forth in the Rome Statute of the International Criminal Court.[4] By diverging from long-established jurisprudence rooted in anthropomorphic tradition, these new rights-of-nature laws and ordinances are broadening the philosophical framework for sustainability initiatives around the world.

This chapter begins by presenting a brief history of human and natural rights, and then describes some standard legal theories used to support rights of nature. The chapter then shows how these have been expressed in specific national laws or local ordinances that give legal standing to nature. (The subsequent chapter – Chapter 11 on Environmental Litigation Involving Municipalities – will summarize landmark legal cases affirming or invalidating such laws and ordinances.)

Genesis and Tradition

Humankind has been contemplating its relationship to the natural world for thousands of years. In fact, more than half of the world's current population ascribe to a monotheistic faith that traces human history back to the very beginning of time, when human beings were believed to live in a garden. Here was the scene of one of humankind's earliest environmental imperatives – the divine command to Adam and Eve to "Be fruitful and multiply: and fill the earth."[5] So states *Genesis*, recorded and preserved by Hebrew writers during the Bronze age some 5,000 years ago. Later wisdom in the same canon of Judaism, known as the Torah, provides guidance for replenishing the earth, such as agricultural directives to let a field lie fallow every seventh year,[6] dietary laws banning certain food sources,[7] and directives for humane treatment of animals.[8] But far from according

https://doi.org/10.1515/9783110689860-010

nature her own rights – as did older and still-enduring belief systems that worship Nature[9] – the *Genesis* imperative makes it clear who is in charge.

In the Biblical account, the Creator asks Adam to "rule" the earth, and "have dominion over the fish of the sea, and over the fowl of the air, and over every living thing that moves upon the earth."[10] And so it is that this ancient sacred text set up a hierarchy with humankind on top – a hierarchy active to this day. Significantly, this man-over-nature concept did not remain isolated within Judaic thought alone: Genesis is also the first book of the Christian Bible, and the Quran of Islam has a similar account of humankind's relationship to nature.[11]

When it comes to the evolution of environmental law, the legacy of the *Genesis* nature paradigm has been profound. After all, law is rooted in morality, which in turn has origins in belief. Modern legal systems in most Western countries have assumed the rightness of human dominance over nature. Laws preserving "property rights" have generally assumed that the human being or beings who own property have a basic right to do what they will with the property.

Payback

Yet over the past 5,000 years, humankind has been a poor steward of nature. While some indigenous populations have lived within their environmental means (see Appendix 7 on Notable Accomplishments of Tribal Governments), the world overall has tended to "get more than it gives" in this respect. Not only are there more people on the earth, but we are consuming more per person in both food[12] and energy,[13] despite some progress in conservation. with some exceptions.[14] And so it is that humanity has overdeveloped the planet, which has experienced growing deforestation and urbanization, a shrinking set of living ecosystems, and loss of biodiversity. Humankind has not sustained "every living thing" but rather have presided over the extinction or diminution of many species.[15]

Myriad scientific studies have seen human actions as the source of many environmental changes, including rising earth temperature and damage to the ozone layer.[16] And it seems as though nature has "struck back" in a kind of brute self-defense. While the number of deaths from natural disasters have declined over the years,[17] presumably due to advancements in technology for prediction and protection, the absolute number of extreme weather events reported has been rising. Adding together drought, floods, extreme weather, extreme temperature, landslides, dry mass movements, wildfires, volcanic activity, and earthquakes, one sees a gradual rise from 1900 to 2019.[18]

A New Consciousness

This undeniable trend toward the loss of natural systems and consequential threats to human existence raises a question: if we humans have not protected the natural environment according to our own earliest legal principles, is it time for us to extend our legal paradigm to include the rights of nature? Can we do more to recognize a fundamental right to life for living beings beyond ourselves? And if so, how can such a recognition anchor itself in existing legal concepts, beginning with the well-known concepts of "natural rights" and "human rights,"[19] which have shaped our modern world.

The news is good. Many jurisdictions are beginning to recognize the rights of nature, forging a new chapter in the evolution of rights, which over the years have extended from a single group to the entirety of humanity and beyond to the natural world. In the past thousand years, Western law has moved from the notion of "rights" for all free adult males; to rights for all adult males; to rights for adult females as well as adult males; to rights for children; to rights for animals in institutional settings; to rights for the unborn; to rights for corporate entities; to rights for domesticated animals; to natural systems in the current era (see Box 10.1).

Box 10.1: Selected Events in the History of Rights
- The Cyrus Cylinder (Persia, 539 BCE) – the world's first charter of rights
- Magna Carta (England, 1215) – rights of free men
- Petition of Right (England, 1628) – rights of free men
- Declaration of Independence (The Thirteen United States of America, 1776) – rights of "all men" applied narrowly
- Declaration of the Rights of Man and of the Citizen (France, 1789) – rights of free men
- US Bill of Rights amending Constitution (United States, 1791) – rights of men applied narrowly
- Oregon Constitution (United States, 1857) – rights of local communities
- Emancipation Proclamation (United States, 1863) – formerly enslaved persons – right to freedom
- Fourteenth Amendment – due process and equal protection of the law extended to "any person," meaning freed slaves too, although in 1883 the Supreme Court ruled this does not apply to women (1868)
- Fourteenth Amendment – US Supreme Court decides corporations are "persons" and thus subject to the amendment's protections for due process (1886) and equal protection of the law (1889)
- Universal Declaration of Human Rights (United Nations, 1948) – various rights for all men and women
- Women's Charter (Singapore, 1961) – various rights for women
- Forest Code (Brazil, 1965) – protection of the Amazon rainforest

- Animal Welfare Act (United States, 1966) – right to protect animals in institutional settings (such as research labs)
- American Convention on Human Rights (Costa Rica, 1969) – right to life for the unborn human
- Dissent in *Sierra Club v. Morton* (United States, 1972) – right of self-defense for threatened nature
- *First National Bank v. Belotti* (United States, 1978) – right to free speech for corporations
- Universal Declaration of Animal Rights (Global, 1978) – right of animals
- Convention on the Rights of the Child (United Nations, 1989) – rights for children
- Borough of Tamaqua, Pennsylvania – municipal ordinance protecting rights of nature (United States, 2006) – rights of nature
- Rights of Nature, Chapter 7, Constitution of the Republic of Ecuador (Ecuador, 2008) – rights of nature
- Law of the Rights of Mother Earth (Bolivia, 2010) – rights of nature
- Statute of the International Tribunal of Mother Earth Rights (Global, 2015)
- *Laudato si'* (Vatican, 2015) – rights of nature as part of creation
- Mexico City Constitution, Rights of Nature (Mexico, 2017) – rights of nature
- Lake Erie Bill of Rights (United States, 2019) – rights of a lake
- National Environment Act (Uganda, 2019) – rights of nature
- The Great Ocean Road and Environs Protection Act (Australia, 2020) – rights of a scenic coastal road to exist
- Resolution in the City of Berkley to Recognize the Rights of Nature (United States, 2021*) – rights of nature
- Law for World Health and Rights of Nature (Switzerland, 2021*) – rights of nature

*Pending at press date.

Note: For a longer timeline, containing more than 60 landmark events over just the past half century, see Advancing Legal Rights of Nature: Timeline https://celdf.org/advancing-community-rights/rights-of-nature/rights-nature-timeline. For more discussion of litigation over rights of nature, see Chapter 11: Environmental Litigation Involving Municipalities.

Rights of Nature Laws

Rights of nature laws are relatively rare, and subject to challenge (as shown in Chapter 11 on Environmental Litigation Involving Municipalities). Nonetheless, they are strong indicators of a new consciousness in favor of the rights of nature. Today the morality implicit in dominant legal systems has begun to shift away from an anthropocentric view to embrace a more holistic vision.[20]

An Existential Perspective

Cultural historian and Catholic priest Fr. Thomas Berry[21] takes an existential perspective in his "Ten Principles of Jurisprudence." His founding principle is that "Rights originate where existence originates. That which determines existence determines rights." Berry suggests that there are three basic rights: the right to be, the right to habitat, and the right to fulfill its role in the earth's "ever renewing processes." Related to this principle, Berry asserts *that all rights are role- or species-specific.* Importantly, he asserts that human rights do not cancel out other rights, and that as such property rights are not absolute. Rights are individual and interdependent. Most eloquently, in his final principle, he describes the value of humanity as dependent on nature rather than superior to it. "In a special manner, humans have not only a need for but also a right of access to the natural world to provide for the physical needs of humans and the wonder needed by human intelligence, the beauty needed by human imagination, and the intimacy needed by human emotions for personal fulfilment."[22]

A Pontiff's Letter to the World

In another chapter of human thought concerning nature, In June 2015, Pope Francis published a papal encyclical on care for the earth, titling it *Laudato si'*, honoring St. Francis of Assisi, known for his love of nature. This was the first encyclical addressed not only to persons of good will, but to "every person living on the planet."[23] Also, it was the first encyclical ever, in a history of hundreds, focused exclusively on environmental issues. Coming from the Judeo-Christian tradition, which gives special priority to humans (and no other creatures) as being made in God's image, Pope Francis does not ascribe any intrinsic rights to nature. But in the opening to his encyclical, he gives nature a human face.

> "LAUDATO SI', mi' Signore" – "Praise be to you, my Lord." In the words of this beautiful canticle, Saint Francis of Assisi reminds us that our common home is like a sister. . . . This sister now cries out to us because of the harm we have inflicted on her by our irresponsible use and abuse of the goods with which God has endowed her.[24]

Furthermore, Pope Francis draws a connection between the human right to life and the existence of a natural resource needed by humans. This forges a bond between the long legal tradition known as natural rights to the new legal paradigm for rights of nature.

Pope Francis cites a predecessor, Pope Paul VI, who in 1971 expressed concerns that "Due to an ill-considered exploitation of nature, humanity runs the risk of destroying it and becoming in turn a victim of this degradation."[25] But the pontiff goes farther, asserting that *our human right to life is rooted in environmental protection*. For example, he asserts that "water is a scarce and indispensable resource *and a fundamental right which conditions the exercise of other human rights.*"[26]

Pope Francis acknowledges that there are laws on the books protecting nature, but expresses doubt that they will be effective if humans fail to see nature as worthy of protection:

> Laws may be well framed yet remain a dead letter. Can we hope, then, that in such cases, legislation and regulations dealing with the environment will really prove effective? We know, for example, that countries which have clear legislation about the protection of forests continue to keep silent as they watch laws repeatedly being broken.[27]

Significantly, as the pontiff was writing this encyclical, a new legal form was arising, a global tribunal dedicated to the defense of nature. In 2015, the International Rights of Nature Tribunal[28] published its Statute of the International Tribunal of Mother Earth Rights.[29] And the following year, the United Nations General Assembly's 71st Session would produce a resolution titled *Harmony with Nature* (Resolution 70/208, August 1, 2016) – the first of many such documents, including most recently a 2020 Pledge for Nature.[30] The purpose of the resolution, crafted by experts in earth jurisprudence worldwide, was to move away decisively from an anthropomorphic view of law and toward a more holistic one.

> In order to forge a balanced and healthy relationship between human activity and the Earth, there is an urgent need for society to *replace the current anthropocentric worldview with a holistic system of governance*, in which humanity plays a different role in how it perceives and interacts with the natural world. In this new role, humanity would accept the reality that its well-being is derived from the well-being of the Earth and that *living in harmony with nature is a necessary means to sustaining human well-being and human rights.*[31]

In the past half-decade since the publication of *Laudato si'* and the passage of the UN Resolution on Harmony with Nature, many more jurisdictions around the world, ranging from town and cities to entire nations, have passed ordinances and laws that accord greater legal standing to nature and to local communities that wish to protect nature.

Key Legal Theories

As mentioned earlier, in the past decade, there has been a broad movement to create legal protections for nature, using a variety of legal principles. The following theories are commonly referenced in national, state, local laws, and/or court decisions asserting rights of nature: natural law, interdependence of human and natural rights, humans as guardians of nature, personhood of nature, rights of animals and/or species, and community self-determination. Of course, these are rarely found in isolation; in many cases jurisdictions or courts rely on more than one (see Box 10.2).

Box 10.2: Three Key Legal Theories for Rights of Nature
- Natural law (including theory of rights)
- Personhood of nature (directly or indirectly through a guardian)
- Community self-determination (including home rule, subsidiarity)

Natural Law

The main legal tradition used to argue for the rights of nature is the legal theory known as natural law, developed during the 17th century in Europe through philosophers such as John Locke. The basic concept is that laws of nature (also called Creation) give certain rights to humans, who do not need laws to create rights; rather, they need laws to protect them.

As stated in the Declaration of Independence that gave birth to the United States of America, "We hold these truths to be self-evident, that all men are created equal, that they are endowed by their Creator with certain unalienable Rights, that among these are Life, Liberty and the pursuit of Happiness. – That to secure these rights, Governments are instituted among Men, deriving their just powers from the consent of the governed . . . ."

Today natural rights principles are being returned home to the very nature that gave rise to them. The Animal Legal Defense Fund cited the right to pursue happiness in its lawsuit to compel federal action on climate change. "By safeguarding the necessary habitats to sustain wildlife, we will also be upholding American's rights to seek happiness, liberty, and solitude in nature."[32] Moreover, the concept that God gave humans rights is now being applied to nature, endowing nature with certain God-given rights.

The pioneering Constitution of Ecuador drew on this concept in 2008, declaring "a new form of public coexistence, in diversity and in harmony with nature."[33] Article 7 of the Constitution sets for the Rights of Nature (see Box 10.3).

Box 10.3: Rights of Nature in the Ecuadoran Constitution
CHAPTER SEVEN
Rights of nature
Article 71. Nature, or Pacha Mama, where life is reproduced and occurs, has the right to integral respect for its existence and for the maintenance and regeneration of its life cycles, structure, functions and evolutionary processes.

All persons, communities, peoples and nations can call upon public authorities to enforce the rights of nature. To enforce and interpret these rights, the principles set forth in the Constitution shall be observed, as appropriate.

The State shall give incentives to natural persons and legal entities and to communities to protect nature and to promote respect for all the elements comprising an ecosystem.

Article 72. Nature has the right to be restored. This restoration shall be apart from the obligation of the State and natural persons or legal entities to compensate individuals and communities that depend on affected natural systems.

In those cases of severe or permanent environmental impact, including those caused by the exploitation of nonrenewable natural resources, the State shall establish the most effective mechanisms to achieve the restoration and shall adopt adequate measures to eliminate or mitigate harmful environmental consequences.

Article 73. The State shall apply preventive and restrictive measures on activities that might lead to the extinction of species, the destruction of ecosystems and the permanent alteration of natural cycles.

The introduction of organisms and organic and inorganic material that might definitively alter the nation's genetic assets is forbidden.

Article 74. Persons, communities, peoples, and nations shall have the right to benefit from the environment and the natural wealth enabling them to enjoy the good way of living.

Environmental services shall not be subject to appropriation; their production, delivery, use and development shall be regulated by the State.

The natural rights theory can provide strong support to philosophical arguments in support of the rights of nature. While the natural rights concept has always had detractors (e.g., by logical positivists who believe that rights come from human-made laws not from any natural or divine source),[34] its influence has been strong, as the history of "rights" in Box 10.3 shows.

It is already established that humans have rights, so one branch of legal thought builds on that. The Inter-American Court of Human Rights has declared the "interdependence and indivisibility of human rights and environmental protection." And further:

> The Court considers it important to stress that, as an autonomous right, the right to a healthy environment, unlike other rights, protects the components of the environment, such as forests, rivers and seas, as legal interests in themselves, even in the absence of the certainty or evidence of a risk to individuals. This means that it protects nature and the environment, not only because of the benefits they provide to humanity or the effects that their degradation may have on other human rights, such as health, life or personal

integrity, but because of their importance to the other living organisms with which we share the planet that also merit protection in their own right. In this regard, the Court notes a tendency, not only in court judgments, but also in Constitutions, to recognize legal personality and, consequently, rights to nature.[35] (At 62)

Interdependence theories in environmental law can make it difficult to choose between human and environmental interests. Recall the concentric circles illustration in chapters 1 and 6 that shows how environment surrounds economy and engineering. In this context, what is the proper philosophy for affordable housing? In some municipalities, the prospect of additional housing is viewed as negative, because even with strict zoning and green architecture, such housing developments are considered antienvironmental, because they can sacrifice trees, disturb ecosystems, and increase traffic (hence air pollution). However, the proponents of high-density housing have employed the word "environment" for their cause as well. The Attorney General of California has characterized the state's Housing Accountability Act as redressing threats to the "economic, environmental and social quality of life."[36] Based on such a principle, a group called the California Renters Legal Advocacy and Education Fund (CaRLA) has filed several lawsuits against cities for failing to approve housing projects.[37]

An interesting line of thought is the connection between human right to own animals as property, the rights of animals not to be owned as property, and the possibility that animals themselves could be recognized as persons who can enjoy property.[38]

Personhood and the Legal Standing of Nature

As the previous section indicates, the concept of personhood is very important in legal theory, because it is attached to the concept of rights. An entity cannot have rights unless it is considered a person. Human beings are considered persons under the law but so are other entities, ranging from corporations to sacred idols.[39]

If nature can be considered a legal person, it may be possible to sue on behalf of nature in federal court based on Article III of the US Constitution, which establishes the judicial branch of the federal government.[40] Professor Babcock notes that while it has taken very long for nature to be recognized as having legal standing, this is a goal worth pursuing. "It is important to give nature the independent legal right to go to court to protect itself from harm because the current system will not allow others to intervene on nature's behalf."[41] She writes:

> While it is difficult to find theoretical support for granting nature direct access to Article III courts, it is not impossible. Indeed, . . . toeholds may be found in Article III itself and in the Court's willingness to accord constitutional standing and protections to nonhumans like corporations. Theories of personhood, which support granting corporations legal status and constitutional rights, might be transferrable to nature, as well as the concept of human dignity, based on notions of fairness and equality.[42]

Nonhuman animals are an important part of nature and these have received focused attention – both through laws to protect endangered species and through laws to protect animals in general. rights, although the word "rights" is rarely used in this domain. In a recent *Harvard Law Review article*, Kristen Stilt noted that whereas environmental law is generally concerned with species, animal law (which is a newer branch of law) is concerned with all animals regardless of characteristics.[43] (Chapter 11 will provide details of a landmark case in this regard.)

The notion of nature as a legal person presents thorny issues. First, whereas humans and even corporations can be considered to have free will and therefore can be held responsible for their actions, nature has no will and therefore cannot or should not be held responsible. A legal person has the capacity to sue and be sued. This could commodify the rights of nature. For example, the Wanganui River in New Zealand now has the status of legal personhood. On behalf of the Wanganui, the Maori people might successfully sue a polluter and receive compensation. But suppose that subsequently the river floods and wipe out a housing development. The developer then might sue the Wanganui, demanding payment from funds awarded to the river from the polluter. Thus, the funds intended to repair the river would go instead to the housing developer. Clearly, rights of nature law must apply one-way, to benefit nature, and not open nature to legal jeopardy.[44]

The Guardian Concept

A related legal theory that is being used to support the rights of nature is the *guardian concept*. Here nature is seen as an entity that has rights but is incapable of representing them in court, and therefore needs a guardian to serve as an advocate. This legal theory is used to protect the rights of individuals with disabilities, the elderly, and animals, among others.

New Zealand has based its environmental laws on this theory.[45] As noted by Craig Kaufman and Pamela Martin, the country has instituted laws creating "statutory guardians charged with promoting and protecting the interests, well-being, and rights of the river Te Awa Tupua and the forest Te Urewera."[46]

When the appointment of a guardian proves challenging, another solution, suggested by Hope M. Babcock of Georgetown University Law School would be to have nature represented by a properly qualified lawyer with "sufficient expertise, resources, and commitment to make arguments on nature's behalf."[47]

Community Self-Determination

Another dominant theory in the rights of nature movement is the notion that a local community has a right to self-government; that higher authorities such as state or federal governments should not have automatic authority to preempt local laws. This concept is often compared to the philosophical principle of subsidiarity, which says that problems should be addressed at the lowest appropriate administrative level. In general, the people who will be affected by decisions should be the ones making them.

While subsidiarity has found expression in many different political forms,[48] at heart it is about local self-determination. Most states in the US have some form of local self-determination enshrined in their constitutions, although in many states such provisions need strengthening to become true "home rule," according to the National League of Cities, which has proposed a Model State Home Rule Constitutional Article.[49] Unless state constitutions clearly allow true home rule, then municipalities can find it difficult to protect their natural assets.

One of the roadblocks to environmental protection is a legal system that puts state and federal laws above local city or town ordinances. While some states have passed laws that support the right of a community to self-governance with respect to the environment, this is the exception to the rule. Many countries, including the US, have a legal system that militates against this. The Ninth Amendment of the US Constitution recognizes a limitation on the federal government's powers to violate the "unenumerated" rights of the sovereign people at the state level, but it remains silent on local rights – which are routinely usurped by states.

The rights of local jurisdictions are described in state laws, and many states have explicit laws that support preemption.[50] Therefore, with few exceptions, municipalities must base their laws in existing state laws – a legal concept known as Dillon's Rule (see Box 10.4). Furthermore, if they pass a law in an area that falls outside existing state law, they must be prepared for legal challenges by state or other litigants citing related state law. For example, the state of Florida recently passed a law (currently being challenged) that specifically prevents local communities from recognizing rights of nature.[51] This is ironic because prior to the 2020 election cycle, the Democratic Party of Florida added rights-of-nature language to its platform[52] – the first time a state political party has ever done so.[53,54] The Democrats' plank combines self-determination with nature rights, stating that the party resolves "to adequately protect our waters, support communities' rights in reclaiming home rule authority and recognizing and protecting the inherent rights of nature." The Republican Party of Florida does not have such a plank, despite a general commitment to preservation in the national Republican platform.[55] Even the (minor) Ecology Party of Florida stops short of declaring rights of nature.[56]

Box 10.4: Dillon's Rule

Dillon's Rule is a legal concept first articulated in a court decision issued by Iowa Judge John F. Dillon in 1868.* The rule says that a municipal government (or other substate government) may exercise only those powers granted to them by their state governments. The rule also states that if there is a reasonable doubt whether a power has been conferred to a local government, then the power has not been conferred.

Dillon's Rule was successfully challenged in 1871, when Judge Thomas Cooley ruled that municipalities have inherent rights.** Courts in Indiana, Iowa, Kentucky, and Texas followed Cooley's rule for more than three decades until the US Supreme Court upheld Dillon's Rule in 1907.***

This line of cases had a last impact on municipal law. As stated by the National League of Cities, "Since then, the following tenets have become a cornerstone of American municipal law and have been applied to municipal powers in most states: A municipal corporation can exercise only the powers explicitly granted to them; Those necessarily or fairly implied in or incident to the powers expressly granted; Those essential to the declared objects and purposes of the corporation, not simply convenient, but indispensable."[57]

*Clinton v. Cedar Rapids & M. R. R. Co., 24 Iowa 455
** People v. Hurlbert, 24 Mich. 44, 95 (1871)
** Hunter v. Pittsburgh, 207 U.S. 161

The Native American Experience

The principle of community self-determination has much in common with another important strain of rights-of-nature advocacy, namely the actions taken by indigenous groups that depend on nature for their livelihood and spiritual practice. In some countries, such as the US, indigenous tribes have their own legal system as sovereign nations within a nation. The National Congress of American Indians states that there are currently 573 "sovereign tribal nations" and defines "sovereignty" as the "authority to self-govern."[58] While at various times and places, this self-governance has been preempted by state or federal government, it is still legally recognized as a meaningful concept.[59] The unique legal standing of native tribes has enabled them to make significant contributions to the rights of nature. So far at least four Native American tribes in the US have passed resolutions affirming the rights of nature.[60] Assisting in such developments are groups like Movement Rights, a California-based group "working with tribes and communities to align human laws with natural laws since 2014."[61] For more on tribal contributions to rights of nature, see Appendix 7 of this book.

Some Developments in the Americas: Ecuador and Mexico City

A watershed event in the rights of nature occurred on September 28, 2008, when, in a popular referendum vote, the nation of Ecuador passed a new national constitution that included natural rights to "Pachamama," or Mother Nature, to its Constitution. As summarized by scholar Kyle Pietari, the text of the Constitution makes harmony with nature a national priority and makes several other changes to existing law. The law grants three distinct rights to nature: the right to integral respect, the right to maintenance and regeneration, and the right of restoration. It grants authority to legal persons to insist that public authorities enforce nature's rights, which authorities are obliged to do by preventing environmentally harmful conduct and by regulating environmental services.

The law recognizes a fundamental right of people to benefit from the environment and prohibits "appropriation of environmental services" (The exact phrase is "Los servicios ambientales no serán susceptibles de apropiación," a phrase intended to prevent landowners from profiteering from preservation.)[62] It places affirmative duties on all Ecuadorians to act in environmentally responsible ways and states that all laws invoking environmental matters should be interpreted to favor nature's protection when there is ambiguity. Finally, it establishes liability for virtually all parties involved when a good or service implicates environmental harm, with no statute of limitations.[63]

Ecuador's example inspired other jurisdictions to act. For example, from 2010 to 2019, various jurisdictions within Mexico have taken steps to protect nature. Mexico's national constitution describes in great detail the natural resources of the country, and then states that "ownership by the Nation is inalienable and imprescriptible, and the exploitation, use, or appropriation of the resources concerned, by private persons or by companies organized according to Mexican laws, may not be undertaken except through concessions granted by the Federal Executive, in accordance with rules and conditions established by law."[64] So it is perhaps not surprising that in January 11, 2017. Mexico City recognized in its charter the rights of nature, among many other rights.[65] In article 13, it states that "The right to the preservation and protection of nature will be guaranteed by Mexico City authorities in the scope of their competence, always promoting citizen participation in this subject." Furthermore, on June 10, 2019, the State of Colima, Mexico recognized rights of nature in its constitution.[66]

These are only two of many examples of rights of nature laws. The Community Environmental Legal Defense Fund maintains a comprehensive timeline of key moments in the evolution of the rights of nature movement.[67]

Some US Municipalities Adopting Rights of Nature

In the US, some 200 jurisdictions have passed their own community bill of rights, including 40 that have used such bills to advance rights of nature.[68] They have amended their governing documents or have passed new ordinances to protect nature, asserting either their own rights to protect nature, or the right of nature to be protected.

Activists have proposed constitutional amendments in Colorado, New Hampshire, Ohio, Oregon, and Pennsylvania, so that the state will refrain from preempting local governments when it comes to environmental protection.[69] As stated in the New Hampshire initiative, the proposed amendment "empowers people and their local governments throughout the state with the authority to enact local laws that protect the rights of people, communities, and their natural environments at the municipal level."[70]

Here are some additional developments in chronological order.

Tamaqua Borough, Pennsylvania. One example of a local ordinance protecting nature can be found in Tamaqua Borough in Schuylkill County, Pennsylvania. A decade and a half ago, in 2006 this town produced what may be the world's first successful local ordinance establishing legal structures to recognize the rights of nature, according to the Community Environmental Legal Defense Fund (CELDF), a global organization helping local communities protect nature. The Tamaqua ordinance established the people's right to self-governance and to a healthy environment, but most significantly, it declares that nature itself has rights:

It shall be unlawful for any corporation or its directors, officers, owners, or managers to interfere with the existence and flourishing of natural communities or ecosystems, or to cause damage to those natural communities and ecosystems. The Borough of Tamaqua, along with any resident of the Borough, shall have standing to seek declaratory, injunctive, and compensatory relief for damages caused to natural communities and ecosystems within the Borough, regardless of the relation of those natural communities and ecosystems to Borough residents or the Borough itself. *Borough residents, natural communities, and ecosystems shall be considered to be "persons" for purposes of the enforcement of the civil rights of those residents, natural communities, and ecosystems.* (Emphasis added.)[71]

Pittsburg, Pennsylvania. In November 2010, after learning that oil and gas companies were leasing land to engage in fracking, the city council of Pittsburgh held a meeting concerned citizens and organizations, adopting a Community Bill of Rights. The new document placed the rights of people, the community, and nature above corporate rights, and contained an absolute ban on the extraction of natural gas using fracking and related activities. Before the Pittsburgh initiative, other jurisdictions had tried to ban or limit fracking, but their solutions were vulnerable to preemption by higher (state or federal) law. The Bill of Rights tried to prevent preemption by asserting the right of self-governance.[72] As of mid-2021, the Bill of Rights still stands, despite getting blunted by a 2012 law preempting local regulation of oil and gas extraction.[73] This example goes to show how difficult it is for localities to determine their own environmental destinies. In most cases, there must be a combination of a state constitution, state laws, and municipal ordinances all in alignment, as well as a political climate that encourages environmental ordinances and discourages challenges to them. In due time, through an ordinance in November 2020, the City of Pittsburgh asserted a right to water, rights of natural communities, right to self-government, and people as sovereign.[74] It is no coincidence that Pennsylvania is host to landmark developments. The state's constitution states that "Pennsylvania's public natural resources are the common property of all the people, including generations yet to come. As trustee of these resources, the Commonwealth shall conserve and maintain them for the benefit of all the people."[75] While this is not a rights of nature statement, it does show a recognition of the value of a healthy environment.

Santa Monica, California. On March 12, 2013, the City Council of the City of Santa Monica passed an ordinance "Establishing Sustainability Rights."[76] This innovative governing document asserted three main rights: (1) the rights of residents to clean water and other natural attributes, including "a sustainable climate that supports thriving human life and a flourishing biodiverse environment"; (2) the "fundamental and inalienable rights" of natural communities and ecosystems to "exist and flourish in the City of Santa Monica"; and (3) the rights of all residents of Santa Monica to self-governance. To make the point of natural rights abundantly clear, the second right states that "residents of the City may bring actions to protect groundwater aquifers, atmospheric systems, marine waters, and native species within the boundaries of the City." The third right notes the following: "All residents of Santa Monica possess the right to self-governance and to a municipal government which recognizes that all power is inherent in the people, that all free governments are founded on the people's authority and consent, and that corporate entities, and their directors and managers, do not enjoy special privileges or powers under the law that subordinate the community's rights to their private interests."[77]

Crestone, Colorado. Continuing the train of municipalities asserting rights of nature, on July 9, 2018, the Board of Trustees in the town of Crestone, Colorado, unanimously approved a resolution recognizing the rights of nature.[78] See Box 10.5 for the resolution.

Box 10.5: Town of Crestone Rights of Nature Resolution
Resolution 006–2018
WHEREAS, an abiding reverence for nature defines and unites the Town of Crestone, whose residents share a deep spiritual connection to the natural world around them . . . the Sangre de Cristo Wilderness, the high alpine desert valley, the old growth cedar and pinon forests, the abundant wildlife, and the life-sustaining waters of the North Crestone Creek.

WHEREAS, town residents have long understood that humans are part of and dependent upon the natural world, which provides the necessities of life – air, water, food, and home – and also nourishes the human spirits, thereby enabling humans not merely to exist, but also to flourish.

WHEREAS, special recognition of the primacy of this relationship exists in the region long before the Town of Crestone was founded, when Native American Tribes considered the area to be sacred land and journeyed here for rites of passage, seeking insight and rejuvenation.

WHEREAS, today, as in the past, visitors and residents alike receive nourishment, inner peace and spiritual renewal from the religious pristine sacred land, and Town residents reciprocate these gifts by serving as stewards of the natural environment.

WHEREAS, the understanding that humans must protect the natural world, though felt with particular intensity in Crestone, is widespread in society, as is demonstrated by the existence of both state and federal laws protecting in environment in general and clean, plentiful water in particular.

WHEREAS, the Board of Trustees therefore wishes to join the growing number of communities, cities and nations around the world that have recognized nature's rights.

NOW, THEREFORE, be it resolved . . . that consistent with this widespread understanding and in furtherance of Crestone's particular commitment to environmental stewardship, the Town of Crestone does officially recognize that nature, natural ecosystems, communities, and all species possess the intrinsic and inalienable rights which must be effectuated to protect life on Earth.

    Kairina Danforth, Mayor

    Attested

    Allyson Ransom, Town Clerk

    Source: Res.+#+006-2018+Recognizing+the+Rights+of+Nature.pdf (squarespace.com); https://static1.squarespace.com/static/55914fd1e4b01fb0b851a814/t/5b4e2ad66 d2a73913cf8416c/1531849430261/Res.+%23+006-2018+Recognizing+the+Rights+of+Nature. pdf

In Colorado, the law SB-181, passed into law April 2019, granting local governments the power to regulate future oil and gas development within their jurisdictions. The law granted Colorado municipalities the power to preempt less restrictive statewide regulations promulgated by the state's conservation authority.[79] While the law does not grant localities the authority to ban development, it gives localities more power to regulate impact of development.

Marion County, Oregon. This community proposed guidance in 2020 to municipalities wanting to write a bill of rights (see Box 10.6). Oregon is one of five states with community rights networks. Others are Colorado, New Hampshire, Ohio, and Pennsylvania.

Box 10.6: Creating a Community Bill of Rights
Provided by Marion County Community Rights, in Marion County, Oregon
　What would a Community Bill of Rights look like?
　It would first and foremost enact the legal civil rights protections that we seek to recognize or elevate, whatever we decide those to be.
　Second, there are several things the Bill of Rights must do to protect those laws:
1. It must describe how the above laws are not subject to federal or state pre-emption because they elevate rights protections.
2. It must strip corporations and all other fictitious entities of any claim to legal personhood so that they do not abuse and hijack such civil rights protections for nefarious purposes that ultimately violate the rights of real persons and communities.
3. It must describe how the rights are self-enforcing, rather than relying on commerce law as their basis for existence.

Source: Marion County, Founding Member, Oregon Community Rights Network 2020. https://marioncommunityrights.wordpress.com/about/ Reprinted with permission.

In Oregon, the language state's constitution supports municipal self-governance. The state's constitution, established in 1857, includes a Bill of Rights that opens as follows:

> *Article I, Section 1. Natural rights inherent in people.* We declare that all men, when they form a social compact are equal in right: that all power is inherent in the people, and all free governments are founded on their authority, and instituted for their peace, safety, and happiness; and they have at all times a right to alter, reform, or abolish the government in such manner as they may think proper.

Furthermore, Article I, Section 33 of the state's constitution mirrors the Ninth Amendment of the US Constitution by recognizing a limitation on the *state* government's powers to violate the "unenumerated" rights of the sovereign people at the *local* level.

Toledo, Ohio. In February 2019, the citizens of Toledo, Ohio, voted to amend their city charter to include protections for Lake Erie (see Box 10.7.). The resulting

Lake Erie Bill of Rights is still hailed as a milestone in the rights of nature, although it has been nullified by all three branches of government in Ohio.[80] For more on this landmark document, see Chapter 11.

Box 10.7: The Lake Erie Bill of Rights

LAKE ERIE BILL OF RIGHTS ESTABLISHING A BILL OF RIGHTS FOR LAKE ERIE, WHICH PROHIB-
ITS ACTIVITIES AND PROJECTS THAT WOULD VIOLATE THE BILL OF RIGHTS

We the people of the City of Toledo declare that Lake Erie and the Lake Erie watershed comprise an ecosystem upon which millions of people and countless species depend for health, drinking water and survival. We further declare that this ecosystem, which has suf-fered for more than a century under continuous assault and ruin due to industrialization, is in imminent danger of irreversible devastation due to continued abuse by people and cor-porations enabled by reckless government policies, permitting and licensing of activities that unremittingly create cumulative harm, and lack of protective intervention. Continued abuse consisting of direct dumping of industrial wastes, runoff of noxious substances from large scale agricultural practices, including factory hog and chicken farms, combined with the effects of global climate change, constitute an immediate emergency.

We the people of the City of Toledo find that this emergency requires shifting public governance from policies that urge voluntary action, or that merely regulate the amount of harm allowed by law over a given period of time, to adopting laws which prohibit activities that violate fundamental rights which, to date, have gone unprotected by government and suffered the indifference of state-chartered for-profit corporations.

We the people of the City of Toledo find that laws ostensibly enacted to protect us, and to foster our health, prosperity, and fundamental rights do neither; and that the very air, land, and water – on which our lives and happiness depend – are threatened. Thus it has become necessary that we reclaim, reaffirm, and assert our inherent and inalienable rights, and to extend legal rights to our natural environment in order to ensure that the natural world, along with our values, our interests, and our rights, are no longer subordinated to the accumulation of surplus wealth and unaccountable political power.

We the people of the City of Toledo affirm Article 1, Section 1, of the Ohio State Constitu-tion, which states: "All men are, by nature, free and independent, and have certain inalien-able rights, among which are those of enjoying and defending life and liberty, acquiring, possessing, and protecting property, and seeking and obtaining happiness and safety."

We the people of the City of Toledo affirm Article 1, Section 2, of the Ohio State Constitu-tion, which states: "All political power is inherent in the people. Government is instituted for their equal protection and benefit, and they have the right to alter, reform, or abolish the same, whenever they may deem it necessary; and no special privileges or immunities shall ever be granted, that may not be altered, revoked, or repealed by the general assembly."

And since all power of governance is inherent in the people, we, the people of the City of Toledo, declare and enact this Lake Erie Bill of Rights, which establishes irrevocable rights for the Lake Erie Ecosystem to exist, flourish and naturally evolve, a right to a healthy environment for the residents of Toledo, and which elevates the rights of the community and its natural environment over powers claimed by certain corporations.

[Remainder of Lake Erie Bill of Rights sets forth specific new laws in seven sections.]

Concluding Reflections

> Who can compare with justice? It creates life.
>
> Sumerian Proverb from the 3rd Century BCE

Humankind has had laws since the dawn of recorded history, but only in modern times have we applied the concept of rights to others beyond ourselves. This chapter has given general examples of such applications in legal theory. The next chapter will show how such issues play out in court when municipalities have been a party – either as plaintiffs or defendants – to litigation over the rights of nature, including the rights of nature generally; the rights of communities (including tribes) to preserve the nature within their boundaries; and the rights of forests, rivers, and lakes to exist and thrive.

Notes

1 https://davidsuzuki.org/wp-content/uploads/2013/11/status-constitutional-protection-environment-other-nations.pdf

2 https://www.bbc.com/future/article/20210316-how-the-human-right-to-a-healthy-environment-helps-nature

3 By October 2020, rivers and ecosystems in at least 14 countries had come under legal protection using one or more of these concepts. See Cary L. Byron, 'Dramatic' global rise in laws defending rights of nature | Reuters; https://www.reuters.com/article/us-usa-environment-lawmaking/dramatic-global-rise-in-laws-defending-rights-of-nature-idUSKBN26M5AQ October 1, 2020. And currently (as of April 23, 2021), the United Nations lists 26 countries with national and/or local laws asserting the rights of nature. Harmony with Nature – Law List (harmonywithnatureun.org); http://www.harmonywithnatureun.org/rightsOfNature/

4 https://www.stopecocide.earth/making-ecocide-a-crime

5 Genesis 1:28, Orthodox Jewish version. The Hebrew word מלאו means to fill. The King James translation says "replenish," perhaps in light of later divine commands to care for the earth, but this is not a literal translation of the Hebrew. For a guide to the full passage see https://biblehub.com/lexicon/genesis/1-28.htm

6 Exodus 23:10–11; Leviticus 25:1–7, 18–22.

7 Dietary restrictions are listed in Leviticus and Deuteronomy, throughout. Why some species are considered edible and other not remains unknown, but it is possible that one purpose may have been preservation of the species identified as nonedible. As Victor Benno Meyer-Rocho says, "Among their purposes. In addition to their religious and health Jewish dietary laws, containing some of the sentiments found also in the Hindu food taboos, have been chosen to illustrate how food taboos with origins steeped in religion, promotion of health, and protection of life combine to create a set of rules that foremost and for all unite a people and create group-cohesion." *Journal of Ethnobiology and Ethnomedicine* (June 29, 2009).

8 *Ex* 23:12, *Dt* 22:4, 6, cited in Laudato Si, section 67.

9 nature worship | Rituals, Animism, Religions, & History | Britannicanature worship | Rituals, Animism, Religions, & History | Britannica; https://www.britannica.com/topic/nature-worship
10 Genesis 1:28, Orthodox Jewish version.
11 https://www.npr.org/sections/thetwo-way/2015/04/02/397042004/muslim-population-will -surpass-christians-this-century-pew-says
12 Economic growth, convergence, and world food demand and supply – ScienceDirect; https://www.sciencedirect.com/science/article/pii/S0305750X20300802
13 Global electricity consumption continues to rise faster than population – Today in Energy – US Energy Information Administration (EIA); https://www.eia.gov/todayinenergy/detail.php? id=44095
14 US energy consumption fell by a record 7% in 2020 – Today in Energy – US Energy Information Administration (EIA); https://www.eia.gov/todayinenergy/detail.php?id=47397
15 A recent study shows that ecosystems are suffering, because while there has not been a loss in the number of species, there has been a shift in type: invasive species are gaining while others are declining. See https://e360.yale.edu/features/are-numbers-of-species-a-true-measure-of-ecosystem -health. For impact on human nutrition, see *The State of the World's Biodiversity for Food and Agriculture*, also http://www.fao.org/state-of-biodiversity-for-food-agriculture/en/
16 See for example this summary from the National Academy of Science titled "Humans Are Causing Global Warming" https://sites.nationalacademies.org/BasedOnScience/climate-change-humans-are-causing-global-warming/
17 https://ourworldindata.org/grapher/number-of-deaths-from-natural-disasters
18 "Global Reported Natural Disasters, By Type," https://ourworldindata.org/grapher/number-of-natural-disaster-events. Included within Hannah Ritchie and Max Roser (2020) – "Natural Disasters". *Published online at OurWorldInData.org*. Retrieved from: https://ourworldindata.org/natural-disasters [Online Resource].
19 For a good discussion of the link between natural rights and human rights in the history of philosophy, see "Natural Law Transformed Into Natural Rights," *Encyclopedia Britannica*, https://www.britannica.com/topic/human-rights/Natural-law-transformed-into-natural-rights
20 As noted by Mihnea Tanasescu, a researcher at the Research Foundation Flanders, Free University of Brussels in Belgium, environmental law has both a legal and a moral dimension. https://www.academia.edu/25399912/The_Rights_of_Nature_Theory_and_Practice
21 Father Berry, a Roman Catholic Priest of the Passionist order, called himself a "geologian," according to a *New York Times* obituary. https://www.nytimes.com/2009/06/04/us/04.berry. htm. For more on his work, see Mary Evelyn Tucker and John Grimm, "Thomas Berry and the Rights of Nature." *Earth Law* (Winter 2019) https://www.kosmosjournal.org/kj_article/thomas-berry-and-the-rights-of-nature/. His complete works are available at this link: Publications Archives – Thomas Berry
22 http://therightsofnature.org/thomas-berrys-ten-principles-of-jurisprudence/
23 Encyclical Letter Laudato si' of the Holy Father Francis on *Care for Our Common Home*, https://w2.vatican.va/content/dam/francesco/pdf/encyclicals/documents/papa-francesco _20150524_enciclica-laudato-si_en.pdf, article 3
24 I Encyclical Letter Laudato si' of the Holy Father Francis on *Care for Our Common Home*, https://w2.vatican.va/content/dam/francesco/pdf/encyclicals/documents/papa-francesco _20150524_enciclica-laudato-si_en.pdf, article 1
25 Apostolic Letter *Octogesima Adveniens* (May 14, 1971), 21: AAS 63 (1971), 416–417. http:// www.vatican.va/content/paul-vi/en/apost_letters/documents/hf_p-vi_apl_19710514_octoge sima-adveniens.html

26 Encyclical Letter Laudato si' of the Holy Father Francis on Care for Our Common Home, ibid., note 2.

27 http://www.vatican.va/content/paul-vi/en/apost_letters/documents/hf_p-vi_apl_ 19710514_octogesima-adveniens.html, article 142. Encyclical Letter Laudato si' of the Holy Father Francis on Care for Our Common Home, ibid.

28 https://www.rightsofnaturetribunal.org/about-us/

29 https://www.rightsofnaturetribunal.org/wp-content/uploads/2018/04/Tribunal-Status.pdf

30 In September 2020, 60 nations signed a "pledge for nature" under the auspices of the United Nations. See 'Dramatic' global rise in laws defending rights of nature | Reuters; https://www.reuters.com/article/us-usa-environment-lawmaking/dramatic-global-rise-in-laws-defending-rights-of-nature-idUSKBN26M5AQ As this book goes to press in the fall of 2021, a United Nations Conference on, and in May 2021, a United Nations Convention on Biological Diversity is pending. UN Biodiversity Conference | United Nations; https://www.un.org/en/food-systems-summit-2021-en/un-biodiversity-conference

31 https://cpb-us-e1.wpmucdn.com/blogs.uoregon.edu/dist/7/13481/files/2016/09/UN-Harmony-with-Nature-Report-on-Earth-Jurisprudence-2016-ttozwg.pdf

32 Historic Lawsuit Targets Government Inaction on Climate Change, Violating Constitutional Right to Liberty – Animal Legal Defense Fund (aldf.org); https://aldf.org/article/historic-lawsuit-targets-government-inaction-on-climate-change-violating-constitutional-right-to-liberty/

33 7 REPUBLICA DEL ECUADOR, CONSTITUCIONES DE 2008 [REPUBLIC OF ECUADOR CONSTITUTION OF 2008], Oct. 20, 2008 Political Database of the Americas, http://pdba.georgetown.edu/Constitutions/Ecuador/english08.html

34 See https://www.heritage.org/political-process/report/the-case-and-against-natural-law

35 https://www.corteidh.or.cr/docs/opiniones/seriea_23_ing.pdf

36 Ryan McCarthy, "AG intervening in San Mateo housing case," The Daily Journal, January 15, 2020.

37 Jared Brey "The YIMBY Group That Is Suing Small Cities," NextCity, August 15, 2019. https://nextcity.org/daily/entry/the-yimby-group-that-is-suing-small-cities. See also https://www.mercurynews.com/2020/01/14/state-intervenes-in-san-mateo-housing-case-that-could-have-major-implications/

38 J. Hadley, *Animal Property Rights: A Theory of Habitat Rights for Wild Animals* (Lexington Books, 2015).

39 In India, in the case of *Yogendra Nath Naskar v. Commission of Income-Tax, Calcutta* (1) SCC 555 (1969), their Lordships of Hon. Supreme Court in *Yogendra Nath Naskar v. Commission of Income-Tax, Calcutta* (1) SCC 555 (1969), held that a Hindu idol is a juristic entity capable of holding property and of being taxed through its Shebaits, who are entrusted with the possession and management of its property. Thus, Shebaits were declared guardians.

40 Article III | US Constitution | US Law | LII / Legal Information Institute (cornell.edu); https://www.law.cornell.edu/constitution/articleiii

41 Ibid., https://scholarship.law.georgetown.edu/cgi/viewcontent.cgi?article=2917&context=facpub

42 Hope M. Babcock, *A Brook with Legal Rights: The Rights of Nature in Court*, 2016; https://scholarship.law.georgetown.edu/facpub/1906

43 Rights of Nature, Rights of Animals – Harvard Law Review; https://harvardlawreview.org/2021/03/rights-of-nature-rights-of-animals/

44 The source of this comparison is Ben Price, author of *How Wealth Rules the World: Saving Our Communities and Freedoms from the Dictatorship of Property* (Berrett Koehler Publishers, 2019), which distinguished between legitimate wealth earned by individuals from wealth that comes from the rights of a propertied elite. In chapter review comments to the author, Price notes "Legal personhood status might be taken advantage of by ever-clever legal representatives for incorporated wealth."

45 (1) (PDF) Constructing Rights of Nature Norms in the US, Ecuador, and New Zealand (researchgate.net); https://www.researchgate.net/publication/328183758_Constructing_Rights_of_Nature_Norms_in_the_US_Ecuador_and_New_Zealand

46 (1) (PDF) Constructing Rights of Nature Norms in the US, Ecuador, and New Zealand (researchgate.net); https://www.researchgate.net/publication/328183758_Constructing_Rights_of_Nature_Norms_in_the_US_Ecuador_and_New_Zealand

47 https://scholarship.law.georgetown.edu/cgi/viewcontent.cgi?article=2917&context=facpub

48 http://jeanmonnetprogram.org/wp-content/uploads/2014/12/JMWP12Follesdal.pdf

49 https://www.nlc.org/wp-content/uploads/2020/02/Home20Rule20Principles20Report WEB-2-1.pdf

50 Many of these laws are written with the help of the American Legislative Exchange Council, which describes itself as a nonpartisan group "dedicated to the principles of limited government, free markets, and federalism" https://www.alec.org/about/ According to comments from Ben Price, cited earlier in note 44, these laws "block municipal interference in profitable activities that harm municipal interests, the environment, and human health."

51 https://wusfnews.wusf.usf.edu/post/environmentalists-sue-gov-desantis-over-clean-waterways-act?fbclid=IwAR0FGYLlEvFET-W-wXPJ5i13NCNz_q4lpkzjxCvhchzggadF6TdLXUZvApg

52 Media Statement: Florida Democrats Adopt Rights of Nature in Party Platform | CELDF; https://celdf.org/2019/10/media-statement-florida-democrats-adopt-rights-of-nature-in-party-platform/

53 Media Statement: Florida Democrats Adopt Rights of Nature in Party Platform | CELDF; https://celdf.org/2019/10/media-statement-florida-democrats-adopt-rights-of-nature-in-party-platform/

54 The Constitution of the Florida Ecology Party declares commitment to "Respect https://celdf.org/2019/10/media-statement-florida-democrats-adopt-rights-of-nature-in-party-platform /and reverence for, preservation and restoration of, the planet and its physical systems, for transparency and accountability at all levels of government," but it does not declare rights of nature. http://ecologyparty.org/?page_id=20

55 The Republican platform on the environment is human centered, stating as follows: "Conservation is inherent in conservatism. As the pioneer of environmentalism a century ago, the Republican Party reaffirms the moral obligation to be good stewards of the God-given natural beauty and resources of our country. We believe that people are the most valuable resources and that human health and safety are the proper measurements of a policy's success." https://www.gop.com/platform/americas-natural-resources/

56 The Constitution of the Florida Ecology Party declares commitment to "Respect and reverence for, preservation and restoration of, the planet and its physical systems, for transparency and accountability at all levels of government," but it does not declare rights of nature. http://ecologyparty.org/?page_id=20

57 https://www.nlc.org/resource/cities-101-delegation-of-power/

58 Tribal Governance | NCAI, https://www.ncai.org/policy-issues/tribal-governance

59 Supreme Court recognizes Native sovereignty in much of Oklahoma (pri.org), https://www.pri.org/stories/2020-10-12/supreme-court-recognizes-native-sovereignty-much-oklahoma
60 An important source for this section https://www.culturalsurvival.org/news/yurok-nation-just-established-rights-klamath-river
61 https://www.movementrights.org/about-us/
62 "Art. 74.- Las personas, comunidades, pueblos y nacionalidades tendrán derecho a beneficiarse del ambiente y de las riquezas naturales que les permitan el buen vivir. Los servicios ambientales no serán susceptibles de apropiación; su producción, prestación, uso y aprovechamiento serán regulados por el Estado." Although as mentioned this provision is intended to prevent landowners from profiteering from preservation, but some have argued that it may have unintended consequences by preventing landowners from selling their lands to the government. See Kyle Pietari, "Ecuador's Constitutional Rights of Nature: Implementation, Impacts, and Lessons Learned," *Williamette Environmental Law Journal*, Fall 2016, pp. 45 ff. https://willamette.edu/law/resources/journals/welj/pdf/2016/2016-f-welj-pietari.pdf
63 For an in-depth discussion of this law and its background, see Kyle Pietari, "Ecuador's Constitutional Rights of Nature: Implementation, Impacts, and Lessons Learned," *Willamette Environmental Law Journal*, 2016-f-welj-pietari.pdf (willamette.edu) 2016-f-welj-pietari.pdf (willamette.edu); https://willamette.edu/law/resources/journals/welj/pdf/2016/2016-f-welj-pietari.pdf
64 https://www.oas.org/juridico/mla/en/mex/en_mex-int-text-const.pdf
65 The original text of the Constitution of Mexico City is here: https://urbanlex.unhabitat.org/sites/default/files/urbanlex//mexico_city_constitution_spanish.pdf https://www.gaiafoundation.org/wp-content/uploads/2018/12/Earth-Jurisprudence-Rights-of-Nature-Come-Alive-in-Mexico-City.pdf
66 Mihnea Tanasescu, "Rivers Get Human Rights: They Can Sue to Protect themselves," *Scientific American*, June 19, 2017.
67 Rights of Nature Timeline | CELDF | Protecting Nature and Communities, https://celdf.org/rights-of-nature/
68 Symposium Exploring the Crime of Ecocide: Rights of Nature and Ecocide – Opinio Juris; https://www.qcode.us/codes/santamonica/
69 http://www.nhcommunityrights.org/uploads/9/0/9/8/90989300/nh_cra_faq.pdf
70 http://www.nhcommunityrights.org/uploads/9/0/9/8/90989300/nh_cra_faq.pdf
71 Borough of Tamaqua, Pennsylvania, Borough of Tamaqua, PA / Part II: General Legislation / Solid Waste, Article III, Corporate Waste and Corporate Control; https://ecode360.com/30184119
72 "Several aspects differentiated the Community Bill of Rights from proposals for regulating fracking through local land use and zoning laws. Not only did it focus on protecting fundamental rights against violation by industrial extraction of gas and those rights as higher law than state administrative law, but it bypassed the entire regulatory system by asserting the authority of the city to protect said rights by exercising the right of local community self-government." https://www.resilience.org/stories/2018-03-13/in-pittsburgh-a-community-bill-of-rights-helped-ban-fracking/
73 https://www.bipc.com/pennsylvania-overhauls-oil-and-gas-act
74 Ordinance supplementing the Pittsburgh Code, Title Six, Conduct, Article 1 Regulated Rights and actions, by adding Chapter 618 entitled Oil and Gas Drilling (foodandwaterwatch.org); https://www.qcode.us/codes/santamonica/
75 http://www.pacourts.us/assets/opinions/Commonwealth/out/126MD17_3-2-20.pdf?cb=2

76 https://www.smgov.net/departments/council/agendas/2013/20130312/s2013031207-C-1.htm

77 12.02.030 Rights of Santa Monica residents and the natural environment. Santa Monica Municipal Code (Santa Monica, CA) (qcode.us); https://www.qcode.us/codes/santamonica/; https://www.smgov.net/departments/council/agendas/2013/20130312/s2013031207-C-1.htm (Added by Ord. No. 2421 CCS § 1, adopted 4/9/13; amended by Ord. No. 2611CCS § 10, adopted by 6/25/19.)

78 https://www.earthlawcenter.org/blog-entries/2018/8/rights-of-nature-take-hold-in-crestone-colorado

79 "Colorado's Sweeping Oil and Gas Law: One Year Later," Gibson Dunn April 30, 2020; https://www.gibsondunn.com/colorados-sweeping-oil-and-gas-law-one-year-later/

80 Kilbert-LEBOR.pdf (utoledo.edu), https://www.utoledo.edu/law/academics/ligl/pdf/2020/Kilbert-LEBOR.pdf

Chapter 11
Rights of Nature Litigation Involving Municipalities

While many nations and communities have asserted the rights of nature though law and ordinance, these are subject to tests in courts. At this time, there is no international law forbidding destruction of nature. As mentioned in the previous chapter, however, "ecocide" may eventually be deemed a crime under Rome Statute of the International Criminal Court.[1] At the present time, cases involving rights of nature have played out in local or national courts, where results have varied depending in part on national legal systems. Some national systems are based largely on civil law, which relies on written legislation,[2] while others are based largely on common law,[3] which relies on case law. Still other national systems combine these systems or rely on other standards.[4] But no matter what kind of legal system governs a country and its municipalities, courts of law often have the "final say" in determining rights of nature – or rights of communities to protect nature. Ultimately, however, rights reside in those that have them, and not in courts, so while particular cases may end, the causes that inspire them continue.

This chapter provides examples of litigation asserting rights of nature in recent years. Of course, such lawsuits play a role in a much larger framework of environmental law and litigation, featuring broad-based themes such as pollution or climate change[5] (see Box 11.1). Plaintiffs and defendants alike should familiarize themselves with this "big picture."

Box 11.1: The Big Picture: Types of Environmental Law and Litigation

Statutory Law – Civil and Criminal
- Laws to ensure clean water
- Laws to ensure clean air
- Laws to protect land or ecosystems
- Laws to protect species or animals
- Laws to protect human health and safety
- Laws asserting rights of nature

Common Law – Torts
- Cases alleging trespass based on environmental contamination
- Cases alleging public and private nuisance
- Cases alleging strict liability for harmful releases
- Cases alleging negligence leading to environmental harm
- Cases alleging violation of rights of nature

---

https://doi.org/10.1515/9783110689860-011

At the same time, however, it is important for cities and citizens to keep sustained attention on emerging victories for rights of nature laws (listed last in Box 11.1). When they get affirmed in courts, these laws are one of the surest ways to protect vulnerable ecosystems and species suit.[6]

Of course, any given legal case will involve a unique set of facts and circumstances and will draw from numerous laws and legal precedents. Nonetheless, it is useful to highlight some key themes in rights of nature litigation as both warning and inspiration to cities and citizens interested in environmental activism.

Recent Legal Developments

In the previous chapter, we saw that there are a few basic theories underpinning or enabling rights of nature laws:
- Natural law
- Inherent rights of nature
- Community self-determination

This chapter will summarize selected legal cases based on these theories.[7] This chapter also includes a general reflection on the outlook for environmental lawsuits involving cities, and a list of some organizations that can help plaintiffs or defendants make environmental arguments.

Cases Addressing Natural Law

Friends of the Earth (2000): Environmentalist group prevails in defending nature based on human harm

In the case of *Friends of the Earth v. Laidlaw Envtl. Servs.* 528 US 167 (2000), the plaintiffs overcame one of the challenges facing environmental lawsuits, which is that courts tend to want proof of direct harm to a human plaintiff. The way around this is to show that the harm done to the environment is related to human harm (and thus traceable to basic principles of natural law). Although this case and others like it are not victories for rights of nature, they can provide useful support for a rights of nature case.[8]

Such was the case with the *Friends of the Earth v. Laidlaw Envtl. Servs.*, which granted legal standing to an environmental organization because a member of the plaintiff organization had a reasonable fear that the river was now too polluted to enjoy.[9] The court stated, "we see nothing 'improbable' about the proposition that a company's continuous and pervasive illegal discharges of pollutants into a river would cause nearby residents to curtail their recreational use of that waterway and would subject them to other economic and aesthetic harms."[10]

Cases Addressing Inherent Rights of Nature

The fundamental right of nature to exist is a common argument used to defend nature against threats. Whether the object of an environmental threat is a forest, a river, a lake, or a species – to name some common beneficiaries of protective litigation – the core issue is their right to live and thrive. The most famous case in this regard was a 1972 case involving the Sierra Club and the Sequoia National Forest, which was decided against the Sierra Club, but became famous for two dissenting opinions that captured the spirit of a movement.

Sierra Club v. Morton (1972): Supreme Court Rejects Rights of Nature in Case Known for Prescient Dissent

The rights of nature concept is based on human rights and often directly related to them. As shown in Chapter 10, Box 10.1, the concept of rights has been evolving over time with ever-wider inclusivity, embracing the idea that if humans have an inherent right to life then so should other living beings. One of the earliest uses of this idea in law was the US Supreme Court case of *Sierra Club v. Morton* (1972). In this close decision, the court affirmed a lower court ruling that the Sierra Club could not sue on behalf of the nature it wished to protect.[11] The court found that the environmental advocates had no legal standing to sue in the matter – which was an attempt to stop the Secretary of the Interior (Rogers Clark Ballard Morton) from permitting development in the Sequoia National Forest. The Sierra Club had argued that the land and ability to enjoy it would be harmed, but the court focused on the Sierra Club as plaintiff and said that it had not proved harm to itself.[12]

Dissenters argued otherwise. Justice Harry Blackmun asked a profound question in his dissent: "Must our law be so rigid and our procedural concepts so inflexible that we render ourselves helpless when the existing methods and the traditional concepts do not quite fit and do not prove to be entirely adequate for new issues?"[13] The great jurist said that the Sierra Club should have standing to sue for environmental issues. His fellow dissenter Justice William O. Douglas, went further, calling for establishment of a "federal rule that allowed environmental issues to be litigated before federal agencies or federal courts in the name of the inanimate object about to be despoiled, defaced, or invaded by roads and bulldozers and where injury is the subject of public outrage."[14] He hoped that popular momentum would lead the way. "Contemporary public concern for protecting nature's ecological equilibrium should lead to the conferral of standing upon environmental objects to sue for their own preservation."[15]

In contrast to the court, which had rejected a rights-of-nature argument, Justice Douglas noted inanimate objects such as ships and corporations are sometimes parties in litigation. "So it should be as respects valleys, alpine meadows, rivers, lakes, estuaries, beaches, ridges, groves of trees, swampland, or even air that feels the destructive pressures of modern technology and modern life. The river, for example, is the living symbol of all the life it sustains or nourishes – fish, aquatic insects, water ouzels, otter, fisher, deer, elk, bear, and all other animals, including man, who are dependent on it or who enjoy it for its sight, its sound, or its life. The river as plaintiff speaks for the ecological unit of life that is part of it."[16]

In support of this argument, Justice Douglas cited a contemporaneous (1972) *California Law Review*, by Christopher Stone, titled "Should Trees Have Standing?" In his landmark article, Stone proposed that rights be granted "forests, oceans, rivers, and other so-called 'natural objects' in the environment, indeed to the environment as a whole."[17] His ideas have had an impact. In a 2010 book based on the article, Stone describes legal cases filed in the name of nonhuman entities, including a river, a marsh, a brook, a beach, a national monument, a tree, and an endangered Hawaiian bird.[18]

Tolosa Villabona (2018): Successful Case Involving the Rights of Forests

In a legal decision that went beyond existing human rights law to assert rights for nature, the Supreme Court of Columbia handed a judgment in favor a of group of 25 young plaintiffs opposing deforestation. The case was *Sentencia 4360–2018 de la Corte Suprema de Justicia, Sala de Casacion Civil, M.P. Luis Armando Tolosa Villabona*, April 05, 2018.

While the young people had sued based on violation of their own rights, the court handed them victory "for the sake of protecting this vital ecosystem for the future of the planet," it would "recognize the Colombian Amazon as an entity, *subject of rights*, and beneficiary of the protection, conservation, maintenance and restoration" that national and local governments are obligated to provide under Colombia's Constitution. Among other directives, the decision requires municipalities in the Amazon to devise and implement territorial land use plans consistent with sustainability.[19]

Series of Successful Cases Involving the Rights of Rivers and Lakes

In May 2021, the Ponca tribe in Oklahoma announced that the Ponca Tribe had adopted a law recognizing the legal rights of two Rivers in their territory: *Ní'skà* (the Arkansas River) and *Ni'ží'dè* (the Salt Fork River).[20] They join other communities in advancing rights of communal waters. In their study of river rights, researchers Erin O' Donnell and Julia Talbot Jones note that "rivers have received their legal rights in different ways and for different purposes." Some were achieved via legislation and others via a judicial decision, while others were based in religious belief or for protection of indigenous values.[21] Another researcher on river rights observes that legal arguments have varied but "an interesting common aspect is that the recognition of the rights of the rivers was in all cases used as a basis to grant innovative remedies."[22] In most cases, however, it was critical to the legal argument that the river be recognized as a *legal person*. Rivers have been treated as legal persons in Bangladesh (the River Turag),[23] Columbia (Rio Atrato), Ecuador, India (Ganges and Yamuna), and New Zealand (Whanganui River, declared by Parliament to be "an indivisible and living whole"), and the US (Klamath River of the Yurok Tribe).[24] The Ganges and Yamuna Rivers in India were declared to be living persons by a lower court, but that decision was overturned, by the Supreme Court of India.[25]

Wheeler and Huddle (2011): Vilcabamba River Protected

In 2011 the owners of a property near the Vilcabamba River in Ecuador, successfully sued the government of the Loja province on behalf of the river, citing Article 71 of the Ecuadorian Constitution, arguing that a planned project would harm the river.[26] In this case, *Richard Frederick Wheeler y Eleanor Geer Huddle c/ Gobierno Provincial de Loja*, juicio 11121-2011-0010 (March 30, 2011), the Provincial Justice Court of Loja ruled in favor of the Vilcabamba River.[27] This was the first time that a court upheld nature's constitutional right to protection. The fact that Ecuador's constitution includes protections for nature helped. (See the following section on Developments in the Americas.)

Turag River, Sukhna Lake, and Paraná River and Wetlands Cases Succeed

In recent years there have been a series of successful rights of nature cases involving rivers and lakes.

On January 30, 2019, the River Turag won distinction from the High Court of Bangladesh as a living entity with legal rights. In Bangladesh Supreme Court,

High Court Division, Writ Petition No. 13898/2016 (2019), the court held that the same would apply to all rivers in Bangladesh.[28] In its decision the Court drew from the "public trust" doctrine in common law, holding that the government had to protect the rivers. In particular, it said that it should be like a parent to a child, under the *parens patriae* doctrine, an old common law doctrine that allows a court to make orders in the best interest of a child.[29] The court gave the Turag River legal rights and ordered the National River Protection Commission (NRPC) to serve as the guardian for it and other rivers. Furthermore, the court banned developers from securing bank loans to develop mandated environmental education for factory workers.

Continuing the trend, in March 2020, the Punjab and Haryana High Court passed an order declaring the Sukhna Lake in the City of Chandigarh as a living entity with intrinsic rights.[30] On November 26, 2020, the Municipality of the city of Rosario, one of the largest cities in the Philippines, adopted a decision declaring its support to recognize the Paraná River and Wetlands a legal person.[31]

Cases Addressing Community Self Determination (Rights of Municipal Communities to Preserve Nature)

A common theme in rights of nature litigation is the right of a community to self-determination. The following landmark four cases include this assertion. Some were unsuccessful (*Rex Capri, Jameison*) but some have held up (*Grant Township, Drewes Farm/Ferner*).

Rex Capri (2017): State Preemption Law Prevails over Self-Determination

In Lincoln County, Oregon, in the case of *Rex Capri, Wakefield Farms, LLC v. Dana Jenkins, Lincoln County*,[32] the preeminence of state over local rights came up as an issue of fundamental state constitutional rights in 2017 when voters approved an ordinance that asserted Freedom from Aerially Sprayed Pesticides in the county. The spray ban cited this language as supporting local self-governance. It also asserted a related right "to clean air, water, and soil not contaminated by aerial spraying of pesticides."[33]

The initiative stated that the right "cannot be achieved when that right is routinely overridden by corporate minorities claiming legal powers to engage in that contamination," and connected this to a "system of preemption which enables corporate decision-makers to wield state governmental power to override local self-government."[34] The spray ban claimed that "the state itself restricts the county's lawmaking powers in ways that prevent the people of the county from protecting the health, safety and welfare of people and natural communities from such harms as aerial spraying of pesticides."[35]

This clause was prophetic, because in fact the ordinance was overturned in a September 23, 2019, court decision when challenged by a local timberland owner and farming corporation.[36] The court's antiban decision relied on a fairly new Oregon state law that asserted state over local authority, essentially overriding the philosophy of the state's constitution. That law was written by a national legal advocacy group called the American Legislative Exchange Committee (ALEC), described by one source as "an industry-sponsored group that pushes a conservative agenda at the state level."[37] Attorney Lindsey Schromen-Wawrin, believes that state preemption is a "weapon of corporate special interests, which can more easily control state legislatures rather than deal with counties and local governments that are closer to the people." One of the plaintiffs joining the appeal was antispray activist Carol Van Strum, who sought legal standing for the Siletz River without success.[38] Despite reports of an appeal, the decision remains unchallenged.

Grant Township: Home Rule Clause in State Constitution Survives Challenge

Another landmark case is presented in *Pa. Dept. of Envtl. Prot. v. Grant Twp.,* No. 126 M.D. 2017 (Pa. Cmwlth. Mar. 2, 2020).

In this case, the community of Grant Township in Western Pennsylvania won a seven-year battle to get the state's Department of Environmental Protection to revoke a permit for an injection well to use for gas fracking. One notable aspect of the litigation is that it was joined by Little Mahoning Watershed, as a party in its own right.[39]

In 2015, the township had adopted a home rule charter supported by a clause in the Pennsylvania Constitution. The Grant Township Community Bill of Rights prohibited certain injection wells and precluded the application of any state laws pertaining to them where those state laws conflict with the charter.[40] The township used a rights of nature argument to achieve the revocation.[41] Over the years, the town's home rule charter has undergone challenge.[42] In the recent case, *Pa. Dept. of Envtl. Prot. v. Grant Twp., No. 126 M.D. 2017 (Pa. Cmwlth. Mar. 2, 2020),*[43] In this case the state environmental protection agency sued Grant Township for preventing it from issuing permits that would allow an injection well in the township.[44]

Jameison: Florida Town Loses Battle to Protect Wetlands Against Development

In the recent case of *James J. Jameison vs. Town of Fort Myers Beach, Florida h 2DCA 731a* (2020),[45] the appeals court sided with a landowner against a town trying to protect its wetlands. Jameison had bought protected wetlands and then complained that the town's ordinances preventing him from developing the land was a violation by the town under Florida's Burt Harris Act.[46] This Florida law has a basis in the US Constitution, which states that "Nor shall private property be taken for public use, without just compensation." The trial court sided with the town, but the appeals court reversed, citing *Palazzolo v. Rhode Island*, 533 US 606, 626 (2001),[47] a case in which the US Supreme Court found that someone who buys a land that was under conservation can claim an illegal taking even when the buyer knew that the land purchased was protected under prior regulation. The Palazzo court stated:

> The theory underlying the argument that postenactment purchasers cannot challenge a regulation under the Takings Clause seems to run on these lines: Property rights are created by the State. So, the argument goes, by prospective legislation the State can shape and define property rights and reasonable investment-backed expectations, and subsequent owners cannot claim any injury from lost value. After all, they purchased or took title with notice of the limitation.

> The State may not put so potent a Hobbesian stick into the Lockean bundle.[48] The right to improve property, of course, is subject to the reasonable exercise of state authority, including the enforcement of valid zoning and land-use restrictions. The Takings Clause, however, in certain circumstances allows a landowner to assert that a particular exercise of the State's regulatory power is so unreasonable or onerous as to compel compensation. Just as a prospective enactment, such as a new zoning ordinance, can limit the value of land without effecting a taking because it can be understood as reasonable by all concerned, other enactments are unreasonable and do not become less so through passage of time or title. Were we to accept the State's rule, the post-enactment transfer of title would absolve the State of its obligation to defend any action restricting land use, no matter how extreme or unreasonable. A State would be allowed, in effect, to put an expiration date on the Takings Clause. This ought not to be the rule. Future generations, too, have a right to challenge unreasonable limitations on the use and value of land.[49]

Based on such an argument, the court found that the trial court erred, and so reversed the final summary judgment entered in favor of the Town, finding instead for the developer. The *Jameison* opinion is part of a long line of cases that sees the most fundamental of rights to be those attached to property ownership. This view may not prevail in the long run if future courts recognize the more fundamental rights of local communities and their individual members.

Drewes Farm Partnership (2020) and Ferner (2020): Lake Erie Bill of Rights Defenders Overcome Invalidation

In an up and down series of developments, a rights of nature charter was passed, invalidated, and then reinstated. In February 2019, voters in Toledo, Ohio, passed the Lake Erie bill of rights as an amendment to the City charter. (For a copy of that historic document, see Chapter 9.) The charter proved a hindrance to a local farm that uses fertilizer, leading to a court challenge that initially succeeded. In *Drewes Farm Partnership and State of Ohio v. City of Toledo* (2020),[50] a federal judge declared that the charter provision was invalid, calling it a "textbook example of what municipal government cannot do."[51] Aside from constitutional arguments, the judge pointed out that Lake Erie's boundaries include portions that lie outside the city, stating "Lake Erie is not a pond in Toledo," and therefore fell outside the city's "constitutional right to self-government." Later in 2020, however, an appeals court in *Ferner v. State*, 2020-Ohio-4698, decided September 30, 2020, found in favor of the city, reversing the decision and remanding back to the trial court, where defenders met with another defeat.[52] The case is ongoing, however, with a new brief filed in May 2021.

The Outlook for Rights of Nature Litigation

Clearly, based on this brief survey of notable rights of nature cases, defending the rights of nature can pose challenges. Considering some of the failures and reversals in this litigation – particularly efforts at self-government – it is clear that there are barriers to such litigation (see Box 11.2).

Box 11.2: The Box of Allowable Activism

According to the Community Environmental Legal Defense Fund, communities are "boxed in by a legal system designed to protect corporate interests and limit their rights to local self-government." Here are the elements of that box:

1. **State Preemption:** State legislatures enact laws that remove authority from communities and define the legal relationship between the state and municipalities as that of a parent to a child. This deprives communities of their own rights.

2. **Nature as Property:** Nature is considered property by law, meaning anyone with title to property has the legal right to destroy it. This allows the actions of a few to impact the entire ecosystem of a community.

3. **Corporate Privilege:** Often referred to as corporate "rights" or corporate "personhood," it means that corporations claim "rights" to protections of free speech (1st amendment/ money as speech), protections from search and seizure (4th amendment), due process and lost future profits (5th amendment Takings clause) and equal protection (14th amendment).

Contracts clause protections, civil rights laws, and commerce laws, further amplify corporate power to override local decision-making.

4. **The Regulatory Fallacy:** The permitting process, and the regulations supposedly enforced by regulatory agencies, are intended to create a sense of protection and objective oversight. By working through regulatory agencies such as the Environmental Protection Agency (EPA) and our state agencies, we're told we can protect our community. We can challenge permit applications and demand regulations be enforced. Except, by their very definition, regulatory agencies regulate the amount of harm that takes place. When they issue permits, they give cover to the applicant against liability to the community for the legalized harm.

Source: CELDF (2021). Reprinted with permission. *Advancing Community Rights | CELDF | Protecting Communities & Nature.*

Cities and citizens need not be discouraged, despite any organized pushback against municipal goals of self-determination and environmental protection.[53] As a final element in its "Box of Allowable Activism," the Community Environmental Legal Defense Fund has warned against falling into the "black hole of doubt." CELDF notes:

> The final blockade to community self-government is the Black Hole of Doubt. We think we're not smart enough, strong enough, or empowered enough – we literally do not believe we have the inalienable right to govern. Sally Kempton, author and feminist, says, 'It's hard to defeat an enemy who has outposts in your head.' CELDF realized it would take a people's movement to establish rights for humans and nature over the systems that control them and is now at the forefront of that movement.

Into Action

The developments described in this chapter vary widely in what they are protecting and how they seek to protect it – both in terms of the legal theories being used and the remedies being sought. Civic leaders and activists committed to the preservation of natural systems and species will find these principles helpful in their work. For the practical purpose of putting these principles to work in advocacy and litigation, there are scores of organizations and resources that can help.

Global Alliance for the Rights of Nature (GARN) is a "network of organizations and individuals committed to the universal adoption and implementation of legal systems that recognize, respect, and enforce the rights of nature."[54] It has 18 founding members and some 150 "expansion members" – all organizations who themselves have nature-rights missions and memberships.[55]

Here are three of these many organizations.

- *The Community Environmental Legal Defense Fund* (CELDF) through grass-roots organizing, public education and outreach, and legal assistance, nearly 200 municipalities across the US have enacted CELDF-drafted Community Rights laws which ban practices – including fracking, factory farming, sewage sludging of farmland, and water privatization – that violate the rights of people, communities and nature. These proposed laws transition local efforts "from merely regulating corporate harms to stopping those harms by asserting local, democratic control directly over corporations."[56]
- *The Earth Law Center* has published a *Community Toolkit for Rights of Nature.*[57] The remainder of this book will provide guidance in more traditional means of action, using nature rights as needed to shed light on other issues.
- *The Indigenous Environmental Network* helps indigenous tribes organize to oppose initiatives harmful to native environments. Its mission statement begins as follows: "IEN is an alliance of Indigenous Peoples whose Shared Mission is to Protect the Sacredness of Earth Mother from contamination & exploitation by Respecting and Adhering to Indigenous Knowledge and Natural Law."[58]

The members of GARN work together to hold systems accountable through an International Rights of Nature Tribunal, which acts as a forum for exchanging ideas on how to prevent natural destruction "often sanctioned by governments and corporations," as well as a tribunal to render judgments on environmental disputes.[59] There have been four Tribunals held with the support of the GARN: Quito (January 2014), Lima (December 2014), Paris (November 2016), and Bonn (November 2017). Cases heard so far address natural destruction in the Amazon, Germany, and Spain, among other locations.[60]

Concluding Reflections

> True law is right reason in agreement with nature.
>
> Marcus Tullius Cicero, The Republic ca 50 BC

Environmental organizations that help with litigation can empower communities strengthen and respect the rights of nature within their jurisdictions – and indeed throughout the globe. Such efforts are bound to generate new legal strategies and solutions, helping citizens and cities alike understand the connection between the rights possessed by the natural entitles to the responsibilities owed by the citizens that enjoy them.[61]

Notes

1 https://www.stopecocide.earth/making-ecocide-a-crime
2 http://www.juriglobe.ca/eng/sys-juri/class-poli/droit-civil.php
3 http://www.juriglobe.ca/eng/sys-juri/class-poli/common-law.php
4 http://www.juriglobe.ca/eng/sys-juri/index-alpha.php
5 For example, 14 US cities have filed lawsuits against energy companies alleging, among other claims, that they knowingly contributed to climate change. The cities include New York City, Baltimore, the City of Boulder and two Colorado counties; King County, Washington; and several California counties and cities (including San Francisco and Oakland). See: Mitigating Municipality Litigation: Scope and Solutions – ILR (instituteforlegalreform.com); https://insti tuteforlegalreform.com/research/mitigating-municipality-litigation-scope-and-solutions/
6 For example 14 US cities have suited 12 other cities and counties, including New York City, Baltimore, the City of Boulder and two Colorado counties, King County, Washington, and several California cities and counties (such as San Francisco and Oakland) have filed lawsuits against energy companies alleging, among other claims, that they knowingly contributed to climate change. Mitigating Municipality Litigation: Scope and Solutions – ILR (instituteforle galreform.com); https://instituteforlegalreform.com/research/mitigating-municipality-liti gation-scope-and-solutions/
7 This chapter draws from primary court documents but also acknowledges secondary sources including Hope M. Babcock (2016), https://scholarship.law.georgetown.edu/cgi/viewcon tent.cgi?article=2917&context=facpub
8 For good article on legal argument, see Similarity, precedent and argument from analogy (uwindsor.ca), https://scholar.uwindsor.ca/cgi/viewcontent.cgi?article=1004&context= crrarpub
9 The exception being Friends of the Earth v. Laidlaw Envtl. Servs., 528 US 167 (2000) (granting standing to an environmental organization because of a reasonable fear that a river formerly enjoyed by a member of the plaintiff organization was now too polluted to be used) https://scholarship.law.georgetown.edu/cgi/viewcontent.cgi?article=2917&context=facpub
10 Friends of Earth, Inc. v. Laidlaw Environmental Services (TOC), Inc.:: 528 US 167 (2000):: Justia US Supreme Court Center; https://supreme.justia.com/cases/federal/us/528/167/
11 https://caselaw.findlaw.com/us-supreme-court/405/727.html
12 "A person has standing to seek judicial review under the Administrative Procedure Act only if he can show that he himself has suffered or will suffer injury, whether economic or otherwise. In this case, where petitioner asserted no individualized harm to itself or its members, it lacked standing to maintain the action." Sierra Club v. Morton:: 405 US 727 (1972):: Justia US Supreme Court Center; https://supreme.justia.com/cases/federal/us/405/727/
13 Ibid., https://caselaw.findlaw.com/us-supreme-court/405/727.html
14 Ibid., https://caselaw.findlaw.com/us-supreme-court/405/727.html
15 Ibid., https://caselaw.findlaw.com/us-supreme-court/405/727.html
16 Sierra Club v. Morton:: 405 US 727 (1972):: Justia US Supreme Court Center; https://su preme.justia.com/cases/federal/us/405/727/
17 https://researchwrit.files.wordpress.com/2011/01/article-c-stone-should-trees-having-standings.pdf
18 *Should Trees Have Standing? Law, Morality, and the Environment*, third edition, by Christopher Stone, (Oxford University Press, 2010). Professor Stone taught law at the University of

California for half a century. For a reflection on his legacy, see "Common Dreams: Remembering Christopher D. Stone," by Ben G. Price, April 21, 2021. https://celdf.org/2021/05/remembering-christopher-stone.

19 For the case, see STC4360-2018-2018-00319-011.pdf (cortesuprema.gov.co); https://cortesuprema.gov.co/corte/wp-content/uploads/2018/04/STC4360-2018-2018-00319-011.pdf For background, see https://www.iucn.org/news/world-commission-environmental-law/201804/colombian-supreme-court-recognizes-rights-amazon-river-ecosystem

20 Who speaks for the Rivers? (mailchi.mp), https://mailchi.mp/efadead8c112/who-speaks-for-the-rivers?e=219f4fcc90

21 Mihnea Tanasescu, "Rivers Get Human Rights: They Can Sue to Protect Themselves," Scientific American, June 19, 2017;

22 https://www.clientearth.org/legal-rights-of-rivers-an-international-trend

23 Strengthening the National River Conservation Commission of Bangladesh | The Daily Star; https://www.thedailystar.net/law-our-rights/law-watch/news/strengthening-the-national-river-conservation-commission-bangladesh-1813927#:~:text=Recently%2C%20in%20a%20ground-breaking%20and%20precedent%20setting%20judgment%2C,river%20Turag%20and%20all%20other%20rivers%20flowing%20throughout

24 https://harvardlawreview.org/2021/03/rights-of-nature-rights-of-animals/. See https://www.hcn.org/issues/51.18/tribal-affairs-the-klamath-river-now-has-the-legal-rights-of-a-person See also https://www.researchgate.net/publication/322592839_Legal_rights_for_rivers_what_does_it_actually_mean

25 https://www.bbc.com/news/world-asia-india-40537701

26 proteccion-derechosnatura-loja-11.pdf (wordpress.com). See http://therightsofnature.org/first-ron-case-ecuador/. See also https://www.scientificamerican.com/article/rivers-get-human-rights-they-can-sue-to-protect-themselves/

27 https://www.elaw.org/content/juicio%2011121-2011-0010

28 https://www.clientearth.org/legal-rights-of-rivers-an-international-trend/

29 In a comment to the au thor, Ben Price notes: "Most of the rights of nature laws CELDF has developed designate the local community, and their municipal government, as trustees who have standing to speak for the local ecosystem. We often compare it to the representation in court that a child lacking legal agency might receive."

30 https://scroll.in/article/965461/do-indias-rivers-have-a-constitutional-right-to-flow.

31 Declaracion de interes publico y apoyo del hcm de rosario para que el rio parana y los humedales tengan personeria juridica upload1049.pdf (harmonywithnatureun.org); http://files.harmonywithnatureun.org/uploads/upload1049.pdf

32 case_17cv23360_judge_bachart_decision_and_opinion_letter.pdf (lincoln.or.us); https://www.co.lincoln.or.us/sites/default/files/fileattachments/county_counsel/page/4891/case_17cv23360_judge_bachart_decision_and_opinion_letter.pdf

33 http://www.lincolncountycommunityrights.org/wp-content/uploads/2015/08/Filed-Ordiance_Freedom-from-Aerially-Sprayed-Pesticides-Ordinance-of-Lincoln-County.pdf

See also Mateusz Perkowski Oregon county's aerial spray ban gets day in court, Capital Press, October 9, 2017. https://www.capitalpress.com/state/oregon/oregon-county-s-aerial-spray-ban-gets-day-in-court/article_6b6a521a-e663-563b-847d-a73ea5171189.html

34 http://www.lincolncountycommunityrights.org/wp-content/uploads/2015/08/Filed-Ordiance_Freedom-from-Aerially-Sprayed-Pesticides-Ordinance-of-Lincoln-County.pdf

See also Mateusz Perkowski Oregon county's aerial spray ban gets day in court, Capital Press, October 9, 2017. https://www.capitalpress.com/state/oregon/oregon-county-s-aerial-spray-ban-gets-day-in-court/article_6b6a521a-e663-563b-847d-a73ea5171189.html

35 http://www.lincolncountycommunityrights.org/wp-content/uploads/2015/08/Filed-Ordiance_Freedom-from-Aerially-Sprayed-Pesticides-Ordinance-of-Lincoln-County.pdf

See also Mateusz Perkowski Oregon county's aerial spray ban gets day in court, *Capital Press*, October 9, 2017. https://www.capitalpress.com/state/oregon/oregon-county-s-aerial-spray-ban-gets-day-in-court/article_6b6a521a-e663-563b-847d-a73ea5171189.html

36 "Lincoln County judge tosses out 2017 voter ban of aerial pesticide spraying" Yachatsnew.com. https://yachatsnews.com/lincoln-county-judges-tosses-out-2017-voter-ban-of-aerial-pesticide-spraying/

37 https://www.hcn.org/issues/51.20/activism-in-oregon-the-fight-for-local-control-upends-western-norms-pesticides

38 Can a campaign for nature and community rights stop aerial spraying in Oregon? By Carl Segerstrom High Country News, October 23, 2019 https://www.hcn.org/issues/51.20/activism-in-oregon-the-fight-for-local-control-upends-western-norms-pesticides

39 Rights of Nature Report: Pennsylvania Ecosystem Fights Corporation for Rights in Landmark Fracking Lawsuit (publicherald.org); https://publicherald.org/grant-township-speaks-for-the-trees-in-landmark-fracking-lawsuit/

40 https://www.mgkflitigationblog.com/ Grant_Township_Environmental_Rights_ERA_SWMA_Oil_and_Gas

41 The case Justin Nobel, "Nature Scores a Big Win Against Fracking in a Small Pennsylvania Town," Rolling Stone, March 2020. https://www.rollingstone.com/politics/politics-news/rights-of-nature-beats-fracking-in-small-pennsylvania-town-976159/

42 Pennsylvania Commonwealth Court Allows Township to Challenge Validity of State Statutes Under the Environmental Rights Amendment: MGKF Litigation Blog, https://www.mgkflitigationblog.com/topic,Zoning

43 Commonwealth v. Grant Twp. | No. 126 M.D. 2017 | Pa. Cmmw. Ct. | Judgment | Law | CaseMine, https://www.casemine.com/judgement/us/5e7391944653d04ff66d9bb9

44 http://www.pacourts.us/assets/opinions/Commonwealth/out/126MD17_3-2-20.pdf?cb=2

45 Jamieson v. Fort Myers https://law.justia.com/cases/florida/second-district-court-of-appeal/2020/19-0238.html

46 Bert J. Harris, Jr., Private Property Rights Protection Act in 1995, known as the Burt Harris Act, most recently amended in 2011. https://law.justia.com/cases/florida/second-district-court-of-appeal/2020/19-0238.html

47 Palazzolo v. Rhode Island:: 533 US 606 (2001):: Justia US Supreme Court Center; https://supreme.justia.com/cases/federal/us/533/606/

48 This refers to the contrasting political views of English Enlightenment thinkers Thomas Hobbes (1588–1679) and John Locke (1632–1704). Hobbes believed in the absolute power of government; Locke believed that government's validity depended on the consent of the governed.

49 *Palazzolo v. Rhode Island*, 533 US 606, 626 (2001) at 626–627 (citations omitted).

50 2020–02-27-Decision-invalidating-LEBOR.aspx (ohioattorneygeneral.gov); https://www.ohioattorneygeneral.gov/Files/Briefing-Room/News-Releases/Environmental-Enforcement/2020-02-27-Decision-invalidating-LEBOR.aspx

51 https://www.ohioattorneygeneral.gov/Media/News-Releases/February-2020/Federal-Judge-Invalidates-Lake-Erie-Bill-of-Rights See also Federal Judge Strikes Down 'Lake Erie Bill of Rights' – Animal Legal Defense Fund (aldf.org)

52 Kilbert-LEBOR.pdf (utoledo.edu), https://www.utoledo.edu/law/academics/ligl/pdf/2020/
Kilbert-LEBOR.pdf. For a critical view of Lake Erie rights, see GRANTING LAKE ERIE ENVIRON-
MENTAL RIGHTS: WILL IT WORK? 26 April 2019 David McRobert and Bianca Salive https://
www.academia.edu/38854554/Granting_Lake_Erie_Environmental_Rights_Will_it_work
53 In some domains, cities are seen as being too litigious. See https://www.instituteforlegal-
reform.com/uploads/sites/1/Mitigating-Municipality-Litigation-2019-Research.pdf
54 https://therightsofnature.org/
55 https://therightsofnature.org/founding-organizations/
56 https://celdf.org/
57 Community Toolkit for Rights of Nature (Earth Law Center, 2019). This can be accessed at
https://www.earthlawcenter.org/towns-cities
58 https://www.ienearth.org/contact-us/
59 https://www.rightsofnaturetribunal.com/
60 https://www.rightsofnaturetribunal.com/cases
61 Katherine J. Iorns, "From Rights to Responsibilities using Legal Personhood and Guardianship
for Rivers" (August 21, 2018), a chapter in *ResponsAbility: Law and Governance for Living Well with
the Earth*, B. Martin, L. Te Aho, M. Humphries-Kil (eds.) (Routledge, London & New York, 2019),
pp. 216–239, available at https://papers.ssrn.com/sol3/papers.cfm?abstract_id=3270391

Chapter 12
Defining Municipal Identity – Beyond Boundaries

What gives a town or city its unique identity? Certainly, legal boundaries – as described in the city charter and demarcated by plats and street signage – provide a clue. Just as human beings' physical bodies help to define who they are, so do municipal maps – despite occasional changes through annexation or merger. Not just any area can be a city; there are standards such as population or density, typically set by state or regional governments.[1]

No matter how small a town or city may be, it has a right to exist, and its existence makes a difference in public life. Indeed, to paraphrase the philosopher Voltaire, if cities did not exist, we would probably have to invent them.[2] For it is through local government that much change is possible; this is the main idea behind the movement call municipalism.[3] Clearly, towns and cities matter politically. One need merely imagine Europe as a vast territory with no cities to understand how important municipalities can be (see Figure 12.1 and Appendix 8).

Municipality Map for Selected European Countries

Germany:	11,500 municipalities and cities, 300 counties, and 16 regions
Italy:	8,014 municipalities, 101 provinces, 20 regions
Poland:	2,479 municipalities, 379 counties, 16 regions
Spain:	8,117 municipalities, 17 communities, and 2 cities
Sweden:	290 municipalities, 17 county councils, and 4 regions
Turkey:	34,305 villages, 2,950 municipalities, 81 provincial administrations
U.K.:	466 local authorities distributed among England, Scotland, Wales, and N. Ireland.

Figure 12.1: A Multitude of Municipalities.
Source: Art by Chris Smith, quarternative.com. Based generally on https://www.ccre.org/docs/Local_and_Regional_Government_in_Europe.EN.pdf For full details, see Appendix 8.

For another example, consider the fact that in the US, there are more than 29,000 named communities, of which more than 19,000 are incorporated as

https://doi.org/10.1515/9783110689860-012

towns, cities, boroughs, or other places with their own governments in one form or another.[4] All of these incorporated areas are defined by municipal boundaries, aka city limits.

Yet city limits, while important, are on the beginning of city identity, not the end. The true identify of a city is what matters most to the people who live in or visit a place. What parks, lakes, businesses, or buildings make a city recognizable and memorable to those who care about it? In some cases, these precious assets are part of a bioregion that extends beyond city limits.[5] The truly sustainable town or city will prioritize the protection and preservation of such "existential" environmental, economic, or engineering assets. They rank high among the key assets identified in this book's Chapter 2 on Mapping Your Municipality. As one researcher has noted, "symbolic spaces affect the urban identify more than the elements."[6]

This brief final chapter will suggest ways to identify municipal identity, starting with the obvious elements of a municipal name and motto and moving on to those existential municipal assets that emerge only very slowly over time. Such identification is important for at least two reasons – one practical and one philosophical. At a practical level, a municipality's unique features can be a source of civic pride as well as tourist appeal, contributing to a town's social climate and economy. More philosophically, municipal identity is arguably the very *raison d'etre* (reason for existence) of its sustainability. If a town loses everything that makes it special, what will there be left to sustain and what citizens will have the motivation to do the sustaining?

More on Boundaries

Boundaries demarcate a city as an incorporated area. People living inside the boundaries are considered residents of the municipality for receiving services, for voting, and for paying taxes. Property owners outside the boundaries do not have these privileges and obligations unless they agree to be annexed.

In addition to annexation, there can be times when cities and counties merge, though this is rare. In most cases, cities and counties coexist. As mentioned in the Introduction, everyone who lives in a city or town (except in the case of an independent municipality) also lives in a county, which means that for those city or township dwellers, there may be some redundancy. One might ask why the redundancy. As one study put it, the answer is "history, politics, and pride"[7] – or, in a word, identity.

Counties have two kinds of territories: incorporated (places designated as a named town, city, borough, or the like, having their own local government) and unincorporated (areas that may go by their own name, but that have no government). An example would be Fairfax County, Virginia, which within its limits has cities such as Falls Church or Alexandria, which have their own governments, but also contains unincorporated areas such as McLean or Vienna. When a person lives within a city's boundaries, that citizen pays taxes to the city as well as to the county, as two governments are providing services. There is inevitable redundancy here – with two governments serving the same slice of population. One might ask why. As one study put it, the answer is "history, politics, and pride"[8] – or, in a word, identity.

Even deeper than municipal identity is the notion of the identity and rights of the people who live within or border the municipality. In this sense, involuntary annexation by a city of a surrounding territory can seem like a threat to liberty. On the other hand, unincorporated areas may wish to form their own governments. The tension here is between the desires of local people and a more general concern for equitable distribution of services and taxation. As stated by Christopher J. Tyson, associate professor of law, Paul M. Hebert Law Center, Louisiana State University, "municipal boundary policy is the lynchpin in the expression of human values through spatial organization and redistributive government."[9]

Being "There"

"Municipal identity" has another meaning that transcends boundaries: namely, the "there" that is meaningfully present for citizens and visitors. For one city it may include be a cathedral and open-air market, for another it might be a marina and a traditional parade, and for yet another it might be a garden show and a sports team.

Such identity factors run high among the possessions of any town or city. Every municipality has a unique story to tell. In the typical case, a municipality's identity will be rooted in a past that inspired not only the name of the city but also the names of city streets and buildings, as well as plazas and landmarks honoring local individuals or events. It will be energized through local teams sporting historic names and colors, captured in three dimensions through local museums and historic markers, and made personal through reminiscences from older residents.

Municipal Names

A brand new, planned town or city may have a clear identity based on the marketing and branding messages of its creators, but most cities – and their names – have identities that have evolved over time – in some cases centuries, and even millennia.

The names of towns, cities, and boroughs contain history that can inspire creativity. Those who foster the long-term survival of particular cities are in some sense also supporting the value of the creations that these city names generate. Consider eau de cologne for the city in Germany (Koln in German, Cologne in French) or Limoges porcelain for the city in France.

There is a long history of brands based on place names that in turn add value to the place. As one brand historian states, "The brand is supported by a location and vice versa."[10] Another researcher notes, "Perception of city brand (commonly referred to as Placemaking or City branding) now drives the potential economic opportunities presented to a city."[11]

Within cities, the names of streets and buildings contain abundant history – as more than one book about place names in New York City have shown.[12] These too are city assets worth preserving and celebrating. Longtime residents of any town or city are likely to recall at least one case of defending and preserving a traditional local name against efforts to rebrand.[13]

Often the names of buildings and streets commemorate local citizens. To be sure, local leaders may occasionally replace a local name to honor a nonlocal hero such as Dr. Martin Luther King, whose name now graces more than 1,000 streets around the world,[14] but these changes usually build on authentically local values.[15] In many cities, street names will reflect values or, even more commonly, local values. In the City of Santa Clara, California, streets are named after a variety of individuals and families, including past mayors, developers, priests, historians, and early pioneers.[16]

The phenomenon of gentrification – defined in Chapter 4 as a process by which longtime residents with low income get replaced by wealthier newcomers – complicates the situation of place names. Gentrification is a pejorative term for what happens when an area that has low real estate values (but which may be rich in other vales) gets purchased by investors who then change its character.[17] In an all-too-typical scenario, buildings that are familiar landmarks to locals get demolished to make way for larger buildings – the story of Doha, capital of Qatar.[18] In a more rural setting, a forest nicknamed after a local landowner may get clear cut to give way to a developer's project with idyllic names designed to attract new residents. (As one pundit has said, "Developers name streets after what they have killed."[19]) The loss in this case is two-fold. Not only does the community lose its natural ecosystem, but it also loses some of its human history as well. City leaders and stakeholders would be wise to defend their environmental and cultural assets against such loss of identity.

Municipal Mottos

Another factor that defines a city is a city's motto – whether it be an ancient Latin phrase selected generations ago or a new, hip slogan. Some cities, such as Baltimore, Maryland, change (or add to) their self-descriptions frequently.

As shown in Box 12.1, on mottos for the City of Baltimore in Maryland, some city mottos are based on objective traits, such as presence of monuments (John Quincy Adam's phrase for 1878) or what was invented there (the revised slogan for 2015, which references the Star-Spangled Banner). Others related to the goals of the city. Mayor Kurt Schmoke wanted to increase literacy with this City that Reads slogan in 1989, and Governor Martin O' Malley's goal with the Believe slogan in 2002 was to inspire hope in relation to overcoming drug addiction and violence.

Box 12.1: Mottos for the City of Baltimore: Selected Examples

1878: The Monumental City (John Quincy Adams)

1970s: I Adore Baltimore; BaltiMORE than you Know; Charm City, USA; Baltimore is Best (Mayor Donald L. Schaeffer)

1989: The City that Reads (Mayor Kurt L. Schmoke)

2000: Greatest City in America (Gov. Martin O' Malley)

2002: Believe (Gov. Martin O' Malley)

2006: Baltimore – Get in On It (Gov. Martin O' Malley)

2015: Baltimore – A Great Place to Grow (Mayor Stephanie Rawlings Blake)

2015: Baltimore – Birthplace of the Star-Spangled Banner (Mayor Stephanie Rawlings Blake)

Source: *The Baltimore Sun.*[20]

Municipal Landmarks

Much of municipal identity is expressed in words – in names – but some existential assets are silent witnesses to history. Anything that serves as a point of reference can be a landmark, and it may not have a proper name. Landmarks are determined subjectively, not objectively. As noted by Richter and Winter in their book on landmarks, "landmarks are a concept of cognizing agents but not of systems."[21]

An important aspect of municipal sustainability lies in preserving and respecting landmarks. On the other hand, there may be a time when landmarks compete. The gas lamps in Beacon Hill in Boston, Massachusetts (mentioned in Chapter 2, Box 2.2), play a part in local identity, but clashed with other unnamed landmarks, namely the tree canopy there in that neighborhood. Working out such paradoxes is an important aspect of municipal identity.

Town squares or plazas form an important part of town or city identity. Nearly every incorporated entity has some spot where people congregate, whether it is as simple as a convenience store at a rural intersection, or a cobblestoned plaza surrounding a cathedral. The recognition and support of such gathering places form an important part in the identity of a municipality.[22]

Ecosystems as Identity

The intersection of environment and identity is the heart of sustainable cities. There are cities where natural systems – be it tree canopies, lakes, rivers, or dunes – form a part of the identity of a town. It is impossible to imagine Paris without Seine, Bonn without Rhine, or Chicago without the Chicago River or Lake Michigan. As such, the city governments and citizens have a natural interest in preserving these natural assets.

In some towns and cities, migratory birds return annually, such as the swallows of San Juan Capistrano.[23] Cities aware of this feature can help by turning their lights out and by planting more trees.[24]

Challenges to Municipal Identity

A town's sense of identity can be challenged by both economic and cultural trends. Each of these forces has the power to demolish local identity – sometimes literally.

Economic decline has changed the character of towns that thrived based on particular industries. Examples in the US include decline of coal towns in Pennsylvania[25] and the past decline of the North End of Detroit, Michigan, which gave birth to the Motown Records community but became home to "graffiti, razor wire, and weeds."[26] In England, numerous towns suffered identity crises with the loss of their industrial base.[27] These may not be "ghost cities," but they are haunted by a more prosperous past.

A converse economic problem is the challenge of gentrification – through which, ironically, the true gentry of an area (original inhabitants that have a cultural claim on an area) get replaced by wealthier newcomers. Under gentrification, ownership of critical assets – whether environmental, economic, or engineering – shifts from longtime residents to newcomers with less commitment to a town's history and therefore identity. This important social term is authoritatively defined by the Urban Displacement Project at the University of California at Berkley as "a process of neighborhood change that includes economic change in a historically disinvested neighborhood – by means of real estate investment and new higher-income residents moving in – as well as demographic change – not only in terms of income level, but also in terms of changes in the education level or racial make-up of residents."[28] Gentrification brings with it a rise in real estate values and tax rates, which can pressure residents to move out, if they are not already displaced by a local government's exercise of eminent domain and/or demolition by neglect based on alleged blight. Those with modest incomes can no longer afford to maintain their homes or to pay the real estate taxes to live in them. The result can be a series of tear downs replaced by McMansions, changing the character of a neighborhood.

An equally strong threat to local identity can comes from a cultural trend such as the so-called cancel culture. Consider the faceoffs in the US concerning the names of cities, streets, buildings, and statues honoring heroes from the losing side of the Civil War.[29] In this trend, a group of protesters, often including individuals from outside an area, call for the removal of a Civil War era monument. The protesters argue that the person honored did not exemplify today's social values and therefore should not be honored.

These events go beyond gentrification and the cancel culture. The erasure of municipal identity is not only the story of the rich replacing the poor or the self-righteous replacing the allegedly sinful. It can be the story of the collective erasing the individual. The urge to destroy history seems to be universal. "Sadly, both the left and the right have succumbed to the urge to destroy heritage at one point or another."[30]

If a city is to be sustainable, its leaders must strive to mitigate the environmental, economic, and engineering risks posed by disregard for local identity. They can leverage internal and external threats to history. Challenges can breathe new life in municipal identity. Rather than taking existential assets for granted, citizens mobilize to defend them. Ultimately, the essence of any city or town emanates from the hopes of its current residents as they look to the future. Town councils, city commissions, and engaged citizens often invoke and protect history only when it is under siege in these ways. The sense of identity can be shattered or strengthened as a result.

Concluding Reflections

> What was the use of my having come from Oakland? It was not natural to have come from there. Yes, write about it, if I like (or anything if I like) but not there, there is no there there.
>
> Gertrude Stein, *Everybody's Autobiography* (1937), Chapter 4, p. 289

In her 1937 book, *Everybody's Autobiography*, the American author Gertrude Stein famously complained about the emptiness of Oakland, California. The "there" that was no longer "there" was her childhood home, but her poignant phrase also bemoaned Oakland itself as a place lacking in landmarks. Her five words have become all too fitting for cities and towns losing their identity to hyper-development. This in turn, can cause its citizens to lose a sense of their own identity.[31]

This closing chapter aspires to encourage and empower city leaders and activists to do all they can to preserve the unique identity of their cities against the commoditization of generic development. The Conclusion to this book will offer principles for doing so.

Notes

1 Municipal Identity as Property (pennstatelawreview.org); http://www.pennstatelawreview. org/118/3/4%20-%20Tyson%20(final)%20(PS%20version).pdf For more on municipal boundaries, see Boundaries – Municipal (uslegal.com), https://municipal.uslegal.com/formation/ boundaries/
2 François-Marie Arouet, *Épître à l'Auteur du Livre des Trois Imposteurs* (November 10, 1770).
3 What's so new about New Municipalism? – Matthew Thompson, 2021 (sagepub.com), https:// journals.sagepub.com/doi/full/10.1177/0309132520909480
4 https://www.census.gov/geographies/reference-files/time-series/geo/tallies.html
5 Bioregions – BIOREGION INSTITUTE, https://www.bioregion.institute/bioregions
6 "Simgesel mekanların öğelerden daha çok kent kimliğini etkilediği de çalışmanın sonuçlarındandır." (PDF) THE EFFECTS OF SYMBOLIC LANDSCAPES ON CITY IDENTITY (researchgate. net); https://www.researchgate.net/publication/334146987_
7 "History, Politics, and Pride: Why Small Cities and Counties Rarely Merge." March 10, 2016, Pew Charitable Trust. https://www.pewtrusts.org/en/research-and-analysis/blogs/stateline/ 2016/03/10/history-politics-and-pride-why-small-cities-counties-rarely-merge
8 "History, Politics, and Pride: Why Small Cities and Counties Rarely Merge," March 10, 2016, Pew Charitable Trust. https://www.pewtrusts.org/en/research-and-analysis/blogs/stateline/ 2016/03/10/history-politics-and-pride-why-small-cities-counties-rarely-merge
9 Municipal Identity as Property (pennstatelawreview.org); http://www.pennstatelawreview. org/118/3/4%20-%20Tyson%20(final)%20(PS%20version).pdf
10 "The Two-way Relationship between a Brand and its Place of Origin," *Knowledge Wharton*, January 23, 2008. The Two-way Relationship between a Brand and its Place of Origin –

Knowledge@Wharton (upenn.edu); https://knowledge.wharton.upenn.edu/article/the-two-way-relationship-between-a-brand-and-its-place-of-origin/

11 https://www.innovation-cities.com/162-standard-indicators/6365/

12 In 2001, Sanna Feirstein wrote, Naming New York: Manhattan Places and How They Got Their Names by Sanna Feirstein | 9780814727126 | Paperback | Barnes & Noble® (barnesandnoble.com); https://www.barnesandnoble.com/w/naming-new-york-sanna-feirstein/1100867310 Twenty years later, a similar book came from Names of New York: Discovering the City's Past, Present, and Future Through Its Place-Names by Joshua Jelly-Schapiro, Hardcover | Barnes & Noble® (barnesandnoble.com); https://www.barnesandnoble.com/w/naming-new-york-sanna -feirstein/1100867310

13 Consider the City of Fernandina Beach, Florida, formerly Fernandina for 400 years, prior to questionable rebranding in 1950. (This City was mentioned earlier in Chapter 2, Box 2.5.) The City hired a consultant in 2015 to advise them on their Parks and Recreation Master Plan. The consultant, who was not from the town, made many recommendations, including changing the name of the main street from Atlantic Avenue to Avenida de las Americas. The recommendation died on the vine due to lack of community support.

14 The Politics Behind Naming a Street After Martin Luther King Jr. Reflects His Unfinished Work | Cities | US News; https://www.usnews.com/news/cities/articles/2020-01-20/for-many-us-towns-and-cities-naming-a-street-after-martin-luther-king-jr-reflects-his-unfinished-work

15 For example, in the City of Fernandina Beach mentioned earlier (note 9) in 1999, Vice Mayor Patricia McGowan Thompson, succeeded in adding the name Martin Luther King to the Elm Street name. Her original idea was to change the name entirely, but the other longtime local citizens wanted to keep the city's pattern of tree names for the streets (Ash, Beach, Cedar, Elm, etc.). The city is on Amelia Island, which has a tree canopy many are dedicated to preserving through groups such as the Amelia Tree Conservancy, ameliatreeconservancy.org

16 Santa Clara Street Names Reflect its History | City of Santa Clara (santaclaraca.gov); https://www.santaclaraca.gov/our-city/about-santa-clara/city-history/santa-clara-street-names

17 For an article about a neighborhood in the crosshairs of gentrification, see How Mount Pleasant quietly became a national model for resisting gentrification – The Washington Post (https://www.washingtonpost.com/magazine/2021/01/25/mount-pleasant-washington-dc-gentrification/) and note the diverse commentary.

18 (PDF) The search for identity in a global world: The case of Doha in Qatar (researchgate.net); https://www.researchgate.net/publication/350386414_The_search_for_identity_in_a_global_world_The_case_of_Doha_in_Qatar

19 Attributed to Jean Pugh of Fernandina Beach, Florida.

20 New Baltimore slogan nods to city's star-spangled history – Baltimore Sun; https://www.baltimoresun.com/maryland/baltimore-city/bs-md-ci-slogan-20150112-story.html

21 book-landmarks-sample-(ch-1).pdf (unimelb.edu.au); https://people.eng.unimelb.edu.au/winter/pubs/book-landmarks-sample-(ch-1).pdf

22 Ten great public squares | CNU; https://www.cnu.org/publicsquare/2019/05/10/ten-great-public-squares

23 Swallows Legend – Mission San Juan Capistrano (missionsjc.com); http://www.missionsjc.com/about/swallows-legend/

24 Cities can help migrating birds on their way by planting more trees and turning lights off at night (phys.org); https://phys.org/news/2021-01-cities-migrating-birds-trees-night.html

25 Coal Towns | Pittsburgh Post-Gazette, https://newsinteractive.post-gazette.com/coal-towns/

26 See Jody Adams Kirshner, *Broke: Hardship and Resilience in a City of Broken Promises*. (St. Martin's Press, 2019), p. 248. (Note: the text gives an incorrect decade for the Motown phenomenon. The decade was the 1960s.)

27 Frontiers | The Long Shadow of Job Loss: Britain's Older Industrial Towns in the 21st Century | Sociology (frontiersin.org), https://www.frontiersin.org/articles/10.3389/fsoc.2020.00054/full

28 UDP Team | Urban Displacement Project, https://www.urbandisplacement.org/about/team

29 Confederate monuments and the problem of forgetting – Benjamin Forest, Juliet Johnson, 2019 (sagepub.com); https://journals.sagepub.com/doi/full/10.1177/1474474018796653

30 The Importance of Historical Heritage and the Fallacy of the Cancel Movement: International Case Studies by Otto Federico von Feigenblatt: SSRN; https://papers.ssrn.com/sol3/papers.cfm?abstract_id=3662939

31 (PDF) City Identity as A Personality Identity Parameter (researchgate.net); https://www.researchgate.net/publication/346338881_City_Identity_As_A_Personality_Identity_Parameter

Conclusion
The Future Is in Our Hands

Will towns and cities learn from the past to create a more sustainable future? The answer depends on what we as concerned citizens and local leaders do today. This brief Conclusion shall serve as both a summary of this book and a call to action.

Slogans for Action

The following slogans bring forth wisdom that anchored the previous 12 chapters:

1. *Name it and claim it.* Every community faces a unique set of environmental issues. Community leaders and activists must identify them, prioritize them, and act on them. Environmental, economic, and engineering risks must be identified and addressed.[1]
2. *Seek and you shall find.* Where are the key assets in your community? Some may be hidden. A first step in preventing loss is finding them and protecting them. With advanced mapping technology, local leaders and activists can create a record of what a locality must protect. This kind of action can help to heal the heartache of communal loss and prevent further degradation.[2]
3. *Write the vision.* Municipal planning documents are more than expensive consulting deliverables dutifully paid for and posted. Ideally, they should reflect the values of the full community.[3]
4. *Claim the rulebook.* Citizens and even city leaders often leave zoning rules up to municipal staff who may not have the same level of commitment to the full scope of the environment as those who live in and lead a municipality. Stakeholder attention to the details of zoning polities makes all the difference.[4]
5. *Translate values into value.* Too often sustainability-minded stakeholders get hushed into submission by those who talk in terms of short-term dollars and cents (costs, budgets, and so forth). But the assets in need of protection often have a value that far exceeds those that are being captured in financial statements by city accounting staff. Imagine being a citizen of Athens if city leaders decide to remove the Acropolis to make room for high-rise luxury apartments based on some short-term profit motive. It sounds like a nightmare, but similar travesties occur every day around the world when citizens abandon their vigils.[5]

https://doi.org/10.1515/9783110689860-013

6. ***Build from and for the earth.*** In planning or approving municipal infra-structure, use sustainable materials to the greatest extent possible, and keep environmental impact in mind.[6]

7. ***Make a promise, keep a promise.*** Municipal green bonds are a powerful tool for financing sustainable infrastructure. The key to them is the capacity and willingness to make and keep a financial promise.[7]

8. ***Broaden your horizons.*** When considering land you wish to conserve, view the land in relation to the big geographic picture. What neighboring land might also need conservation? How can local land trusts help? Can your city contribute to or benefit from the funding of a local land trust?[8]

9. ***Lean on a kind stranger.*** Do you have a conservation or preservation proj-ect that your locality can not afford? Do not forget that there is a world of kind and caring people out there well beyond your municipal borders who may be able to help. Nonprofit and government grants are an excellent ex-ample of this.[9]

10. ***Get off your pedestal.*** As a local leader or activist, have you had a bias – conscious or unconscious – toward your status as a human, rather than see-ing yourself as part of a wider creation that includes living ecosystems? If so, it is time to get off your manmade pedestal and consider and respect the rights of nature.[10]

11. ***Fight for what is right.*** Process, procedure, and politics are important. There are many ways to participate in government and policymaking. But this takes us only so far in the effort to conserve and preserve assets in the natural and built environments. Sometimes it is necessary to take legal action.[11]

12. ***To thine own self be true.*** What is the core identity of your town or city? Is it captured in an old oak tree that sparks memories for many? A farmer's market where young and old gather? An abandoned mill with picturesque stone walls? Discovering and protecting that identity may be your greatest single task as a sustainability activist. You can make sure that there will al-ways be a "there there" for your hometown – however large or small, rich or poor, it may be.[12]

Never Give Up

The greatest lesson is, never give up in advocating for sustainable solutions grounded in the environmental, economic, and engineering needs of your mu-nicipality. Participate in politics as best you can. In the words of *New York Times* authors Philbrick and Leonhardt, "Think issues, not parties."[13] They

suggest a series of actions: vote, lobby, show up, converse, donate, and last but not least run for office. All these actions can empower municipal sustainability.
The future is in your hands.

Notes

1 For more information, see this book, Alexandra R. Lajoux, *Empowering Municipal Sustainability: A Guide for Towns, Cities, and Citizens* (De Gruyter: 2022), Chapter 1.
2 Ibid., Chapter 2.
3 Ibid., Chapter 3.
4 Ibid., Chapter 4.
5 Ibid., Chapter 5.
6 Ibid., Chapter 6.
7 Ibid., Chapter 7.
8 Ibid., Chapter 8.
9 Ibid., Chapter 9.
10 Ibid., Chapter 10.
11 Ibid., Chapter 11.
12 Ibid., Chapter 12.
13 https://www.nytimes.com/guides/year-of-living-better/how-to-participate-in-government

Appendices

Appendix 1
UN Sustainable Development Goals

The United Nations (UN) Sustainable Development Goals, which grew from deliberations at a 2012 UN Conference on Sustainable Development in Rio de Janeiro, Brazil, were adopted by all member states in 2015.[1] Conference delegates from all over the world worked together to produce goals to meet shared environmental, economic, and social challenges. The effort was an outgrowth of an earlier initiative in 2000 that had set Millennium Development Goals (MDGs), which conducted a global effort in 2000 to eradicate poverty and disease.[2]

Sustainable Development Goals
- Goal 1. End poverty in all its forms everywhere
- Goal 2. End hunger, achieve food security and improved nutrition, and promote sustainable agriculture
- Goal 3. Ensure healthy lives and promote well-being for all ages
- Goal 4. Ensure inclusive and equitable quality education and promote lifelong learning opportunities for all
- Goal 5. Achieve gender equality and empower all women and girls
- Goal 6. Ensure availability and sustainable management of water and sanitation for all
- Goal 7. Ensure access to affordable, reliable, sustainable and modern energy for all
- Goal 8. Promote sustained, inclusive and sustainable economic growth, full and productive employment and decent work for all
- Goal 9. Build resilient infrastructure, promote inclusive and sustainable industrialization and foster innovation
- Goal 10. Reduce inequality within and among countries
- Goal 11. Make cities and human settlements inclusive, safe, resilient, and sustainable
- Goal 12. Ensure sustainable consumption and production patterns
- Goal 13. Take urgent action to combat climate change and its impacts*
- Goal 14. Conserve and sustainably use the oceans, seas, and marine resources for sustainable development
- Goal 15. Protect, restore, and promote sustainable use of terrestrial ecosystems, sustainably manage forests, combat desertification, and halt and reverse land degradation and halt biodiversity loss

https://doi.org/10.1515/9783110689860-014

- Goal 16. Promote peaceful and inclusive societies for sustainable development, provide access to justice for all and build effective, accountable, and inclusive institutions at all levels
- Goal 17. Strengthen the means of implementation and revitalize the global partnership for sustainable development

*Acknowledging that the United Nations Framework Convention on Climate Change is the primary international, intergovernmental forum for negotiating the global response to climate change. See Transforming Our World: The 2030 Agenda for Sustainable Development | Department of Economic and Social Affairs (un.org).[3]

Notes

1 Sustainable Development Goals | UNDP; https://www.undp.org/sustainable-development-goals
2 The Millennium Development Goals Report 2015 | UNDP; https://www.undp.org/publications/millennium-development-goals-report-2015
3 https://sdgs.un.org/2030agenda

Appendix 2
Subsidiarity

Towns and cities often argue that they should have the power to determine their own destiny through political self-determination, rather than having to follow the dictates of higher authorities such as states or countries. In philosophy and law, this political value is based on the principle of subsidiarity – a concept going back to medieval times.[1] This principle has been adopted officially by the Roman Catholic Church in modern times as part of its social doctrine. The following Vatican document on "The Principle of Subsidiarity"[2] can have relevance to any town or city. (Author)

The Principle of Subsidiarity

Origin and Meaning

Subsidiarity is among the most constant and characteristic directives of the Church's social doctrine and has been present since the first great social encyclical.[3] It is impossible to promote the dignity of the person without showing concern for the family, groups, associations, local territorial realities; in short, for that aggregate of economic, social, cultural, sports-oriented, recreational, professional, and political expressions to which people spontaneously give life and which make it possible for them to achieve effective social growth.[4] This is the realm of *civil society*, understood as the sum of the relationships between individuals and intermediate social groupings, which are the first relationships to arise and which come about thanks to "the creative subjectivity of the citizen."[5] This network of relationships strengthens the social fabric and constitutes the basis of a true community of persons, making possible the recognition of higher forms of social activity.[6]

186. *The necessity of defending and promoting the original expressions of social life is emphasized by the Church in the Encyclical Quadragesimo Anno, in which the principle of subsidiarity is indicated as a most important principle of "social philosophy."* "Just as it is gravely wrong to take from individuals what they can accomplish by their own initiative and industry and give it to the community, so also it is an injustice and at the same time a grave evil and disturbance of right order to assign to a greater and higher association what lesser and subordinate organizations can do. For every social activity ought of its very nature to furnish help to the members of the body social, and never destroy and absorb them."[7]

https://doi.org/10.1515/9783110689860-015

Based on this principle, all societies of a superior order must adopt attitudes of help ("subsidium") – therefore of support, promotion, development – with respect to lower-order societies. In this way, intermediate social entities can properly perform the functions that fall to them without being required to hand them over unjustly to other social entities of a higher level, by which they would end up being absorbed and substituted, in the end seeing themselves denied their dignity and essential place.

Subsidiarity, understood *in the positive sense* as economic, institutional, or juridical assistance offered to lesser social entities, entails a corresponding series of *negative* implications that require the State to refrain from anything that would de facto restrict the existential space of the smaller essential cells of society. Their initiative, freedom, and responsibility must not be supplanted.

Concrete Indications

187. The principle of subsidiarity protects people from abuses by higher-level social authority and calls on these same authorities to help individuals and intermediate groups to fulfil their duties. This principle is imperative because every person, family, and intermediate group has something original to offer to the community. Experience shows that the denial of subsidiarity, or its limitation in the name of an alleged democratization or equality of all members of society, limits and sometimes even destroys the spirit of freedom and initiative.

The principle of subsidiarity is opposed to certain forms of centralization, bureaucratization, and welfare assistance and to the unjustified and excessive presence of the State in public mechanisms. "By intervening directly and depriving society of its responsibility, the Social Assistance State leads to a loss of human energies and an inordinate increase of public agencies, which are dominated more by bureaucratic ways of thinking than by concern for serving their clients, and which are accompanied by an enormous increase in spending."[8] An absent or insufficient recognition of private initiative – in economic matters also – and the failure to recognize its public function, contribute to the undermining of the principle of subsidiarity, as monopolies do as well.

In order for the principle of subsidiarity to be put into practice there is a *corresponding need* for: respect and effective promotion of the human person and the family; ever greater appreciation of associations and intermediate organizations in their fundamental choices and in those that can not be delegated to or exercised by others; the encouragement of private initiative so that every social entity remains at the service of the common good, each with its own distinctive characteristics; the presence of pluralism in society and due representation of its vital components; safeguarding human rights and the rights of minorities; bringing about bureaucratic and administrative decentralization; striking a balance between the public and private spheres, with the resulting recognition of the *social* function of the private sphere; appropriate methods for making citizens more responsible in actively "being a part" of the political and social reality of their country.

188. *Various circumstances may make it advisable that the State step in to supply certain functions.*[9] One may think, for example, of situations in which it is necessary for the State itself to stimulate the economy because it is impossible for civil society to support initiatives on its own. One may also envision the reality of serious social imbalance or injustice where only the intervention of the public authority can create conditions of greater equality, justice, and peace. Considering the principle of subsidiarity, however, this institutional substitution must not continue any longer than is absolutely necessary, since justification for such intervention is found only in the *exceptional nature* of the situation. In any case, the common good correctly understood, the demands of which will never in any way be contrary to the defence and promotion of the primacy of the person and the way this is expressed in society, must remain the criteria for making decisions concerning the application of the principle of subsidiarity.

Notes

1 The Pre-History of Subsidiarity in Leo XIII (stjohns.edu); https://scholarship.law.stjohns.edu/cgi/viewcontent.cgi?article=1162&context=jcls
2 Compendium of the Social Doctrine of the Church, Pontifical Council for Justice and peace, Part IV, Subsidiarity, The Vatican, Rome, June 29, 2004.
3 Cf. Leo XIII, Encyclical Letter *Rerum Novarum: Acta Leonis XIII, 11* (1892): 101–102, 123.
4 Cf. *Catechism of the Catholic Church*, 1882.
5 John Paul II, Encyclical Letter *Sollicitudo Rei Socialis, 15: AAS* 80 (1988): 529; cf. Pius XI, Encyclical Letter *Quadragesimo Anno: AAS* 23 (1931): 203; John XXIII, Encyclical Letter *Mater et Magistra: AAS* 53 (1961): 439; Second Vatican Ecumenical Council, Pastoral Constitution *Gaudium et Spes, 65: AAS* 58 (1966): 1086–1087; Congregation for the Doctrine of the Faith, Instruction *Libertatis Conscientia, 73, 85–86: AAS* 79 (1987): 586, 592–593; John Paul II, Encyclical Letter *Centesimus Annus, 48: AAS* 83 (1991): 852–854; *Catechism of the Catholic Church*, 1883–1885.
6 Cf. John Paul II, Encyclical Letter *Centesimus Annus, 49: AAS* 83 (1991): 854–856; John Paul II, Encyclical Letter *Sollicitudo Rei Socialis, 15: AAS* 80 (1988): 528–530.
7 Pius XI, Encyclical Letter *Quadragesimo Anno: AAS* 23 (1931): 203; cf. John Paul II, Encyclical Letter *Centesimus Annus, 48: AAS* 83 (1991): 852–854; *Catechism of the Catholic Church*, 1883.
8 John Paul II, Encyclical Letter *Centesimus Annus, 48: AAS* 83 (1991): 854.
9 Cf. John Paul II, Encyclical Letter *Centesimus Annus, 48: AAS* 83 (1991): 852–854.

Appendix 3
LEED-ND Scoring Tool

The Leadership in Energy and Environmental Design (LEED) standards have expanded to include a model for Neighborhood Development (ND). These standards are developed and approved by the US Green Building Council,[1] a member of the World Green Building Council.[2]

The following categories are rated in the LEED-ND standards:

Integrative Process

Integrative Planning and Leadership[3]
Green Building Policy and Incentives[4]

Natural Systems and Ecology

Ecosystems Assessment*
Green Spaces[5]
Natural Resources Conservation and Restoration
Light Pollution Reduction
Resilience Planning

Transportation and Land Use

Transportation Performance*
Compact, Mixed Use and Transit Oriented Development
Access to Quality Transit
Alternative Fuel Vehicles
Smart Mobility and Transportation Policy
High-Priority Site

Water Efficiency

Water Access and Quality*
Water Performance
Integrated Water Management

https://doi.org/10.1515/9783110689860-016

Stormwater Management
Smart Water Systems

Energy and Greenhouse Gas Emissions

Power Access, Reliability and Resiliency*
Energy and Greenhouse Gas Emissions Performance*
Energy Efficiency
Renewable Energy
Low Carbon Economy
Grid Harmonization

Materials and Resources

Solid Waste Management*
Special Waste Streams Management
Responsible Sourcing for Infrastructure
Material Recovery
Smart Waste Management Systems

Quality of Life

Demographic Assessment*
Quality of Life Performance*
Trend Improvements
Distributional Equity
Environmental Justice
Housing and Transportation Affordability
Civic and Community Engagement
Civil and Human Rights
Innovation

Regional Priority

Regional Priority
*Classified as prerequisite.

Source: Based on the Leadership in Energy and Environmental Design (LEED) Rating System for Neighborhood Development (ND). Adapted from the LEED Standard of US Green Building Council (USGBC)[6] 2021.

Notes

1 http://www.usgbc.org

2 US Green Building Council | World Green Building Council (worldgbc.org); https://www.worldgbc.org/member-directory/us-green-building-council

3 To support high-performance, cost-effective outcomes through an early analysis of the inter-relationships among city or community system.

4 To encourage the design, construction, and retrofit of buildings using green building practices.

5 To provide accessible green spaces that positively impact physical, mental, and psychological health and well-being of the community while also enhancing the environmental quality of the city or community.

6 https://www.usgbc.org/leed/v41#cities-and-communities

Appendix 4
Sustainable City Planning Resources

The following author-curated list features global planning organizations that focus on environmental sustainability for cities and towns.

AIVP (Association Internationale des Villes et des Portes) http://www.aivp.org/en/
AIVP is an international organization connecting public and private development stakeholders in port cities.

C40 https://www.c40.org/
A network of the world's megacities committed to addressing climate change.

Cities Alliance https://www.citiesalliance.org/
This organization focuses on eradicating poverty, but also cooperates with others in addressing climate change.

City Fix https://thecityfix.com/
An online resource for news and analysis on urban sustainability and development.

City Mayors Foundation http://citymayors.com/
A think tank and association for city mayors around the world.

City on the Move https://www.ville-en-mouvement.com/en
A global think tank focused on socializing and transportation.

A2R Resilience Initiative http://www.a2rinitiative.org/
An outgrowth of the 100 Resilient Cities Initiative (2013–2019), this initiative supports chief resilience officers in the network. The new initiative builds on the 80 Resilience Strategies, more than 4,000 actions and initiatives launched by 100 Resilient Cities.[1]

Community Development Society https://www.comm-dev.org/
An international network of community development researchers, practitioners, and policy makers with an interest in community development.

Community Planning http://communityplanning.net/
A website aimed at helping people shape the future of their cities, towns, and villages in any part of the world.

EcoCity Builders https://ecocitybuilders.org/
Curated access to 10,000 vetted green city websites.

https://doi.org/10.1515/9783110689860-017

Economic Development Directory http://ecodevdirectory.com/
An online director of development organizations around the world.

Foundation for the Urban Environment https://www.ffue.org/
*A think tank focusing on land use and planning, including cultural heritage con-
servation and improvement; transport and mobility; and environment/climate at
global and local level.*

Future of Places Research Network https://foprn.org/
*A collaborative platform for research, implementation, networking, and advocacy,
centered on key issues of public space as a fundamental component of sustainable urban development.*

urban development.

Global Alliance for Buildings and Construction http://globalabc.org/
*With over 130 members, including 29 countries, the GlobalABC is a platform for
governments, the private sector, civil society, and intergovernmental and international organizations to increase action toward a zero-emission, efficient and resilient buildings, and construction sector.*

Global Development Research Center http://gdrc.org/
*A research center with a variety of resources, including those focused on urban
environmental management.* http://gdrc.org/uem/index.html. *The GDRC framework for urban environmental management is found here:* https://www.gdrc.org/
uem/doc-intro.html

Global Environmental Facility https://www.thegef.org/partners/countries-
participants
*This World Bank Group organization, which involves 183 countries, includes an
initiative on sustainable cities.* https://www.thegef.org/topics/sustainable-cities

Global Exchange https://globalexchange.org/about-us/
*An international human rights organization promoting social, economic, and envi-
ronmental justice.*

Global Green Growth Institute https://gggi.org/
*A treaty-based international, inter-governmental organization dedicated to foster-
ing sustainable growth in developing countries and emerging economies. It has a
Green Cities initiative.*
https://gggi.org/theme/green-cities/

Global Grid https://theglobalgrid.org/about/
A website with urbanist news from local sources.

Global Planning Network http://www.globalplannersnetwork.org/
A membership organization for planning association. Supports the Vancouver Declaration. http://www.globalplannersnetwork.org/wp-content/uploads/2017/08/WPC-declaration-2006-updated-June-2017.pdf *and UN Sustainable development goals* https://sdgs.un.org/goals

Global Planning and Educational Association Net (GPEAN) http://www.gpean.org/content/publications
A website that enables urban planning organizations to communicate with one another. Has international membership. http://www.gpean.org/content/pages/organization

IBM Smarter Cities https://www.ibm.com/smarterplanet/us/en/smarter_cit ies/solutions/planning_mgt_solutions/
A sponsoring source for resources and events focused on information technology for cities.

Innovation Cities Program https://www.innovation-cities.com/
A think tank that generates metrics for cities and published ranking. 162 metrics are compared for 500 cities.

Institute for Sustainable Development (ISD)
ISDUS.org

The ISD works working with chambers, entrepreneurship organizations, economic development organizations and corporate citizens to ensure resiliency.

International City/County Management Association (ICMA) https://icma.org
ICMA is a global association of city and county managers and other employees serving local governments.

International Council for Local Environmental Initiatives – aka Local Governments for Sustainability
https://iclei.org/
A global network of more than 1,750 local and regional governments in more than 100 countries. Members are committed to urban development that is sustainable, described as "low-emission, nature-based, equitable, resilient, and circular."

International Downtown Association
https://downtown.org/
Association for professionals who help "transform cities into healthy and vibrant urban places."

International Economic Development Council https://www.iedconline.org/
A nonprofit, nonpartisan membership organization serving economic developers.

International Federation of Consulting Engineers https://fidic.org/node/756
The global representative body for national associations of consulting engineers, representing over one million engineering professionals and 40,000 firms in 100 countries worldwide.

International Federation for Housing and Planning https://www.ifhp.org/
An association for urban planners with resources that include a "greenmaps."[2]

International Institute for Environment and Development https://www.iied.org/
A think tank conducting research to promote sustainable development and protect the environment, with 350 partners in 60 countries.

International Institute for Sustainable Development
https://www.iisd.org/
A global think tank that works toward fair economies, fresh water, and a stable climate by working through powerful partnerships.

International Institute for the Urban Environment https://www.iied.org/about
A research institute that helps to support sustainable development and protect the environment. It aims to identify local solutions that can work at scale and introduce these to global forums.

International New Town Institute http://www.newtowninstitute.org/
INTI studies the role of new towns in a world moving toward more urbanization. It defines new towns as "cities or towns that are designed from scratch and built in a short period of time." They are different from a "normal" city that gradually grows and evolves over time.

International Society of City and Regional Planners (ISOCARP) https://isocarp.org/
A global association of city and regional planners who can join as Individuals or institutions. Maintains a data bases of planning organizations and events.

International Union for Conservation of Nature (IUCN) https://www.iucn.org/about/
A membership organization composed of government and civil society organizations, with 1,400 member organizations and input of more 15,000 experts.

International Urban Development Association
https://inta-aivn.org/en/
A global network for urban development: policymakers of national, regional, and local government; business leaders in real estate development, construction, engineering, service provision, product development; thought leader, research institutes; and influential architecture and urbanism firms, to jointly establish new parameters for sustainable and integrated development of urbanized areas.

International Urban Planning and Environmental Association (IUPEA)
https://www.iupea.org/
A membership association that aims to resolve conflicts between forces of economic development and environmental preservation by fostering dialogue and generating practical solutions.

Metropolis https://www.metropolis.org/
A global network of major cities and metropolitan areas focused on a wide range of issues including metropolitan governance. Operates the World Organization of United Cities and Local Governments (UCLG) – see below.

New Urbanism http://newurbanism.org/
A website with resources dedicated to "new urbanism," defined as a development strategy that addresses issues such as sustainable development.

Planners Network http://www.plannersnetwork.org/
An association of professionals, activists, academics, and students involved in physical, social, economic, and environmental planning in urban and rural areas.

Planum http://www.planum.net/partners
A global association open to scientific journals, academic and research institutes, practitioners and scholars, policy makers, stakeholders, and the wider arena of those involved in the fields of urbanism, urban planning, architecture, urban studies, urban development, and environmental preservation.

Project for Public Spaces https://www.pps.org/
A nonprofit organization dedicated to helping people create and sustain public spaces that build strong communities.

Resilient Cities Catalyst https://www.rcc.city/about-rcc
A new nonprofit advancing the urban resilience movement, linking government, civil society, and the private sector.

Urban Design Resources http://www.urbandesignresources.org/tools/
A global website with a variety of resources for urban designs.

SlimCity https://www.weforum.org/reports/slimcity-cross-industry-public-private-initiative-urban-sustainability
An online marketplace hosted by the World Economic Forum for cities and the private sector to exchange best practices and deliver resource efficiency within cities worldwide.

Smart Communities Network https://www.smartcitiesnetwork.net/
A global platform for thought leadership, business intelligence, knowledge sharing, and creating business opportunities for the smart city's global community.

Society for Urban Ecology
https://www.society-urban-ecology.org/
A community that strives to foster and develop knowledge and implementation of urban ecology worldwide by strengthening contacts and enriching the dialogue between researchers and practitioners, by representing the interests of the academic community within the wider international institutional context and by making the collective expertise of SURE available, where appropriate, in furthering the discussion of urban ecological issues.

Symbiotic Cities Network (SURE) https://www.symbioticcities.net/
A networking website promoting economic, political, technological, and cultural engagement toward maintaining a regenerative symbiotic relationship with the city's surrounding environment.

United Cities and Local Governments (UGLG) https://www.uclg.org/
A global network of cities and local, regional, and metropolitan governments and their associations, committed to representing, defending, and amplifying the voices of local and regional governments.

United Nations Department of Economic and Social Affairs

https://www.un.org/development/desa/en/about/who-we-are.html
This UN department is the home of the UN's Sustainable Development Goals,[3] *which include the goal of "sustainable cities and communities."*

United Nations Environmental Program (UNEP) https://www.unenviron ment.org/about-un-environment
An arm of the UN that works closely with UN member states and stakeholders in the public and private sectors to leverage partnerships in sustainable development. Has a sustainable cities initiative.[4]

Urban Land Institute https://uli.org/
A worldwide network of real estate and land use experts.

Urban Matters http://urban-matters.org/
A countercultural community exploring "unplanning," stating that the pragmatics of conventional or "neoliberal" planning, which is investor oriented, no longer seems an adequate response to "a multilayered society permanently on the move."

World Business Council for Sustainable Development https://www.wbcsd.org/
A group of nearly 200 global companies committed to advance the sustainability agenda.

World Organization of United Cities and Local Governments (UCLG) https://www.metropolis.org/
A global network of major cities and metropolitan areas focused on a wide range of issues including metropolitan governance. Operates the World Organization of United Cities and Local Governments. Operated by Metropolis (see above).

WRI Ross Center for Sustainable Cities https://wrirosscities.org/
A global nonprofit helping cities become more sustainable. Practice areas include urban climate resistance (see https://wrirosscities.org/our-work/topics/urban-climate-resilience).

Notes

1 https://www.rockefellerfoundation.org/news/rockefeller-foundation-launches-new-climate-resilience-initiative-commits-initial-8-million-continue-supporting-global-network-cities-chief-resilience-officers/
2 https://www.greenmap.org/maps-projects/explore-green-maps
3 https://www.un.org/sustainabledevelopment/sustainable-development-goals/
4 https://www.unenvironment.org/regions/asia-and-pacific/regional-initiatives/supporting-resource-efficiency/sustainable-cities

Appendix 5
Statute of the City: A National Law for Urban Planning in Brazil

Brazil's national law, Statute of the City, articulates why and how to plan for the collective good and the future of the environment.[1] (Author)

Chapter I

General Guidelines

Art. 1 – the implementation of urban policy, which deals with arts. 182 (http://www.planalto.gov.br/ccivil_03/Constituicao/Constituicao.htm#art182) and 183 of the Federal Constitution, the provisions of this Law will be applied; (http://www.planalto.gov.br/ccivil_03/Constituicao/Constituicao.htm#art183).

Single paragraph. For all purposes, this Law, called The Statute of the City, establishes rules of public order and social interest that regulate the use of urban property for the collective good, security and well-being of citizens, as well as environmental balance.

Art. 2 – the objective of urban policy is to order the full development of the social functions of the city and urban property, by the following general guidelines:

I – guarantee of the right to sustainable cities, understood as the right to urban land, housing, environmental sanitation, urban infrastructure, transport and public services, work and leisure, for present and future generations

II – democratic management through the participation of the population and representative associations of the various segments of the community in the formulation, implementation and monitoring of urban development plans, programs, and projects

III – cooperation between governments, private initiative, and other sectors of society in the urbanization process, in service to the social interest

IV – planning the development of cities, the spatial distribution of the population and the economic activities of the municipality and the territory under its area of influence, in order to avoid and correct the distortions of urban growth and its negative effects on the environment

https://doi.org/10.1515/9783110689860-018

V – provision of urban and community equipment, transport, and public services appropriate to the interests and needs of the population and local characteristics

VI – ordering and controlling land use, to avoid:

(a) the inappropriate use of urban real estate

(b) the proximity of incompatible or inconvenient uses

(c) land parcelling, overconstruction, or use or misuse in relation to urban infrastructure

(d) the installation of undertakings or activities that can function as traffic generating poles, without the provision of the corresponding infrastructure

(e) the speculative retention of urban property, which results in its underuse or nonuse

(f) the deterioration of urbanized areas

(g) pollution and environmental degradation

(h) the exposure of the population to disaster risks [2]

VII – integration and complementarity between urban and rural activities, in view of the socioeconomic development of the municipality and the territory under its area of influence

VIII – adoption of patterns of production and consumption of goods and services and urban expansion compatible with the limits of environmental, social, and economic sustainability of the municipality and the territory under its area of influence

IX – fair distribution of benefits and burden stemming from the urbanization process

X – adequacy of economic, tax and financial policy instruments and public spending to urban development objectives, to privilege investments that generate general well-being and the enjoyment of goods by different social segments

XI – recovery of government investments that have resulted in the valuation of urban real estate

XII – protection, preservation, and recovery of the natural and built environment, cultural, historical, artistic, landscape, and archaeological heritage

XIII – hearing of the municipal government and the population interested in the processes of implementation of enterprises or activities with potentially negative effects on the natural or built environment, the comfort or safety of the population

XIV – land regularization and urbanization of areas occupied by low-income population through the establishment of special standards of urbanization, land use, and occupation and building, considering the socioeconomic situation of the population and environmental standards

XV – simplification of land parcelling, land use and occupation legislation and building standards, with a view to reducing costs and increasing the supply of lots and housing units

XVI – isonomy of conditions for public and private agents in the promotion of enterprises and activities related to the urbanization process, granted the social interest

XVII – stimulus to the use, in land parcels and urban buildings, of operating systems, construction standards, and technological contributions that objective the reduction of environmental impacts, and the saving of natural resources[3]

XVIII – priority treatment to the works and buildings of energy infrastructure, telecommunications, water supply, and sanitation.[4]

XIX – guarantee of decent conditions of accessibility, use and comfort in the internal premises of urban buildings, including those intended for housing and the service of domestic workers, observed minimum requirements of dimensioning, ventilation, lighting, ergonomics, privacy, and quality of the materials employed.[5]

Notes

1 Brazil http://www.planalto.gov.br/ccivil_03/leis/LEIS_2001/L10257.htm
2 Included in Law No. 12,608, 2012. http://www.planalto.gov.br/ccivil_03/_Ato2011-2014/2012/Lei/L12608.htm#art24
3 Included in Law No. 12,836, 2013; http://www.planalto.gov.br/ccivil_03/_Ato2011-2014/2013/Lei/L12836.htm
4 Included in Law No. 13,116, 2015; http://www.planalto.gov.br/ccivil_03/_Ato2015-2018/2015/Lei/L13116.htm#art30
5 Included in Law No. 13,699, 2018; http://www.planalto.gov.br/ccivil_03/_Ato2015-2018/2018/Lei/L13699.htm#art1

Appendix 6
Tree City USA Standards

The following is reprinted with permission from Tree City USA Standards, Arbor Day.[1]
To qualify as a Tree City USA community, you must meet four standards established by the Arbor Day Foundation and the National Association of State Foresters. These standards were established to ensure that every qualifying community* would have a viable tree management program and that no community would be excluded because of size.

Four Standards for Tree City USA Recognition

Standard 1

A Tree Board or Department

Someone must be legally responsible for the care of all trees on city- or town-owned property. By delegating tree care decisions to a professional forester, arborist, city department, citizen-led tree board, or some combination, city leaders determine who will perform necessary tree work. The public will also know who is accountable for decisions that impact community trees. Often, both professional staff and an advisory tree board are established, which is a good goal for most communities.

The formation of a tree board often stems from a group of citizens. In some cases a mayor or city officials have started the process. Either way, the benefits are immense. Involving residents and business owners creates wide awareness of what trees do for the community and provides broad support for better tree care.

Standard 2

A Tree Care Ordinance

A public tree care ordinance forms the foundation of a city's tree care program. It provides an opportunity to set good policy and back it with the force of law when necessary.

A key section of a qualifying ordinance is one that establishes the tree board or forestry department – or both – and gives one of them the responsibility for

https://doi.org/10.1515/9783110689860-019

public tree care (as reflected in Standard 1). It should also assign the task of crafting and implementing a plan of work or for documenting annual tree care activities.

Qualifying ordinances will also provide clear guidance for planting, maintaining and/or removing trees from streets, parks and other public spaces as well as activities that are required or prohibited. Beyond that, the ordinance should be flexible enough to fit the needs and circumstances of the particular community.

For tips and a checklist of important items to consider in writing or improving a tree ordinance, see Tree City USA Bulletin #9.[2]

Standard 3

A Community Forestry Program with an Annual Budget of at Least $2 Per Capita

City trees provide many benefits – clean air, clean water, shade and beauty to name a few – but they also require an investment to remain healthy and sustainable. By providing support at or above the $2 per capita minimum, a community demonstrates its commitment to grow and tend these valuable public assets. Budgets and expenditures require planning and accountability, which are fundamental to the long-term health of the tree canopy and the Tree City USA program.

To meet this standard each year, the community must document at least $2 per capita toward the planting, care and removal of city trees – and the planning efforts to make those things happen. At first this may seem like an impossible barrier to some communities. However, a little investigation usually reveals that more than this amount is already being spent on tree care. If not, this may signal serious neglect that will cost far more in the long run. In such a case, working toward Tree City USA recognition can be used to reexamine the community's budget priorities and redirect funds to properly care for its tree resources before it is too late.

Standard 4

An Arbor Day Observance and Proclamation

An effective program for community trees would not be complete without an annual Arbor Day ceremony. Citizens join to celebrate the benefits of community trees and the work accomplished to plant and maintain them. By passing and reciting an official Arbor Day proclamation, public officials demonstrate their support for the community tree program and complete the requirements for becoming a Tree City USA!

This is the least challenging – and probably most enjoyable – standard to meet. An Arbor Day celebration can be simple and brief or an all-day or all-week observation. It can include a tree planting event, tree care activities, or an award ceremony that honors leading tree planters. For children, Arbor Day may be their only exposure to the green world or a springboard to discussions about the complex issue of environmental quality.

The benefits of Arbor Day go far beyond the shade and beauty of new trees for the next generation. Arbor Day is a golden opportunity for publicity and to educate homeowners about proper tree care. Utility companies can join in to promote planting small trees beneath power lines or being careful when digging. Fire prevention messaging can also be worked into the event, as can conservation education about soil erosion or the need to protect wildlife habitat.

Notes

1 https://www.arborday.org/programs/treecityusa/standards.cfm?detail=2
2 https://shop.arborday.org/9-how-to-write-a-municipal-tree-ordinance. See Chapter 4 of this book for a summary of this publication.

Appendix 7
Notable Accomplishments
of Tribal Governments in the Advancement
# of Sustainability

From the Trojan War to the battle over Keystone XL Pipeline, human history can be seen as a continuing confrontation between a new world of exploration represented by conquerors of wealth versus an old world of stewardship represented by local defenders. In many cases the defense has been for nature, and the defenders have been the governments of indigenous tribes.[1]

The many accomplishments of indigenous leaders in the advancement of sustainability over the years can not be captured in a mere appendix. To learn about these contributions, readers can turn to comprehensive studies on the topic.[2] Indeed the purpose of this brief essay is to inspire them to do so. Leaders of today's towns can and must learn from those whose sustainable traditions preceded them in time, yet endure.

Guardians of Nature

Indigenous people are earth's guardians – by definition. They are "distinct social and cultural groups that share collective ancestral ties to the lands and natural resources where they live, occupy or from which they have been displaced,"[3] says the World Bank. For such people, natural ecosystems are "inextricably linked to their identities, cultures, livelihoods, as well as their physical and spiritual well-being."[4]

> Given this linkage, towns have much to learn from tribes. More specifically, today's incorporated municipalities, built as they are on modern concepts of individual property and political power can learn strategies from tribes that practice a more communal and traditional type of governmental structure – one that offers some significant advantages in the tackling of environmental issues.

According to one recent scientific study, human presence on earth is not the cause of biodiversity loss; the cause of loss is over-exploitation by some humans. The sustainable practices of indigenous tribes have helped preserve what little wild nature we still have today.[5]

https://doi.org/10.1515/9783110689860-020

With rare exceptions, current biodiversity losses are caused not by human conversion or degradation of untouched ecosystems, but rather by the appropriation, colonization, and intensification of use in lands inhabited and used by prior societies. Global land use history confirms that empowering the environmental stewardship of Indigenous peoples and local communities will be critical to conserving biodiversity across the planet."[6]

A Living Force Today

Although the forces of history have thinned their ranks – today only about 5 percent of the world population is characterized as indigenous[7] – indigenous people and their tribes remain an important force in our world economy, particularly in defense of the planet itself. Although displacement has disrupted governance for some indigenous people, others do have tribal structures that have endured. In the US, for example, 574 tribes are sovereign nations with a formal relationship to the US government.[8] More broadly, the United Nations has a dedicated program to preserve the rights of indigenous peoples.[9]

Tribal governments shoulder a wide range of responsibilities, including but not limited to management and protection of environmental resources, advancement of the tribal economy, and maintenance of infrastructure.[10]

Many tribes have a shared belief in the value of nature, so the tribal value system begins a priori as sustainable. As a combination of their legal structure and their value systems, many tribes have been able to do more than the average locality in maintaining sustainability of lands, waters, and the wildlife they support. Today leaders within and beyond tribal sovereign states are drawing on the wisdom of indigenous tribes to adapt to the dynamics nature, including climate change.[11]

This appendix lists selected accomplishments[12] in chronological order, with only sparse commentary. The stories speak for themselves.

Representative Timeline of Tribal Accomplishment

The National Conference of State Legislatures observed that "a handful of states and American Indian tribes have experimented with implementing sustainable development practices to ensure a future for their citizens."

2007. The National Conference of State Legislatures observed that "a handful of states and American Indian tribes have experimented with implementing sustainable development practices to ensure a future for their citizens."[13] The publication lists accomplishments of the following tribes: the Nez Perce tribe (for salmon habitat conservation, watershed management, wetlands restoration, pollution reduction, and erosion control); the Confederated Tribes of the Warm Springs in central Oregon (for sustainable forest management); Shakopee Mdewakanton Sioux Community of the Dakota people located near Prior Lake, Minnesota (for renewable energy, water reclamation, and land conservation).

2010. The Swinomish tribe, locate in the Northwester US, in Washington State, became the first tribe to develop a climate action plan.[14] Fifty states would follow.

2014. The Tūhoe people succeeded in getting the New Zealand Parliament to pass the *Te Urewera Act*, finalizing a settlement between the Tūhoe people and the government. The Act recognizes a large geographic area known as the Te Urewera – formerly a national park – as having "legal recognition in its own right."

2016. The Ho-Chunk Nation, with territories that span several states in the American Midwest, took a first vote for a Rights of Nature tribal constitutional amendment. It was the first tribal nation in the US to do so. the Ho-Chunk Nation amended its Tribal constitution to assert the Rights of Nature to mitigate environmental damage from frac sand mining, oil transport, and industrial agriculture.[15] The provision declared that "Ecosystems and natural communities within the Ho-Chunk territory possess an inherent, fundamental, and inalienable right to exist and thrive." In addition, it bans frac sand mining, fossil fuel extraction, and genetic engineering as violations of the Rights of Nature.[16]

2016. Colombia's Constitutional Court ruled that the Rio Atrato possesses rights to "protection, conservation, maintenance, and restoration," and established joint guardianship for the river shared by indigenous people and the national government. That same year, 200 US and Canadian tribal nations signed a treaty that formally recognized the right of the grizzly bear to exist in a healthy ecosystem.

2017. The Ponca Nation in Oklahoma passed a statute recognizing the rights of nature after suffering from effects of fracking.[17] The new law came out of concern for natural systems that needed protection. Casey Camp-Horinek, a member of the Ponca Tribal Business Council evoked the legal theory of guardianship when she said that "It is going to take all of us humans because we're speaking for those without voices, for the deer, the cattle, those that fly."[18] Also in 2017, an association of three indigenous peoples[19] succeeded in having the New Zealand Parliament pass the *Te Awa Tupua Act,*[20] granting the Whanganui River legal status as an ecosystem.[21] Also in this year, the Ponca Nation of Oklahoma adopted a customary law recognizing the rights of Nature.

2018. The White Earth band of the Chippewa Nation (also known as Ojibwe and Anishinaabe people) adopted the "Rights of the Manoomin" law, based on an 1855 Treaty Authority. This law secured the legal rights of manoomin, or wild rice, to protect the legal rights of this grown wild plant as well as the water and habitat it needs to survive as a traditional staple crop. According to the Center for Community Environmental Legal Defense Fund, this was the first law to secure legal rights of a particular plant species. The Tribal resolution explained that it adopted the Rights of Manoomin law because "it has become necessary to provide a legal basis to protect wild rice and freshwater resources as part of our primary treaty foods for future generations."[22]

2019. The Yurok Tribal Council, which has territory in northern California, voted unanimously in favor of a resolution establishing the rights of the Klamath River. According to the Yurok Tribe, which is based in Northern California, the resolution "establishes the Rights of the Klamath River to exist, flourish, and naturally evolve; to have a clean and healthy environment free from pollutants; to have a stable climate free from human-caused climate change impacts; and to be free from contamination by genetically engineered organisms."[23]

2020. The Menominee Indian Tribe of Wisconsin asserted that the Menominee River has the right to exist naturally, flourish, evolve, remain unpolluted, and carry out its natural ecosystem functions. That same year, in the North American Northwest, the Nez Perce Tribe General Council passed a resolution recognizing the Snake River as a living entity that has "the right to exist, the right to flourish, the right to evolve, the right to flow, the right to regenerate, and the right to regeneration."[24] 2020 was also the year when the Tŝilhqot'in Nation (in the Canadian Northwest) enacted a "ʔEsdilagh Sturgeon River Law." It states: "The Aboriginal title and rights of the Tŝilhqot'in people includes the *tu* [waters] in our territory, including ʔElhdaqox [the Sturgeon River]. *Nen* [lands] and *tu* cannot be separated but are interconnected." It recognizes that "People, animals, fish, plants, the *nen*, and the *tu* have rights in the decisions about their care and use that must be considered and respected."[25]

2021. For the first time, a river is granted official rights and legal personhood in Canada Quebec, Canada, February 23, 2021 – The Muteshekau-shipu Alliance today announced the granting of legal personhood to the Magpie River, through the adoption of two parallel resolutions by the Innu Council of Ekuanitshit and the Minganie Regional County Municipality (RCM).[26] The press release about the event notes that "The initiative is part of a global movement – particularly active in New Zealand, the United States and Ecuador – to recognize the rights of Nature."[27]

Notes

1 While individual members of tribes such as elders can have a major impact, it is important to recognize the importance of tribal councils or organizations. The US Federal Code defines

them as follows: " 'tribal organization' means the recognized governing body of any Indian tribe; any legally established organization of Indians that is controlled, sanctioned, or chartered by such governing body or which is democratically elected by the adult members of the Indian community to be served by such organization and which includes the maximum participation of Indians in all phases of its activities." 25 U.S.C. § 450b (2015) – Definitions:: Title 25 – Indians (Sections 1–4307) – US Code:: Justia; https://scholarship.law.tamu.edu/cgi/viewcontent.cgi?article=2307&context=facscholar

2 See, for example, Clan and Tribal Perspectives on Social, Economic, and Environmental Sustainability (Emerald Publishing, 2021). Clan and Tribal Perspectives on Social, Economic and Environmental Sustainability: Indigenous Stories from Around the Globe: -, James C. Spee, Adela J. McMurray, Mark D. McMillan: 9781789733662: Amazon.com: Books; https://www.amazon.com/Tribal-Perspectives-Economic-Environmental-Sustainability/dp/1789733669/ref=tmm_hrd_swatch_0?_encoding=UTF8&qid=1620490810&sr=1-1 Ecological Sustainability in Traditional Sami Beliefs and Rituals (Peter Lang GmbH, 2016). Amazon.com: Ecological Sustainability in Traditional Sámi Beliefs and Rituals (Moderne – Kulturen – Relationen) (9783631665985): Boekraad, Mardoeke: Books; https://www.amazon.com/Ecological-Sustainability-Traditional-Beliefs-Rituals-dp-3631665989/dp/3631665989/ref=mt_other?_encoding=UTF8&me=&qid=1620491557

3 Indigenous Peoples Overview (worldbank.org); https://www.worldbank.org/en/topic/indigenouspeoples

4 Indigenous Peoples Overview (worldbank.org); https://www.worldbank.org/en/topic/indigenouspeoples

5 People have shaped most of terrestrial nature for at least 12,000 years | PNAS; https://www.pnas.org/content/118/17/e2023483118

6 Ellis et alia, PNAS April 27, 2021 118 (17) People have shaped most of terrestrial nature for at least 12,000 years | PNAS; https://www.pnas.org/content/118/17/e2023483118

7 Indigenous Peoples Overview (worldbank.org)Indigenous Peoples Overview (worldbank.org); https://www.worldbank.org/en/topic/indigenouspeoples

8 https://www.ncai.org/about-tribes. For legal aspects of tribal government, see Cohen's Handbook of Federal Indian Law | LexisNexis Store; https://store.lexisnexis.com/products/cohens-handbook-of-federal-indian-law-skuusSku57318?gclid=CjwKCAjw7diEBhB-EiwAskVi195iIKsf6oYP_VNumLeVg4VbTPtiFmqY-oiGscDwOMJHWuDRbUeIBoCi10QAvD_BwE

9 OHCHR | Special Rapporteur on the rights of indigenous peoples, https://www.ohchr.org/EN/Issues/IPeoples/SRIndigenousPeoples/Pages/SRIPeoplesIndex.aspx

10 https://www.ncai.org/about-tribes

11 Indigenous Knowledge for Climate Change Assessment and Adaptation (cambridge.org), https://www.cambridge.org/core/books/indigenous-knowledge-for-climate-change-assessment-and-adaptation/040C74883218D38652166413CF0E5FB1

12 This timeline includes items from the Community Environmental Defense Legal Defense Fund: Rights of Nature Timeline | CELDF | Protecting Nature and Communities; https://celdf.org/advancing-community-rights/rights-of-nature/rights-nature-timeline/ For a fuller list, see this source.

13 States and Tribes: Building New Traditions (National Conference of State Legislatures 2007); https://www.ncsl.org/print/statetribe/Sustainabledev.pdf

14 How the Swinomish tribe has pioneered the fight againt climate change – The Washington Post – https://www.washingtonpost.com/climate-solutions/2020/11/24/native-americans-climate-change-swinomish/

Appendix 8
European Governance Structures

Albania 308 communes 65 municipalities
Austria 2357 municipalities, 9 regions
Belgium 589 municipalities, 10 provinces, 3 regions, 3 communities
Bosnia and Herzegovina 63 and 74 municipalities, 10 cantons
Bulgaria 264 municipalities
Croatia 429 municipalities, 106 towns, 21 cities, 21 counties
Cyprus 484 communities, 39 municipalities
Czech Republic 6,250 municipalities, 14 regions
Denmark 98 municipalities, 5 regions
Estonia 193 municipalities, 33 cities
Finland 336 municipalities and 2 regions
Former Yugoslav Republic of Macedonia 84 municipalities and one city
    (composed of 10 of the municipalities)
France 36,682 municipalities, 96 departments, plus a unique structure for
    Corsica as a dependency
Georgia 64 municipalities and 5 self-governing cities
Germany 11,500 municipalities and cities, 300 counties, and 16 regions
Greece 325 municipalities, 13 self-governed regions
Hungary 3,175 municipalities (varying), 19 counties
Iceland 76 municipalities
Ireland 5 boroughs, 80 towns, 5 cities, 29 counties
Italy 8,014 municipalities, 101 provinces, 20 regions
Latvia 110 municipalities and 9 cities
Lithuania 60 municipalities
Luxembourg 106 municipalities
Malta 68 local councils
Montenegro 21 municipalities
Netherlands 418 municipalities, 12 provinces
Norway 430 municipalities, 19 counties
Poland 2,479 municipalities, 379 counties (including 65 of the municipalities),
    16 regions
Portugal 4,259 parishes, 308 municipalities, 2 regions
Romania 2,861 municipalities, 207 towns, 103 cities, 41 counties
Serbia 174 municipalities and cities, 2 provinces
Slovakia 2,792 municipalities, 138 cities, and 8 regions
Slovenia 211 municipalities

https://doi.org/10.1515/9783110689860-021

Spain 8,117 municipalities, 17 communities, and 2 cities
Sweden 290 municipalities, 17 county councils, and 4 regions
Switzerland 2,551 municipalities, 6 half-cantons, and 20 cantons
Turkey 34,305 villages, 2,950 municipalities, 81 provincial administrations
Ukraine 10,278 villages, 782 towns, 457 cities, 488 districts, 24 regions, and 1
  republic in the United Kingdom's capital city of London, there are 32
  boroughs as well as the Corporation of the City of London, which is the
  city's financial district
United Kingdom 466 local authorities distributed among England, Scotland, Wales,
  and Northern Ireland

Index

accounting, public sector 8, 9, 12, 13, 19,
   27, 38, 39, 65, 66, 67, 68, 69, 70,
   128, 182
activists, community XXVII, 9, 12, 16, 19, 26,
   38, 53, 77, 146, 166, 179, 182, 201
ad valorem tax 8
aesthetic zoning 57, 63
American Institute of Architecture 84
American Chestnut Foundation 25
American Institute of Certified Planners
   46
American Planning Association 16, 18
assessed value of property 8, 70, 71
assets of a municipality XII, XVII, XXI, XXVI,
   XXVIII, 7, 9, 10, 11, 12, 16, 19, 20, 21, 22,
   24, 25, 26, 27, 28, 29, 30, 43, 53, 60,
   68, 69, 73, 79, 94, 97, 111, 128, 140,
   143, 155, 173, 175, 176, 177, 178, 182,
   183, 210
American Legislative Exchange
   Committee 163
American Road and Transportation Builders
   Association XXVI
American Society of Civil Engineers 76
American Society of Heating, Refrigerating
   and Air-Conditioning Engineers 79

Berry, Fr. Thomas 137
bondholders 95, 98, 99
bonds, municipal XVIII, XXVIII, 59, 65, 71,
   93–98, 100, 101, 102, 104–105, 111, 114,
   120, 183
boundaries, municipal XXI, XXIX, XXX, 3, 13,
   24, 25, 38, 53, 58, 75, 147, 165, 172, 173,
   174, 176, 178, 179
brick-and-mortar jobs 7
brownfield 80, 123
Brundtland Report 3
budgets, municipal 7, 37, 66, 67, 68, 69, 79,
   128, 182, 210
buffer ordinance 59
buffers 22, 24, 59
building codes 79, 81–83

cancel culture 178
Central Emergency Relief Fund 127
chief resilience officer 35
citizens, municipal participation by III, V, XI,
   XII, XXI, XXII, XXIII, XXV, XXVI, XXVIII,
   XXIX, 3, 4, 6, 7, 11, 13, 21, 22, 23, 25, 26,
   34, 35, 38, 39, 53, 62, 65, 66, 69, 70,
   75, 77, 78, 83, 97, 103, 111, 120, 147,
   149, 158, 166, 167, 173, 174, 175, 177,
   178, 182, 191, 199, 205, 209, 210, 214.
   See also *residents.*
city's motto 176
civil engineers 75, 76, 85, 88
civil law 157
cladding 81
climate change XI, XXI, 4, 5, 6, 34, 45, 82,
   83, 139, 150, 188, 190, 197, 214,
   216–218
Climate Pact, European Green Deal 40
collaboration 58, 77, 109
collateral for green financing 28, 97
common law, role in environmental
   litigation 157, 162
community, role in sustainability VI, XI–XVI,
   XXII, XXV, XXVIII, XXXII, 21, 26, 27, 35,
   36, 37, 39, 42, 55, 57, 77, 111, 112, 113,
   114, 116, 117, 123, 124, 125, 126, 127,
   139, 143, 144, 146, 147, 149, 150, 155,
   158, 162, 163, 165, 166, 167, 176, 177,
   182, 189, 190, 194, 195, 197, 202, 203,
   205, 209, 210, 211, 215, 216, 217
Community Environmental Legal Defense Fund
   (CELDF) XVI, 146, 165, 166, 167, 216
Congressional Budget Office 76
constitutional law 8, 30, 41, 141, 143, 162,
   165
contracts 53, 99, 100, 122, 166
cost of growth 7
county governments XXVII, 65, 121
Covenant of Mayors for Climate and
   Energy XXVII
COVID-19 XXI, XXIII, XXIX, XXXII, 45, 105, 122
credit rating agencies 97, 98, 99ff.

https://doi.org/10.1515/9783110689860-022